RICHARD E. BERGER, M.D., is an associate professor of urology at the University of Washington Medical School, and chief of urology at Seattle's Harborview Medical Center. A board-certified urologic surgeon, Dr. Berger has written extensively on potency disorders and teaches residents and medical students how to diagnose sexual problems.

DEBORAH BERGER, M.S.W., is a journalist whose work has appeared in *Parade*, *Ladies' Home Journal*, and numerous other publications. She has been a health and medical reporter for many years, as well as a consumer columnist for radio and newspapers.

Avon Books are available at special quantity discounts for bulk purchases for sales promotions, premiums, fund raising or educational use. Special books, or book excerpts, can also be created to fit specific needs.

For details write or telephone the office of the Director of Special Markets, Avon Books, Dept. FP, 105 Madison Avenue, New York, New York 10016, 212-481-5653.

BIO-POTENCY

YOUR GUIDE TO SEXUAL FULFILLMENT

RICHARD E. BERGER, M.D.
―― AND ――
DEBORAH BERGER, M.S.W.

AVON BOOKS • NEW YORK

This book is dedicated to Benjamin

AVON BOOKS
A division of
The Hearst Corporation
105 Madison Avenue
New York, New York 10016

Copyright © 1987 by Richard E. Berger and Deborah Berger
Published by arrangement with Rodale Press, Inc.
Library of Congress Catalog Card Number: 86-24789
ISBN: 0-380-70816-7

All rights reserved, which includes the right to reproduce this book or portions thereof in any form whatsoever except as provided by the U.S. Copyright Law. For information address Rodale Press, Inc., 33 East Minor Street, Emmaus, Pennsylvania 18049.

First Avon Books Printing: June 1990

AVON TRADEMARK REG. U.S. PAT. OFF. AND IN OTHER COUNTRIES, MARCA REGISTRADA, HECHO EN U.S.A.

Printed in the U.S.A.

RA 10 9 8 7 6 5 4 3 2 1

Contents

Notice	vii
Acknowledgments	viii
Introduction	ix

1 What's Normal?   1
How to tell if you have a potency problem . . . myths and facts about impotence . . . normal changes in sexual potency

2 The Magic: What Happens When You Get an Erection   19
How the penis, testicles, veins, arteries and nerves work to give you an erection . . . the sexual response cycle . . . sleep erections

3 How *Not* to Get an Erection   37
Lifestyle habits that cause potency problems . . . common saboteurs . . . performance anxiety . . . drugs that can poison your sex life . . . proper diet

4 Keep Illness from Undermining Potency   66
Diabetes . . . blood vessel disease . . . kidney problems . . . hormone imbalances . . . testicular problems . . . nerve diseases . . . diseases of the penis . . . surgical treatments that cause erection problems

5 It Takes Two to Tango   90
Why men don't talk about erection . . . how women react to impotence . . . good talkers make great lovers . . . waiting can be hazardous to your relationship . . . the woman's needs

Contents

6 Self-Help: A 12-Week Potency Program You Can Try at Home — 109
Stopping self-sabotage . . . reducing stress, building confidence . . . preventing premature ejaculation . . . all about sexual aids and devices

7 Who to See and What to Expect — 129
Finding a competent professional . . . exactly what the doctor will do . . . all about potency tests . . . checking the mechanics . . . psychological tests

8 Medical Solutions for Physical Problems — 152
Penile shots: the latest treatment . . . penile implants . . . artery repair . . . sealing leaky veins

9 Sex Therapy for Sexual Success — 193
Are you suited for sex therapy? . . . learning to talk . . . learning to focus on pleasure . . . self-help sex therapy . . . sex therapy and the single man

10 For Women Only: How to Help Yourself (As You Help Your Partner) — 211
Potency isn't just a man's issue . . . working together for pleasure . . . is his erection a sign of your attractiveness?

11 Staying Potent: Six Guidelines for Future Sexual Success — 220
Enjoy sex your whole life . . . the power of potent thinking . . . suggestions for sexual success

References — 228

Index — 252

Notice

All names have been changed.

We are very grateful to the men and women whose personal experiences have added so much to our book. In all cases, we have changed names and any other identifying information. In some cases, we have combined the characteristics of several different individuals into one person in the book.

Great progress has been made in diagnosing and treating erection problems. The vast majority of men and their partners do not have to adjust to life without intercourse—solutions are available. This book is not a substitute for individual professional health care. A change in a man's ability to get or maintain an erection can be caused by many different things, including an illness. If a potency problem persists, you should always see a physician for a complete medical evaluation.

Acknowledgments

We are truly grateful to many people. While we don't have the space to mention everyone, some individuals deserve special mention.

First of all, we want to thank our agents, Connie Clausen and Guy Kettelhack, for their professional expertise and encouragement.

And we appreciate Jane Adams's valuable advice on the book proposal.

Many experts generously agreed to be interviewed. We especially appreciate the comments of Domeena C. Renshaw, M.D., Tom F. Lue, M.D., Saul Breit, Ph.D., Julia R. Heiman, Ph.D. and Robert Knopp, M.D. Our sincere thanks also to John L. Hampson, M.D., Susan Tollefson, R.N., M.A., Roger E. Nellans, M.D., Denise Kramer-Levien, R.N., Varda Hanson, R.N., M.S.N., Suszette Brady, R.N., B.S., Marilyn McIntyre, M.S.W. and Michael Kelch, M.S.W.

To Bruce and Eileen MacKenzie of Impotents Anonymous and Cindy Meredith, R.N., M.S.N., of Recovery of Male Potency (ROMP), we owe a special debt of gratitude.

Donna Hadland and the staff at American Medical Systems were quick to respond with information, and very helpful.

Our editor, Stephen Williams, was with us from the beginning of the book. His enthusiasm, critical eye and support were invaluable. Our thanks also to the publisher and staff at Rodale Press.

We have a very special appreciation for those we interviewed, whose names and identities have been changed. Their willingness to share their very personal and private experiences, in the hope that others might benefit, added immeasurably to our book.

And last, but certainly not least, we want to thank our friends and colleagues for their encouragement, loyalty and patience.

Introduction

We wrote this book so that men and their partners would not have to endure an erection problem in silence and despair, thinking there was nothing to be done.

The fact is that now, about 90 percent of all men with erection problems can be treated successfully. In recent years, there has been a virtual revolution in the ways erection problems can be diagnosed and solved. If there's one message we want to convey to our readers—men and women—it's that you don't have to be deprived of the pleasure of intercourse. We tell you how to find the expert assistance you need, and what you can do to help yourself—and your partner.

An erection problem is not a sentence to life without intercourse. Very often, impotence is the body's way of signaling a health problem which needs to be properly treated. Sometimes, the solution is as simple as changing some daily habits. Other times, medical treatment is needed—treatment which may include a combination of sophisticated tests and procedures. But almost always, the problem can be solved and the man and his partner can go back to enjoying a full, complete sex life.

Most of us have grown up with myths about sexuality, and certainly misinformation about erection is widespread. The complexity—and the delicacy—of the erection process are explained in our book. Once you understand what goes on, and how easy it is to disturb the system, you'll be better equipped to avoid self-sabotage. And you'll know the importance of getting help early, so a simple difficulty doesn't develop into something more complicated.

We also explain why growing older does not mean

sex must become a thing of the past. Impotence is not a normal part of aging. Whether you are 50, 60, 70 or older, you don't have to be deprived of sexual enjoyment.

Potency is an issue for men *and* women. As you read this book, you'll meet men and women who encountered a potency problem. Some faced the problem, sought help, discovered a solution and even found their relationship became stronger as a result of their shared experience. Some were afraid of facing the problem, but, happily, were able to overcome their anxieties and obtain proper treatment. And some, sadly, only got help after many years of pain, after emotional estrangement from their loved ones and self-blame had taken their toll. We think their stories will move you, hold your attention and educate you.

Finally, this is a book to share. Whether you are a man or a woman, young or old, married or single, we hope you'll share the information with those closest to you. Use it where it can do the most good.

AIDS and Other Sexually Transmitted Diseases

Some men think that if they have an erection problem and cannot have intercourse, they won't get a sexually transmitted disease. This is *not* true. You can get AIDS or another sexually transmitted disease if you share bodily fluids with an infected person, by vaginal, oral, or anal sex. Also, having an implant provides no protection whatsoever from contracting a sexually transmitted disease, or from giving it to anyone else.

Apart from celibacy, the only way to protect yourself from being infected is to have a monogamous relationship with a person who is not infected with any sexually transmitted disease. If there is any doubt about either partner's health, a condom will provide good (but not absolute) protection. Consult your physician or local health department for more information.

1

What's Normal?

Male potency is one of the last sexual topics in America left in the closet. Men who have trouble getting an erection have told us over and over that no one knew about their problem. "I've never even told my best buddy," says one man. Confides another: "I discussed it briefly with some male friends. But I couldn't carry it any further. Men just aren't comfortable discussing it."

It's not surprising that most men don't discuss sexual potency among themselves except to brag about their exploits or their size. For many men, being potent is an essential, basic ingredient of their self-image: what makes a man a *man*. But men should have a reliable, accurate source of information about potency. They should know that impotence, whether temporary or long-term, is a very common problem. That being "normal" isn't being a superstud, able to perform on command. That few men get great erections every time. That if there is a long-term problem, there's a 90 percent chance it can be treated successfully.

Most changes in potency aren't a problem, but do require some adjustment. "When I was in college I could play a couple of games of soccer, run a few laps around the track and make love three times in the same day—no problem!" says Gene, a stocky, muscular 40-year-old man. Smiling a bit wistfully at the memory he adds, "Of course, that was 20 years ago. Times have changed and so have I." Joseph, a divorced college professor, says, "When I was in my 20's, I could take a woman out after a long day at work, have dinner and a few drinks, go dancing and then go home with her and make love." He shakes his head incredulously and says, "Now, in the same scenario, 25 years later, there's a big difference. By the time I get her home, I'm exhausted from work, dinner and making a good impression—never mind the dancing. I just want to go to sleep! But," Joseph continues, grinning, "the next morning I'm ready. Really ready."

Joseph's behavior is common among men, and nothing to worry about. A man's sexual response changes as he matures, along with other physical attributes like eyesight, hair color and skin tone. But the emphasis is on the word "change," because with good health and a willing partner, a man should be able to enjoy sex no matter what his age.

There's Reuben, for example, a spry retired military man who's taken such good care of himself over the years that he passes for 70 even though he's pushing 86. He's active and involved with many things—not the least of which is romance. But still he showed up at a clinic worried about his love life. And unlike some men, who have difficulty discussing such matters, Reuben wasn't interested in small talk. He got right to the point: "I'm worried about not being able to get an erection sometimes," he told his doctor. "I have three girlfriends, and I usually visit each one a couple of times a week." While many men would envy this performance record, Reuben found himself unable to make love as often as he wanted. He was afraid his body might be "giving out" on him.

As it turned out, there was nothing wrong with Reuben or the way his body was working. Far from it, in fact. At 85 he was able to have intercourse quite often. His only problem was that he wanted his body to function a little better than most men of any age can rightfully expect. He's a good example of a man with unrealistic expectations worrying unnecessarily about erection. And he's not unusual. Many men don't really know what is meant by the word "impotence."

It's Not What You Think

When we use the terms *impotence* or *erection problem* in this book, we simply mean that the erection is absent, or that it can't be maintained firmly enough to have sexual intercourse. We don't like referring to a man as "impotent" because that's attaching a label that can make him feel powerless or ineffectual. Unfortunately, impotence is a word loaded with meanings which have nothing to do with a man's ability to get and maintain an erection. A dictionary defines impotent as "lacking in power, strength or vigor: helpless." But the common association of sexual impotence with powerlessness is nonsense. A man can be successful, happy and in charge of many aspects of his life and still have erection problems, just like he can have any other health problems. When it happens, impotence is a problem, but it's one that usually can be solved. You can take charge of the erection problem in much the same way you deal with other types of health and life problems—by getting informed and getting help. The important thing is to see it as a health problem, not a statement about your worth as a man or a lover.

Doctors use the term *primary impotence* to mean that a man has never been able to have and maintain an erection that's sufficiently firm for intercourse; *secondary impotence* is the term used for patients who have had healthy, normal erections, but now find themselves with erection problems. You may also hear medical people describing impotence as "erectile dysfunction." It's important for doctors to have these definitions, but it is equally important for you not to let the words stop you from seeking help. One man avoided going to a sexual dysfunction clinic at a major medical center because he was so turned off by the word "dysfunction." He felt that showing up at the clinic would be an announcement to the world that he was something less than a man. (Some health professionals recognize this problem and have given their clinics more encouraging names.)

The Ignorance Trap

Whatever the specific type of erection problem, it can make a man feel like an essential part of his identity is gone. He can become very depressed, critical of himself and insecure about his partner. Without a doubt, for many men erection difficulties can cause far more stress than other health problems.

And men often suffer that stress alone, since the whole subject of potency is taboo. Joseph, the divorced college professor, has friends who can talk about almost anything—but the subject of erections is still off limits. "After all, a guy who's impotent doesn't say, 'Hi, just call me limpy,'" jokes Joseph.

Fred would certainly agree. A 39-year-old married man, Fred has never talked about sex or potency with male friends. "I don't know men who really talk about sex. One summer I worked in a factory to make money for school, and the guys on the assembly line would brag about all the women they had. But it was just showing off." Fred believes most men are not comfortable showing their vulnerability to another man. "Men are taught to be self-reliant, not to complain a lot. A lot of men think talking about problems is just complaining. And sex is one of the most difficult areas to talk about in any kind of meaningful way." This reticence makes it difficult for a man to get accurate information.

Many women, sad to say, share the same misconceptions about potency. Here's what one divorced, middle-aged man has to say about women: "They don't understand that, just like a woman can really have a headache, a man can really be tired. A lot of women react to that by having their feelings hurt. I've had women tell me I must not find them attractive—when I was just honestly exhausted." In this scenario, the penis is seen as some sort of ultimate lie detector, showing a man's true feelings by not acknowledging a woman's attractiveness with an erection.

Ignorance about potency among women also plays a big role in the communication snafu. Many women simply never learned anything about male physiology. "I had no formal sex education, none!" says Lyla, an attractive 37-year-old woman who runs the personnel department for a large state agency. "My assumption was just that a man got hard on demand. I thought he could say, 'I want an erection' and there it would be. That simple!" Growing up, Lyla got her information about sexuality from her girlfriend—"she was much more experienced than me, she was considered fast"—and her older sisters. "They told me you could look at a man's hand and tell how big his penis was. I believed that. They believed that. Why not?" She laughs. "I just didn't have any basis for believing that a man couldn't just make an erection happen. Later, when I got older, I felt sometimes that I was in control, that a man would get an erection in reaction to how sexy I was. But I didn't really understand the process. In fact, when I was younger, I thought men were hard all the time. I didn't even know they were usually soft, and had to get an erection."

Even people who are knowledgeable and worldly about many things may nonetheless continue to be very ignorant of the basic facts of potency. There's Peter, for example, a 63-year-old, successful businessman with two grown children. He was married for 30 years and enjoyed a good emotional and sexual relationship with his wife before she died last year. Usually a calm, somewhat formal gentleman, he becomes noticeably agitated when asked about his understanding of erection. "I never had any sex education from anywhere! I had very little knowledge of erection. Until recently, I didn't even know it was blood entering the penis that made the erection."

And it's not just men of Peter's generation who don't know important information about how the male body works. Adam is 39, a college-educated hotel manager, married for 12 years. "We grew up on a farm, so we learned some things just from seeing the animals. But not enough. When I was 15 I started having 'wet dreams,' and I was sure I was terribly abnormal in some way. I used to have this one dream about a naked woman swinging through the air on a trapeze. I had the same dream and the same results for several months." He smiles at the recollection, clearly enjoying the picture in his mind. "Finally I went to my older brother—he was about 23 at the time—and he explained what was happening to me. He was helpful and supportive. At that point in time I had no understanding of the basic physiology of erection, and I'm pretty sure I don't know too much to this day. I went to a big state university and belonged to a fraternity. We never talked about sex seriously, just about it as a conquest. We never talked about any *problems* with sex." Even now, Adam acknowledges, the subject makes him nervous.

Sometimes, lack of knowledge can lead to years of anxiety. Frank remembers some difficult times: "I had an operation on my testicles when I was about 6 years old," says this insurance company vice president. He lowers his voice and continues: "My testicles were filling up with fluid. The thing I didn't know for years was that they didn't operate on my penis. I thought my penis was shaped funny because of the surgery. I thought they cut my penis. When I saw other guys in high school gym class I knew my penis was okay, that the 'seam' on the backside of the penis was normal, not the line where they cut me. But thinking I had a scar, that I had been cut, that I was sort of lopsided, that caused me a lot of anxiety for a long time."

Frank didn't have a brother in whom he could confide or compare his penis to see if his was normal. So he never told anyone of his fears. Sex education was not a big part of his home life. "Once my dad brought home a book—he got it from the doctor, I think. Anyway it was very technical and anatomical. I was supposed to read it and then meet with him later in the day if I had any questions." He stops, and almost snorts the next sentence. "I didn't have any questions.

My dad seemed very embarrassed—more so even than me."

Frank, married for 15 years to a woman who is a social worker, believes that he's learned to be more open about sex, and it's an easier topic for him than it used to be. "But," he says, "I still wouldn't initiate such a conversation."

Doctors Don't Always Know

Surprisingly, even many physicians don't have a good grasp of the subject of erection, although they've been exposed to some basic physiological facts. Nowadays, many medical schools include some information about human sexuality in their curriculum, but doctors already in practice may not have received such training. And they may not be comfortable with the subject. The end result of all this can be a physician susceptible to the myths about erection.

Just a few years ago, most physicians were taught that the vast majority of impotence cases were caused by psychological factors. Now that we know more about erection and researchers have begun studying the effects of illness on erection, it's thought that at least 50 percent of all impotence has a physical cause or a physical contributing factor. But this information has been slow in reaching many physicians and other health care professionals already in practice. Doctors who don't specialize in erection problems may remain ignorant of the new information.

For example, one internist who sees a lot of elderly patients told us she thought most cases of impotence were caused by psychological problems. And although sexuality was a concern of her patients, she didn't think much could be done to help men with erection problems.

Thinking like that can cause a lot of needless unhappiness and confusion. Take, for example, Bill's experience. About a year ago, he began having a problem with potency. At the age of 49, happily married for the second time, Bill felt secure in his relationship with his wife, Janice. Still, he sometimes could not get an erection, although he felt very aroused and wanted to make love. Bill had never had a problem with sex before, and he was puzzled and troubled. So was Janice.

They didn't know what to do. Bill felt rather uncomfortable about asking anyone about his problem. But, in what he regarded as a fortunate circumstance, he became ill and had to go see his family doctor. There, he mustered his courage and told the doctor matter-of-factly: "I can't get an erection like I used to." The physician responded, "Well, you're not as young as you used to be." And that was that. Bill was too embarrassed to say anything else. But he was angry: 49 was far too young to put sex on the shelf. He didn't think Janice wanted to live without sex, either. Bill believed there had to be more to his problem, and after some anxious and uncomfortable weeks he decided to find another doctor.

Bill was right to doubt his doctor. His age was no explanation for the changes he was experiencing. It would be normal for it to take Bill a little longer to get an erection than it did ten years before. But even with direct stimulation and allowing plenty of time, Bill just could not get an erection.

Fortunately, Bill searched persistently until he found a urologist who specialized in sexual potency. The doctor was able to find—and treat—the cause of his difficulty.

Unfortunately, Bill's experience is not unique. Doctors aren't immune to the prejudices in our society, and one of the strongest of those prejudices says that older men inevitably lose their ability for and interest in sex—and they should just accept this as a sad but inevitable fact. Researchers at Oregon Health Sciences University found that some doctors reacted to older men with sexual problems differently than they did to younger patients. Their work suggests that doctors are more likely to write off the potency problems of older men, while those of younger men are taken seriously.

This medical ignorance can be tragic. Ask Ralph, a 43-year-old co-owner of a small business. He's been married for 17 years, and has been a diabetic for 15. (Diabetes sometimes can cause impotence, as we explain in chapter 4.) He had erection problems—and doctor problems—for a long time. "You've got supposedly sophisticated, knowledgeable medical people who think impotence is primarily psychological. My wife's doctor told her it was all in my head. I thought it was all in my head. I want to know why we can't have a campaign to educate doctors."

Initially, Ralph paid a high price for this misinformation. "Thinking it was in my head caused stress and I went through a lot of problems." Fortunately, Ralph didn't settle for the first information he received. He did some reading on his own, and found a doctor who was able to help him.

In addition to knowledge, the attitude of the professional helping you is important. (We explain how to find someone who can help you in chapter 7.) Mason learned this the hard way. A 42-year-old government worker, he went to many different professionals for help with a long-term potency problem. "In general," he says, "there's a lack of knowledge. Some didn't care. My wife and I went to a minister who said he had done impotence counseling. Well, we wanted to discuss difficulties with erection. He wanted to talk about everything else, to go all around the subject. He didn't really want to get into impotence."

Professionals aren't the only source of help. Support groups, while no substitute for individual diagnosis and treatment, can provide valuable information. Local chapters of these groups are available in many areas, and more are springing up around the country (see chapter 6 for more information).

Shattering the Myths

There are many common myths that cause a lot of problems for the men and women who believe them. It's time to lay these myths to rest.

Myth: Impotence is the normal result of aging.
Fact: Impotence is not normal. Men do experience *changes* in their erections as they age, but a healthy man can still enjoy a fulfilling sex life well into old age.

Many men associate their 40's with the beginning of an "inevitable decline" in potency. Because their erections are different than when they were younger, they may see themselves as on the decline sexually. This is wrong. (Certainly, they wouldn't expect to run a mile with the same speed as they did in high school—but they could still expect to cover the distance. And they might enjoy the scenery more.)

It is true that you're more likely to develop diseases as you age. Therefore, the chances of developing erection problems do increase with age. But these erection difficulties are the result of disease, not aging itself. Many of the health problems which can cause impotence can be prevented.

Myth: Impotence is usually a psychological, not a physical problem.
Fact: If you think this is true, you're certainly not alone. Many health professionals still believe "it's all in your head." We've talked with many patients who were told just that, despite a history of health problems that could easily account for the impotence.

Michael, for example, is a 70-year-old with a history of vascular problems. A complete examination and tests revealed that these blood-flow difficulties made it impossible for him to have an erection. After some discussion with his wife and physician, Michael decided to have a penile implant. (We discuss these in detail in chapter 8.)

Shortly before the surgery, Michael visited another physician on an unrelated matter. Upon hearing that Michael was having the operation, the doctor tried to discourage him. "It's unnecessary surgery," he insisted. "The problem is in your mind." Michael wisely ignored this inaccurate information. Since having the surgery he's enjoyed a very satisfying sex life.

Myth: Men who have been very active sexually while

young will wear out faster than men who have conserved their resources.

Fact: There's no evidence to support the belief that we are given a finite amount of sexual energy when we're born, and once we use it up, it's gone forever. Instead, research indicates that sexual energy may be a renewable resource; after you use it, you replenish your supply so it will be available again. The more sexually active you are when young, the more likely it is that you will continue to enjoy sex in your later years. After all, sexuality is an important and vital part of life.

"I had a very good sexual relationship with my wife," says Russell, a 69-year-old widower who was married for 26 years. "In fact, there was a period of several months when I was in my late 40's when my sex drive actually increased. I don't know what to attribute this to. I really didn't notice any difference as I've aged—I've always enjoyed it."

The belief that you will lose your sexuality as you age, however, can have a powerful negative effect. And thinking that your active sex life will continue as long as you so desire can have a correspondingly positive influence.

Myth: Occasional impotence always develops into a chronic problem.

Fact: Most men experience occasional impotence at some point in their lives, and while it's unwelcome, it's not usually a sign of a chronic condition. Occasional erection problems are often caused by alcohol, medication, stress (don't underestimate the power of pressure) or exhaustion. Knowing what can trigger an episode of impotence often enables you to take steps to prevent it (see chapter 3). And self-knowledge can save you lots of needless anxiety.

One night, for example, Thomas, a 32-year-old electrician, could not get an erection. It was the first time he and his new girlfriend, Julie, were trying to make love. Thomas cared for her, but getting involved with Julie was complicating his life in many ways. He felt confused about the new attachment he was forming.

That first time, Thomas blamed his erection problem on the bottle of wine he'd just polished off. But later in the week, he found himself again without an erection, although he felt aroused and Julie was clearly eager to have sex with him. This time he had had nothing to drink, and felt he had no excuse for not getting an erection.

Although Thomas usually had a good sex life, he had experienced occasional problems, and he knew how to handle the situation. He calmly explained to Julie, "Sometimes this happens. It just takes a little patience. After a while, it will go away." He wasn't happy about his erection difficulties, but he wasn't going to go crazy because of the problem, either. Julie, sensitive to his feelings, decided not to push the issue. "I didn't want to harp on it," she says. "I didn't want to make it into a huge problem."

As it turned out, the next afternoon everything changed. "We had a wonderful time," Julie remembers, smiling. "Everything was fine. I really think it was just an issue of trust and security, of feeling accepted."

Myth: Alcohol plus sex equals better sex.

Fact: A small amount of alcohol may relax you, but anything more can leave you willing but unable. Bert, for example, a young, healthy man who had never experienced any problems with erections, went out drinking with some old friends. He spent several hours guzzling beer, almost nonstop. Then, feeling very friendly, he went back to his girlfriend's apartment. But his body wouldn't cooperate. No erection at all. A lot of alcohol every once in a while may result in temporary impotence, but when you recover from the binge, your potency should return. In fact, this may happen before your headache disappears.

Alcoholics, on the other hand, may find that impotence is a *chronic* problem. (We discuss this in detail in chapter 3.) The bottom line: Men who drink a lot are playing Russian roulette with their ability to enjoy intercourse.

Myth: Medications rarely cause impotence.
Fact: This is false. Many men fail to make the connection between medications and impotence, but there is a strong one—a fact that many physicians neglect to tell their patients (see chapter 3).

It's important to realize, though, that individuals react differently. A drug that causes problems in Harry may have little or no effect on Paul. And although certain types of medications are well known as possible impotence-causers, knowledge in this area is changing and increasing so that in the future perhaps even more drugs will be identified as causing potency difficulties. In general, stopping the medication that's causing the problem will clear it up. (Always consult your doctor first.)

But remember that drugs in *combination* with other drugs and everyday substances can have an effect far more powerful than the drug alone. A man who takes a pill for his cold, has a beer, puts drops in his eyes and smokes a cigarette is ingesting a large number of chemicals. Any one of them may work against his potency. Together, they can wreak havoc on his ability to get or maintain an erection.

Myth: Vasectomies cause impotence.
Fact: When a surgeon performs a vasectomy, he makes an incision in the scrotum and cuts the tube which carries the sperm from the testicle to the penis. This operation does not affect the arteries, veins, and nerves which cause erections. However, if a man does not want to have a vasectomy and gets one anyway, it's possible that the psychological distress he suffers could cause erection problems.

Myth: The smaller your penis, the more likely you are to experience erection problems.
Fact: There's no evidence that this is true. The size of the penis bears no relation to predicting erection problems. Arteries, veins and nerves are the crucial elements for erection, and these can function properly, or cause problems, regardless of the size of the penis. In fact, the size difference between erect penises is usually

quite insignificant. And many women, while recognizing that men care about size, think the quality of lovemaking, not the length of the penis, is the issue.

Myth: Masturbation causes impotence.

Fact: This comes from the erroneous belief that we're given a limited amount of sexual energy, and once we use it up, it's gone. This is not true. Masturbation is normal and pleasurable, and does not lead to erection problems. For people without a partner, masturbation may be the only sexual outlet available.

Normal Changes in Sexual Potency

Now that we've punched holes in some common myths, let's look at the changes a man should expect, and how he can turn them to his and his partner's advantage.

As you age, you undergo changes—normal changes. The differences will not be apparent overnight. You won't notice a sudden change in performance when you turn 40, or 50 or 60—unless, perhaps, you persuade yourself that such will be the case. The changes occur gradually, and each individual has his own particular pattern, with some men noticing changes earlier than others. But some changes are almost universally associated with aging:

- A longer period of time is needed to reach an erection. (Some interesting work has been done to actually measure this change. Two researchers at the University of Southern California showed the same erotic movie to two groups of men and measured their responses. The men who were between 19 and 30 years of age developed erections almost six times faster than the men between 48 and 65 years old.)
- The erection may be slightly less firm than when a man was younger.
- It's easier to delay orgasm and ejaculation.
- Ejaculation is less forceful. (For some men, the ejaculation is also slightly less pleasurable.)

- Less fluid is ejaculated.
- After orgasm, erection is lost more quickly.
- And, perhaps the most noticed change: There's a longer period of "down time" between erections.

A man will usually experience these changes over a period of many years, generally beginning in his 30's. Typically, they come on gradually, and sometimes are so subtle they won't be noticed for a long time. Many of these changes will be insignificant; some will be welcome; some will require some adjustment. If you and your partner know what's normal for your particular age group, you'll know when something's amiss. And if you do develop an erection problem that persists, you'll know when to get help.

Adolescence and Early 20's: Erection Ease

A healthy young man in his teens and early 20's should have no trouble getting erections. In fact, he may embarrass himself with erections in awkward situations.

Paul can remember what that feels like. Now 39 and married for more than a decade, Paul recalls his adolescent potency with a mixture of fondness and humor: "I'd be sitting in class with an erection—I'd sometimes have an erection all day long. And it could be embarrassing—you'd have to lose it before you could stand up. I was actually looking for the day when that didn't happen." His tanned face breaks out in a big grin. Maturity hasn't diminished his sense of humor. "Now, Lord knows, I can sit for hours."

A man who's in late adolescence or early adulthood can have intercourse two or three times within a fairly short period of time. (One man recounted with great pride a memorable afternoon in which he had intercourse four times in four hours.) At this age, a man's sexual appetite is strong, and so is his ability to get an erection. Consequently, on a purely physical level, foreplay may not be tremendously important. In fact, for some men this age, foreplay doesn't exist.

The Middle Years:
Less Urgency, More Enjoyment

In just a few years, this quick-as-lightning erection response will have slowed down. A man in his 30's is not likely to suffer the embarrassment Paul so fondly recalled. It takes the more mature man a bit more time to become erect. In healthy men, this is a gradual change, and the slowed response can lead a man to be more interested and involved in foreplay, to the benefit and pleasure of himself and his partner.

Jennifer has been married to Douglas for 15 years. They met while both were in college, and married 2 years after graduation. She's noticed a change in Douglas, but for her, it's a positive one: "Doug has always been a good lover," she says, smiling. "But I have to say that he's become less—well, hurried, in the last few years. He's much more willing to hold me and caress me. When we were in school, he was much more task oriented. Now, he'll spend lots of time with me before starting intercourse—and our sex life is terrific."

As a man gets older, it will usually take him a longer time to reach orgasm and ejaculate. A man may find it easier to control his ejaculation, and to delay it. Jennifer has noticed this change in Doug, and both of them are happy about it. "It's much easier to last longer," Doug says. "In some ways, sex is better now than it was a few years ago. I used to have a greater sense of urgency. Now I can relax and enjoy myself without consciously having to try so hard to delay my orgasm." For many men in their early 20's, this would be difficult or impossible.

Generally, as a man gets older, he'll notice that his orgasms may be somewhat less intense. And the amount of fluid he ejaculates is somewhat less. The orgasm may last a shorter period of time. The amount of force which propels the semen out of the penis is reduced. Even men in their 30's may notice this last change: "I notice a difference in ejaculation. It's not as strong as when I was 18. I squirt less far. When I was younger there'd be this tremendous pressure," says Paul. (This change in the forcefulness of ejaculation may be due to a slight weakening in the muscles at the base of the penis, as we explain in chapter 2.)

The Later Years: The Need for More Stimulation

As a man ages, more stimulation and time may be required before he attains a firm erection. Caressing the penis may become a necessary (and pleasurable) prelude in order for an older man to achieve an erection.

For example, George, a 65-year-old, came to a urologist saying, "Nothing happens down there. I used to be able to get an erection just by looking at a pretty woman. My wife is a very beautiful woman, and in the past I've always been able to just look at her and get an erection. Now I'm still very attracted to my wife, but I look at her, and nothing happens. I can watch her getting undressed, I feel excited, but my penis just lies there." However, George did report that he was able to get a satisfactory erection with oral sex.

George needed to know whether this change was normal. The urologist told him that some foreplay would be necessary for him to get an erection. At this age, visual stimulation wasn't enough. He needed some "hands-on" encouragement. George was surprised to learn that his changes were normal. He wasn't entirely pleased by the information, but he was willing to make the necessary adjustments. And his sex life improved considerably.

As a man goes into his later years, he may find a difference in the firmness of erections. Men over age 60 frequently have slightly less firm erections. By itself, this small change usually poses no problem. Older women, however, often have less vaginal lubrication, another natural result of aging. The combination of a slightly less firm penis with a drier vagina can make intercourse difficult. But a solution is readily at hand: use of a water-based lubricant. The problem we're describing is definitely not impotence.

Unlike men in their mid-years who ejaculate with less force, some older men may find they have intercourse with no ejaculation at all. Some men are bothered by this change; for others, it's of little consequence. The plus to this situation, of course, is that these men can enjoy intercourse for longer periods of time.

After ejaculation, the older man will lose his erection more quickly than he did in his younger years. A young man might find himself with an erection even after ejaculation, but this is certainly not typical of a man in his 50's or older.

One change which comes naturally with age is especially significant. The time period between erections increases. Noticeably. Understandably, this is probably the most disturbing and unwanted change. For some men in their 60's, it may be hours between erections, even with stimulation. For others, it may be days. There's a lot of individual variation, but the general trend is more time between erections. This is normal and does not mean the man is impotent. Try thinking of this as a resting time from intercourse, but *not* from other types of sexual activity.

These changes appear gradually in healthy men, over time. For some men, they come on so slowly they are hardly noticeable.

So, for the most part, these changes shouldn't pose a problem for the well-informed man and his partner. And understanding how the penis becomes erect can actually add to your enjoyment—and that of your partner.

2

The Magic: What Happens When You Get an Erection

What is the magic behind the mystery? While erections seem to just "happen," erection is really a very complicated process that involves hidden nerves, arteries, veins, hormones and, of course, some more visible parts of a man's body like the penis and testicles. Although a lot is known about the intricacies of erection, it is still veiled in mystery.

Lifting the veil is important, because understanding how erections happen can help explain why they sometimes don't. And this knowledge will also help you and your partner understand why it's normal for a man's erections to vary somewhat in size, firmness and duration—or even, on occasion, fail to appear.

Since the subject is anatomy, you may find it helpful to examine yourself or your partner while reading this chapter. In fact, couples might benefit from reviewing the material together to see for themselves just what we are describing.

The Penis

The *penis* is where erection all comes together, but the penis isn't acting alone. Looking at one, it might be difficult to imagine that it contains thousands of tiny blood vessels and a sophisticated network of nerves. The mystery deepens when you consider that all this complicated biological machinery must work together to control the flow of blood which produces an erection.

Long cylinders called the *corpora cavernosa* run down each side of the penis. These paired cylinders have to fill with blood for a man to obtain an erection.

The Penis

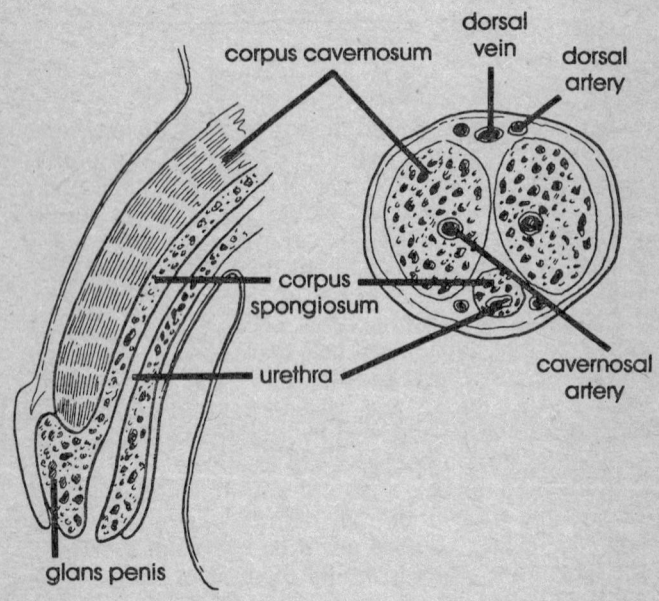

They are like long balloons: When pumped up with blood they are erect; when vacant, they are not erect. And they hold a lot of blood. When erect, the penis holds about eight times as much blood as when flaccid.

A tube called the *urethra* runs along the bottom of the penis. The urethra carries sperm and urine, but not, thankfully, at the same time. When a man ejaculates, a valve between the urethra and the bladder closes off the bladder and allows only sperm to pass. Although some sperm may be washed out when a man urinates, in general the same sophisticated valve system prevents sperm from traveling down the urethra when a man is urinating.

Surrounding the urethra is other spongelike tissue called the *corpus spongiosum*. This area also fills with blood during an erection. It is connected to the most sensitive part of the penis, the tip or head, called the glans penis.

The *glans penis* is a little bonus from nature, an extra source of sexual enjoyment for the man. It normally becomes firmer and larger when a man is aroused. And a man will respond more quickly to stimulation at this point than anywhere else along the penis.

The skin of the penis slides easily over the entire penile shaft. All males are born with an extension of this skin, called the *foreskin*, which covers the glans penis. However, it has been very common for American men to have had the foreskin removed shortly after birth with a minor surgery called circumcision. (There is usually no medical reason for circumcision, and these days many parents choose not to circumcise their baby boys.)

Despite what you may have read or heard, the penis itself has no muscles. (Consequently, exercise or activity will not permanently change the size or the shape of the penis.) However, there are important muscles at the base of the penis that rhythmically contract and propel the semen down the urethra and out the penis.

These muscles are somewhat unusual, because they operate both automatically and under a man's conscious control. For example, during ejaculation, a man does not decide to contract these muscles; it just happens. However, a man does have conscious control over these muscles sometimes. If a man contracts the muscles at the base of his penis when he has an erection, he can increase the firmness of his erection for a few seconds. (Some sex therapists recommend exercises to increase the strength of these muscles, as we explain in chapter 6.)

As a man ages, the muscles become less powerful, and his ejaculation may have a little less force. Also, because these muscles help him void urine completely, an older man with somewhat relaxed muscles may find himself dribbling a small amount of urine after he thinks he's finished.

The Testicles

Behind the penis are the *testicles,* two ball-shaped glands that are vitally important to erection. Normal testicles feel something like hard-boiled eggs when you touch them. Men usually learn at a fairly early age that their testicles are vulnerable and quite sensitive to pain. (Falling off a bike or being kicked in the groin during a game of touch football can reinforce that knowledge quite effectively.)

In the womb, a male fetus's testicles actually change location. They form near the kidneys, but during the last three months of pregnancy descend into the bag that holds them, the *scrotum*. It's not uncommon for a baby boy to be born with a testicle that has not completely descended into the scrotum. During the first year of life, an undescended testicle may actually fall into place on its own. If it doesn't, a simple operation can place the testicle in the scrotum. Still, two normal, functioning testicles aren't essential for healthy sex. Men with one normally functioning testicle don't have any more problems with potency than their doubly endowed counterparts.

If you examine yourself (or your husband), you'll notice a soft swelling on the back of the testicles. This sensitive area is called the *epididymis,* and it's the home for the sperm as they mature. Lots of things—injuries, infections (such as mumps), certain other types of disease—may cause problems with sperm production, thus affecting a man's ability to father a child.

But nature has done a good job of protecting the hormones that play a major role in a man's ability to have a healthy, firm erection. The production of *male hormones* in the testicles is separate from sperm production, and far more resistant to damage. That's why the vast majority of infertile men have no more difficulty with erections than their fertile counterparts. In fact, there's a big difference between fertility and potency.

Fertility refers to a man's ability to father a child. Generally, in order for a man to do that, he has to ejaculate normal sperm. Potency means a man can get and maintain an erection. *Erection is a separate process from ejaculation, so erection and fertility do not go hand-in-hand.* It's fairly common knowledge that a man can have an erection and not ejaculate; however, many people are not aware that a man can have an ejaculation without an erection. Many men who lose their ability to have an erection still become aroused and, with stimulation, can ejaculate.

This means that a man with erection problems can still get a woman pregnant. He can father a child using artificial insemination. Or, if he ejaculates in the entrance of a woman's vagina, it's possible that she could become pregnant. The chances of this happening, of course, are significantly less than with intercourse, when a man ejaculates very close to the entrance of the womb.

Testosterone, one of the hormones produced by the testicles, deserves special mention. Just how testosterone influences erection is still something of a mystery. There are men with erection problems who have low testosterone levels, and they can be successfully treated with injections of this hormone. What's confusing is that there are also men with low levels of the hormone who have no problems getting and maintaining erections. So it appears that there's a fair amount of individual variation in how much testosterone the body needs.

Some testosterone, however, is essential to sexual desire. When there's just a bare minimum of testosterone in his body, a man's sexual interest is greatly reduced or disappears completely. Along with this discouraging change comes a decreased volume of ejaculate and persistent low energy. The transformation that can occur when low-testosterone men are treated properly is truly remarkable. Men with low testosterone

---

Self-Exam

It's important to examine your testicles regularly for cancer, even though testicular cancer is relatively rare. Men 18 to 32 years old and over 60 run a higher than average risk of getting testicular cancer. But anyone can be vulnerable.

If left untreated, this cancer can lead to death. Fortunately, removal of the diseased testicle often halts the cancer. Removal of one testicle will not affect potency. If both testicles are removed (a very rare occurrence), potency problems can result. While potency can be restored with testosterone shots, it's best to catch the cancer early. That's why self-examination is so important. Here's how to do it.

Hold the testicle with both hands, so it doesn't slip around. (It's important in doing this exam that you know the location of your epididymis, since you could mistake it for trouble. The epididymis is normally a soft, sausage-shaped organ, running up and down the back of the testicle. It feels like a bump when you touch it. There's a slight groove between the testicle and the epididymis.) Lightly massage the whole surface of each testicle, using both hands. You should not feel any hard lumps. If you do feel one, see your family physician or a urologist immediately. If found early, testicular cancer is virtually 100 percent curable.

Play it safe and give yourself an exam once a month. It only takes a couple of minutes, but it can save your life.

levels who are listless, sexually uninterested and withdrawn can undergo a major personality change when they receive the correct care.

Take Mark, for example, who lost both testicles to cancer when he was 27. The surgery saved his life but left him without the ability to get or maintain an erection. Because he had no testicles, his body made no testosterone, except for the insignificant amount produced by his adrenal glands. Mark was told to take testosterone pills to offset the loss. But unknown to Mark, the prescribed dosage was too low. He was left with no sexual desire and only token explanations.

For years, Mark accepted his doctor's assurances that everything possible was being done to help him. Other doctors told him his impotence was psychologically caused, that he had not recovered mentally from the trauma of having his testicles removed. This went on for ten long years, until finally Mark heard about some new treatments for impotence. He made a decision that turned his sex life around: He sought another opinion. After evaluating Mark, the urologist injected him with a much larger dose of testosterone. Three weeks later, Mark was a new man. He was energetic and enthusiastic, and happily reported that his sex drive was back—and very strong. Mark will always have to give himself testosterone shots on a regular basis. And he'll have to come in for routine checkups. But that's a small price to pay for a normal life after a decade of bad advice and no sexual intercourse.

It's important that testosterone not be seen as a miracle substance or a cure-all. Increasing testosterone so that it's above the normal level doesn't turn a man into a sexual superstud. In fact, too much testosterone can actually throw a monkey wrench into a man's sexual functioning, and possibly cause other health problems. A man with normal testosterone levels can find himself in a no-win situation if he takes the hormone.

A case in point is Jerry, a college athlete who took testosterone for more than a year to help build up his muscles. Jerry's body responded to the extra (unneeded) amounts of the hormone by shutting down his own testicles' production of testosterone. Unfortunately, when Jerry stopped taking the shots, his body didn't get the message. Several months after he stopped the injections, Jerry's system was still out of whack. His pituitary gland was taking a very long time to send messages to his testicles to start producing testosterone again. After six months, Jerry's sexual desire began gradually returning, and his testosterone level started its slow climb back to normal. Jerry was lucky; he gambled with his health and his sexuality, but he recovered. Not surprisingly, he vowed never to take the hormone again.

Unfortunately, particularly in the case of older men, some physicians still prescribe testosterone to patients with erection problems without first doing tests to see if the hormone is abnormally low. (More about the tests you should expect is found in chapter 7.) We believe this is a real disservice to the men who do have adequate testosterone levels because their problem remains undiagnosed and untreated. Moreover, their testicles may stop producing testosterone and take time to revert to normal after the shots have stopped.

Two other male hormones also influence potency. *Luteinizing hormone* (LH) is made by the pituitary gland in the brain; it stimulates the testicles to produce testosterone. Low levels of LH caused by pituitary disease can lead to low testosterone and potency problems. The other hormone, *prolactin,* is also made by the pituitary gland. Very high levels of prolactin, sometimes caused by tumors in the pituitary gland, can block the effectiveness of testosterone in the body and decrease sexual desire. Simple blood tests can measure the levels of these hormones in the body.

The Blood-Pumping System

The penis, testicles and other organs can't do everything on their own. They need help. Vital to erection are the *arteries* that expand and carry extra amounts of blood to the penis when a man is sexually aroused. Without increased flow, there can be no erection. The crucial locations for this blood-flow activity are the corpora cavernosa, those two long cylinders which run down each side of the penis. Inside the corpora cavernosa are thousands of small, balloonlike cavities called sinuses. Important arteries run into the corpora cavernosa and connect with these sinuses. When a man gets an erection, the arteries supply the sinuses with blood, causing them to expand. The penis then becomes larger and firmer.

Also located in the corpora cavernosa are thousands of tiny, thin-walled veins which normally drain blood from the sinuses. These veins play a far more important role in this process than many physicians have thought. New research shows that veins have to function properly for a man to get and maintain a good, firm erection. Research by Tom Lue, M.D., urologist, and his colleagues at the University of California, indicates that pressure from the expanding sinuses compresses the thin-walled veins and thus slows down the blood flow out of the penis. But, if things don't work properly and the veins are not squeezed enough by the arterial sinuses, the increased blood flowing into the penis will only flow back out, leaving a man with no erection, or a poorly sustained one.

To imagine this process, think of a bathtub which is filling up with water. The amount of water in the tub depends on how fast the water is flowing into it—and how quickly it's leaving. If you have a faucet on full blast, but there is a large open drain in the tub, you'll never get enough water to take a bath.

It appears that there are at least three reasons why the veins won't work properly, and shut down: There's not enough arterial blood getting into the sinuses to completely expand them and get them to squeeze the veins partially shut; the sinuses are too stiff to be expanded by the incoming blood; the veins were abnormally formed at birth so they can't be squeezed

The Penile Sinuses: Before Erection

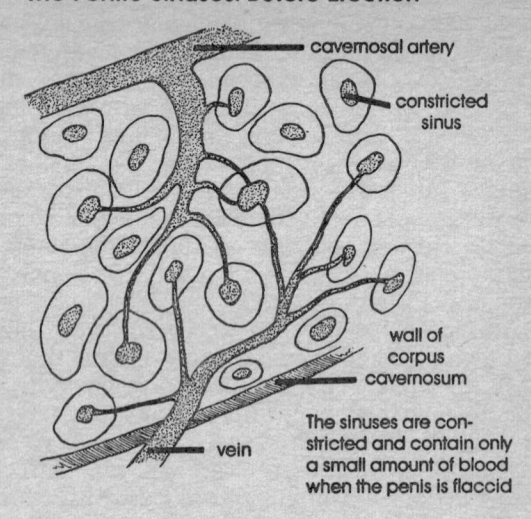

- cavernosal artery
- constricted sinus
- wall of corpus cavernosum
- vein

The sinuses are constricted and contain only a small amount of blood when the penis is flaccid

The Penile Sinuses: During Erection

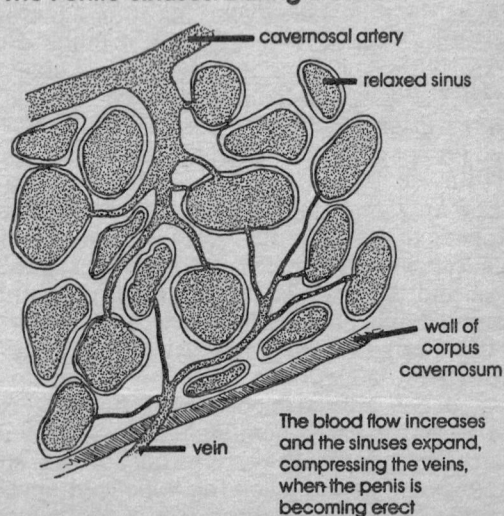

- cavernosal artery
- relaxed sinus
- wall of corpus cavernosum
- vein

The blood flow increases and the sinuses expand, compressing the veins, when the penis is becoming erect

shut. The end result of all this is that a man won't get a good erection, or if he gets one, he will lose it too quickly for intercourse to take place. Vein problems can be treated (see chapter 8).

The Male Genitals

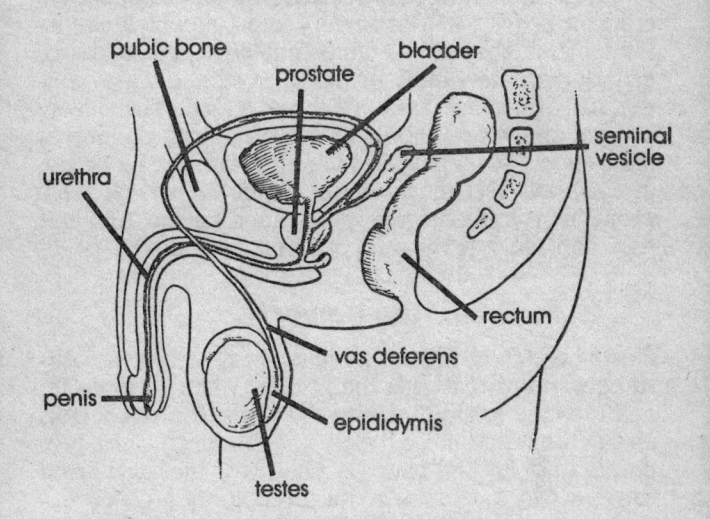

Labels: pubic bone, prostate, bladder, seminal vesicle, urethra, rectum, vas deferens, penis, epididymis, testes

The Prostate

The *prostate,* which sits inside the pelvis behind the pubic bone, produces about half the fluid in a man's ejaculate. Behind and above the prostate are two glands shaped like rabbit ears. Called *seminal vesicles,* they also produce liquid which is part of a man's ejaculate.

As far as erection is concerned, the only importance of the prostate and seminal vesicles rests in their location. They can be crucial to erection because they are strategically placed near vital nerves that may be injured during some operations.

One of those operations is the removal of the prostate itself, usually because of prostate cancer. (Common prostate infections usually do not affect potency though they may diminish desire.) Many men have their prostate removed with absolutely no harm to their potency. And new operating techniques mean that even more prostate surgery patients will continue to enjoy intercourse. However, some patients do have erection problems after surgery, most of which can be treated (see chapter 4). Unfortunately, the chances of getting prostate cancer or other prostate diseases dramatically increase as a man gets older. That's why every man over 40 should have a rectal examination at least once a year. During such an exam, the physician can actually feel the prostate and detect any possible problem. (Granted, such procedures are no fun, but they don't take long—and can save your life.)

The Nerves

During erection, the body's nervous system is the central computer that tells the arteries when to open up and increase blood flow into the penis. It also controls ejaculation. But the nervous system doesn't just give orders to open and close. It also sends messages from the penis to the brain. A man becoming aroused has his nervous system operating in full gear. The taste of his lover's mouth, the touch of her hand, the sound of her voice, the smell and sight of her body all send messages to the brain, which then orders the arteries to send more blood to the penis. And the sensations of pleasure in his penis and throughout his body are transmitted through the nervous system to the brain.

Your emotions and your state of mind affect your physical ability to get an erection. Here's where the nervous system plays such an important role. There are two parts to the unconscious (or autonomic) nervous system which control erections: the parasympathetic network, which relaxes you, and the sympathetic system, which puts your whole body on alert.

During erection, the parasympathetic nervous system is in full gear, sending messages to the arteries and sinuses to expand and let more blood into the penis. The parasympathetic nervous system also plays a crucial role in food digestion and in relaxation.

In contrast, the sympathetic nervous system is the uptight partner in this operation. These nerves tell the arteries and sinuses in the penis to constrict and decrease blood flow. They go into full gear when you are anxious or tense, shifting blood away from your penis and digestive system into your muscles. Therefore, a man who is tense and anxious might be physically unable to get an erection because the overactivity of his sympathetic nervous system is clamping down on the blood flow into his penis.

The Erection

All jokes and worries aside, penises are remarkably similar in size when erect. This means that the smaller the penis is when relaxed, the larger proportionally it will get when erect. Erections actually follow a pattern: First the penis increases in length, then in circumference and finally it elevates—one might say it raises itself up in greeting. Because of the increased blood flow, the penis gets warmer as it gets friendlier.

How much time does all this action take? A teen-aged boy may go from no erection to complete erection so fast it appears to be almost instantaneous, while a man in his 60's may find five to ten minutes is required. Generally, as a man ages, it takes longer for him to get an erection. This is normal, so don't worry. As we've explained, it is not the first sign of impotence. Just use the extra time to enjoy your partner.

A man cannot will an erection to happen, although he can "set the stage" by being receptive to the sensations he is feeling. But a man *can* prevent an erection from happening by being too concerned about making love. In the same way that a man can give himself indigestion by worrying about business problems while eating a sumptuous meal, a man who's worried (perhaps about his ability to satisfy his partner), upset, distracted or otherwise "not in the mood" may find his body uncooperative if he tries to have intercourse. Instead of allowing his body to respond naturally to the pleasurable sensations of lovemaking, he is trying to force an erection. Such efforts will often fail.

This does not mean the man will develop a persistent problem with erections. His body may just be reacting normally to stress, fatigue or other distractions. Sex should not be, and often cannot be, just another task or chore to perform. Sex isn't a duty or an obligation. For men as well as women, it's okay to say no. (Erection difficulties caused by trying to force an erection are unfortunately all too common, as we explain in chapter 3. But they are also, thankfully, preventable much of the time.)

The Sexual Response Cycle

Women and men go through distinct stages called the sexual response cycle (SRC) when they have sex. Here's how the cycle progresses in a man: Mike enjoys a good sexual and emotional relationship with Susie, his wife. It's the end of a relaxing Saturday spent together, and Mike is lying next to Susie. Mike's testosterone and the hormones manufactured in his brain contribute to his feelings of desire as he watches Susie read a book. She glances at him out of the corner of one eye, kindling a spark, and he remembers past pleasurable experiences making love. Mike's in the first part of the SRC, *desire*. The time spent in this phase varies according to what else is going on in the situation, and how each person responds. In this case, Mike proceeds within a few minutes to the next phase, *excitation*.

Mike begins to feel aroused. Susie smiles at him, and puts down her book. She touches his thigh. Under the influence of testosterone, Mike's brain and spinal cord send messages through his nervous system to the blood vessels in his penis. These messages tell the blood vessels to increase the blood flow into Mike's corpora cavernosa, the cylinders in his penis. His heart rate increases as his heart works to pump the extra blood into his penis. Meanwhile, the increasing pressure in the sinuses partially shuts down the flow of blood out through the veins. All this activity results in Mike's penis becoming longer and thicker as it starts to stand up. The head of his penis, that highly sensitive area called the glans penis, begins to swell and becomes even more responsive to sensations. Susie helps this excitement along by rubbing the tip of Mike's penis with her hand, and kissing his belly. The skin of Mike's scrotum starts to thicken and becomes tighter around his testicles, which rise up toward his groin.

The time spent in the *excitement* phase varies considerably. Mike is still a fairly young man, 42 years old, so it only takes him a few minutes to get a full, firm erection. During this time, Mike and Susie begin having intercourse. The blood pumping faster through Mike's body makes his chest and face a little flushed. His breathing is deeper. His heart beats faster. He's enjoying himself. He's totally immersed in making love.

Mike is now in the *plateau* phase, which is a steady maintenance of the excitation stage. During the plateau, Mike's testicles will actually increase in size, although he probably won't be aware of this change. The head of his penis will swell even more, and secretions from glands in his urethra may start to flow out of his penis. (This is not an ejaculation, but a very small amount of sperm may be part of this flow.) He will spend several minutes in the plateau phase, but at other times, this phase may last a much longer or a much shorter period of time.

Many men try to prolong intercourse during the plateau to make the lovemaking last longer. Mike may deliberately slow down his thrusts and movements in order to stave off his orgasm and increase his and his wife's pleasure. Twenty years ago, staying in the plateau phase was more difficult for Mike, but now in his 40's he finds it easier to do. Sometimes the plateau is very brief, leading to early ejaculation (see chapter 6). Mike's plateau lasts for several minutes before he reaches the next stage, *orgasm.* Orgasm lasts for only a few, extremely pleasurable, seconds, and it usually signals the end of the erection. Still, orgasm has little else to do with erection because it is controlled by a different part of the nervous system. Remember, a man can have an erection without an orgasm, and an orgasm without an erection.

Though brief, orgasm actually has two distinct stages. During the first part, emission, the fluid from Mike's seminal vesicles, prostate and testicles flows into his urethra. The sphincters which prevent this fluid from traveling back up into the bladder also close down. These sensations are experienced by Mike as ejaculatory inevitability—he feels that any second he will ejaculate and he won't be able to stop it.

The second part of the climax is Mike's actual ejaculation. The muscles around Mike's urethra contract every 0.8 seconds, combining with contractions from muscles in his pelvis and anus. This generates a great amount of force that pushes the semen in his urethra out of his penis. Mike experiences a powerful feeling of release. The excitement he feels gives way to relaxation. His desire to continue thrusting disappears. Mike is now in the *resolution* phase (which also happens if stimulation stops before orgasm and ejaculation). The increased blood flow to his penis, which caused the erection, stops. The sinuses become smaller, and the veins open up to their normal levels, allowing the extra blood to drain out of Mike's penis. His scrotum becomes less tense, and the testicles drop to their normal, lower position. Mike loses his erection.

When Mike was younger, there were occasions in which he did not lose his erection even after an ejaculation. This is not uncommon in men of high school or college age, but it's much less typical for older men. As a man ages, he loses his erection more easily during the resolution phase. Once the penis becomes flaccid, Mike enters the final stage of the erection cycle, the so-called *refractory period*. This is the period of time after resolution when Mike is unable to enter the excitement phase and get an erection, although he may still feel desire. Typically, this period lasts longer as a man ages. Some young men have virtually no refractory period at all, but it's not uncommon for a man in his 40's, like Mike, to have this period last hours.

Why does the body have this enforced rest from intercourse? Scientists do not fully understand why nature has programmed this time for a sabbatical from intercourse. Maybe it's to allow time for sperm to move into position where they can be ejaculated. (Sperm are made in the testicles, travel to the epididymis, which has a remarkable 15 feet of tubing, all wound up, and then move into the vas, the tubes which carry the sperm to the urethra where they can be ejaculated.)

Desire may return before the body's ability to get an erection is restored, causing a certain amount of frustration, but this situation is not impotence.

Sleep Erections

So far we've talked about erections which result from arousal when a man is conscious of the sensations and the pleasure. But there's another type of erection which has important implications for the diagnosis and treatment of erection problems. Researchers have found that men get erections about five to six times a night during sleep, with each episode lasting as long as 25 minutes. These nocturnal events take place when a man is dreaming, but not necessarily because the man is enjoying some particularly arousing X-rated scenarios. In fact, his dreams may have no erotic content at all. So far, scientists can't explain just why men get erections at night, but some think it's the body's way of exercising the erection process.

Waking up with an erection is usually due to waking up in the middle of the dream. Normal sleep erections show that a man's physical systems are functioning normally. If a man does not get nocturnal erections, his erection problems are probably caused by some physical condition. (Rarely, it can mean that he is not sleeping normally.) If he does get sleep erections but, when awake, cannot be aroused, psychological factors, possibly triggering spasms in the blood vessels supplying the penis, are probably at work. Simple home tests can help determine if a man has sleep erections, and more sophisticated tests are available at sleep laboratories and medical centers (see chapter 7).

You don't need to remember all these fine points of the erection process. And you certainly don't want to think of them when you're making love. But understanding the basics of this process can help you avoid sabotaging yourself—and your partner.

3

How *Not* to Get an Erection

Why would anyone want to know how not to get an erection? Actually most men already know how not to—they just don't *know* that they know. And this ignorance can mess up their love lives, cause them needless stress and generate emotionally painful (though preventable) problems. Many men cause their own erection problems, often due to lack of information and a basic misunderstanding of just how the male body works. This self-sabotage can be stopped. Learning what can cause a man not to get an erection will allow him to more easily avoid that problem.

An erection is not something a man consciously decides to do, like flexing his biceps, kicking a ball or raising his arm. Instead, erection is a complicated physical and emotional response. The stage is best set with a willing (hopefully, enthusiastic) partner, a comfortable setting free from distractions and enough time not to feel pressured. Assuming all systems are go—that he has no medical problems that affect his ability to get or maintain an erection, isn't too tired, depressed or distracted and is sufficiently aroused—the man will probably find himself with an erection. But because erection is such a complex, delicate process, there are many things that can prevent it from happening. Some are within a man's control.

One key to sexual success is to know how to avoid sabotaging yourself so you don't unknowingly create situations that make having and maintaining potency difficult, or downright impossible.

Setting Yourself Up for Failure

Let's look at an example of unconscious and extremely effective self-sabotage. William, 43 years old, is a hard-working engineer for an aerospace company. He has been married to his second wife, Sharon, for the last four years. Like any couple, they have their ups and downs, but for the most part, this is a happy marriage of two career-oriented, busy, productive people. William is somewhat more formal than his gregarious wife; more precise in his speech and meticulous about his appearance. Sharon, eight years younger than her husband, is more relaxed and casual in her attitudes and manners. Together, they make an interesting study in contrasts, and value their differences as well as their shared beliefs in hard work and persistence. William and Sharon have no children, but William's two daughters from his first marriage visit frequently.

During the last few months, William has been under a lot of pressure at work. His responsibilities have increased and he's had to put in long hours. He is in the running for a hotly contested promotion, and is determined to beat out his younger competitor.

William's doctor has been after him for years to quit smoking, so William has cut down on the number of cigarettes he smokes, but he hasn't stopped completely. The doctor recently told William he has high blood pressure, and that he must take medication for the problem every day. And William has to admit that recently he just hasn't been feeling his usual energetic self. Some changes in work assignments mean that he now spends most of his time at his desk. And although for years William could eat anything and remain almost skinny, in the last six months he's put on an extra 30 pounds. Secretly, he hates the weight and thinks it makes him look older, but he's uncomfortable admitting that it bothers him. His doctor also wants him to exercise regularly, follow a low-fat diet and lose weight. William tries to follow these recommendations but pressures at work seem to make it difficult. Often he doesn't take a lunch break and just has a sandwich at his desk, so his once enjoyable noontime squash games have become a thing of the past. When he comes home from work, he's so tired he just wants to rest, not jog or play tennis. And although he knows a low-fat diet will help him lose the extra pounds, he's a meat and potatoes (smothered in sour cream) eater of long standing. Trying to change his eating habits just adds one more stress to his life.

Because Sharon also has had a rough schedule at her city planning office, the couple has been spending little time together during the work week. Saturday and Sunday are "their" days together—once they do the household chores, sort through a stack of mail, pay bills and spend some time with William's daughters.

During most of their marriage, William and Sharon have enjoyed sex together. But lately Sharon has wanted some changes in the bedroom. She's been reading books about women's sexual fulfillment, and wants her husband to read them—and try some of the suggestions. But William finds it difficult to read or talk about sex. Like many people his age, he received virtually no sex education as a child, and although he takes pride in the fact that he's overcome the puritanical aspects of his background, the subject of sex still makes him uncomfortable. He secretly believes that sex shouldn't be talked about unless there's a problem, so if Sharon wants to talk, something must be wrong.

To make matters even more disturbing to William, what Sharon wants to talk about is orgasm. William "knows" that, as the man, he is supposed to "give" his wife an orgasm, and he fears that he has failed. And although he would deny it if asked, William has been influenced by what he sees in movies and on television: A "real" man is always ready to perform, eager for sex and able to satisfy any woman.

William believes he should always be ready to perform; his preoccupation with work, his health problems and his fatigue are irrelevant to this demand.

These concerns just add to his anxiety and guilt. William is treating his body worse than one of the machines he designs—it's never supposed to wear down, especially when it comes to sex. In William's mind, the responsibility for fulfilling his desires, and his wife's, rests squarely on him.

One Friday night, William comes home exhausted from a grueling day at the office and finds his wife taking a nap before dinner. He lies down beside her and falls asleep. When Sharon awakes, she wants to make love. As they cuddle and kiss, William gets excited, but a troubling conversation he had with his boss keeps popping into his mind. He loses his erection while making love and becomes embarrassed, angry and ashamed. He's always been able to maintain an erection before. Sharon is clearly frustrated, although she tries to be understanding. She kisses him and murmurs a few words of encouragement. After a few minutes of lying quietly next to him, she asks him to please read the books on sex she has been mentioning for the last several weeks. William wants, more than anything, not to talk about his "failure." He wants to escape into sleep, and he finally does.

During the next week, William and Sharon do not talk about what happened Friday night. But William thinks about it almost constantly and worries that it will happen again. He's determined not to repeat his erection "failure." So he plans a special night for the two of them.

The next Friday, William puts in a hard day at the office. He spends the morning feeling frustrated and angry over some problems at work, and to relieve his tension he smokes almost nonstop. In the afternoon he has a two-hour, unsatisfactory meeting with his boss, which just adds to his tension. Finally it's time to leave, and William struggles to get home in rush-hour traffic. He barely has time to change his shirt before he and Sharon leave for dinner at their favorite restaurant. At the restaurant, William, worried about making love later, tries to relax with two martinis. Then, deciding it's a special night and his diet doesn't apply, he treats himself to a big steak with all the trimmings. After dinner the couple goes for a stroll. It's after midnight by the time they get home.

By now, William has been looking forward for several hours to making love with his wife. Sharon undresses slowly, but William doesn't waste any time. Although it's been a long day and he is tired, William has decided this is the night to make love, and he doesn't want anything—even fatigue—to interfere. He strips and gets into bed. Lying there, he watches his wife get ready for bed, and feels himself becoming aroused. Sharon also has been anticipating the end of the evening. She is warm and willing, eager to have intercourse. William *wants* to make love, but he's nervous, tired and afraid he will fail. His mind keeps returning to the last time, when he lost his erection. After several minutes of caressing his wife, he does not have an erection and begins to panic. Sharon is upset too. She asks if he still finds her attractive—what else could be the problem? William is tired, angry and discouraged. He snaps back that Sharon is not the problem, and stomps off to the kitchen, where he tries to console himself by drinking some Scotch.

Unfortunately, this isn't an unusual example of sexual failure. It describes the experiences of many couples. Some overcome their problems in the early stages; others try to ignore the situation and find that their occasional difficulty turns into a chronic condition. It is important to realize that William set himself up for failure in a number of ways—many of them correctable. Here's what's wrong between William and Sharon, and how it could be set right.

Performance Anxiety

First, William has *performance anxiety*. Simply put, a man can prevent an erection just by being so anxious and nervous about having sex that he can't let himself become aroused. William, quite understandably, has performance anxiety because he lost his erection the last time he tried to make love. He doesn't know why it happened, and he feels very guilty about it. He thinks it is his "fault." And he feels worse now that it's happened again. He failed this time because instead of enjoying the sensual pleasure of being close to his wife and allowing nature to take its course in producing an erection, he tried to force it mechanically. He treated his penis as a "tool" that could function according to his demands. This is certainly not a rare attitude, but it can easily lead to self-sabotage. William mistakenly tried to use the "willpower" that had served him well in other areas of his life to overcome his lack of potency. William also feels pressure from Sharon, generated by her own needs and insecurities. And Sharon believes that William's loss of erection says something about his feelings about her and her attractiveness—not anything about his health, or the stresses in his life. Sex for her is becoming more and more a reassurance of her desirability than a pleasurable, loving act.

William and Sharon could correct their misunderstanding with a frank discussion about their needs and desires. William could explain that he does in fact find his wife desirable, and Sharon could clear up the mystery of just what it is William is supposed to learn by reading the sex books. She could make clear what changes she wants in the relationship and what she thinks they can do to help each other relax and enjoy their time together more.

But so far, this husband and wife have demonstrated a *failure to communicate,* which has been exacerbated by their demanding work schedules. William and Sharon have let their relationship slide. They don't spend much time together, and when they do, they don't discuss openly and honestly what is going on. They haven't maintained the intimacy that once made their relationship so strong and rewarding. The bedroom just happens to be the spot where the communication breakdown is most obvious. William is afraid to discuss his erection problem; his fears fuel his anxiety and make the difficulty even worse. *At this point, the problem is not his two experiences with potency problems, but the messages he's been giving himself about them.*

What's the solution for William and Sharon? They might want to make a commitment to spend 30 minutes, every night, together. They might take a walk, lie quietly and cuddle, or just sit side by side, holding hands. They need to re-establish the intimacy in their relationship by giving each other time that's free from other demands. (For more suggestions, see chapter 6.) But it's important to recognize that in William's case, physical factors are also at work, so rejuvenating the closeness of the relationship may not solve his erection problem. Combined with other changes, however, William and Sharon can have a sexually successful and happier relationship.

Pick Your Anxiety

Performance anxiety can take many different forms. For some men, it is linked to the degree of intimacy in a relationship. One man, 33 years old, could only get an erection in an impersonal setting. He would visit topless bars where, for a fee, a dancer would rub up against him. He could have a full, firm erection this way and ejaculate. But when he liked a woman and developed a friendship with her, he was unable to get an erection.

Sometimes the reverse is true and performance anxiety is only a problem when a man tries to have sex with someone who is a virtual stranger to him. Hal, for example, dated several different women in a short period of time, but he was unable to get an erection with any of them. The common thread in each of these situations was that he didn't know the woman very well, and he really didn't feel comfortable with her. Hal's performance anxiety had to do with wanting to feel secure and accepted as a person, not just as an instrument of sexual satisfaction. Once Hal developed a serious relationship, erections were not a problem. In this case his penis was mirroring his emotional state.

Sometimes performance anxiety is based on beliefs that prove almost intractable to change. Lee, for example, a 26-year-old, developed an infection in the urinary tract which resulted in a painful drip from his penis. Very concerned and in some pain, he came to a hospital clinic for help. A physician properly prescribed some tetracycline, an antibiotic commonly used to clear up the problem. But a so-called friend of Lee's told him that if he took the medicine, he'd never get an erection again.

After some anxious rumination, Lee decided to take the pills anyway, to rid himself of the painful infection. The medicine cleared up his problem in a week, and Lee should have been back to normal.

But the next time he tried to make love with his girlfriend he was unable to get an erection. This had never happened to him before. And he was not even able to get an erection when he masturbated. These developments threw him into an emotional tailspin, which only worsened when his girlfriend decided to leave him, saying he was no longer "a real man." Lee was frantic.

About four weeks later, this terrified young man again showed up at the clinic, seeking help. He had not had an erection since he took the medicine, and was absolutely frantic with anxiety. The doctor reassured him correctly that there was no way the antibiotic could have caused his impotence, and suggested that the worry, not the medicine, was at the root of his problem.

Unfortunately, such advice had no effect on Lee's lack of erection. In his heart, he believed that his "friend" had spoken the truth. He felt doomed to impotence. Hoping to counteract his beliefs, the physician gave him a placebo shot, promising that this "medicine" would clear up any problem Lee had with erections. Alas, the "cure" did not work. Though there was no physical reason for his sudden inability to get an erection, Lee remained impotent. His beliefs were powerful enough to override his sexual desires and his body's ability to respond.

Lee was referred to a community mental health center for help in overcoming his fears. Although Lee's case is somewhat extreme, this story is a perfect example of performance anxiety and the enormous power of the mind.

Anxiety can also lead to a potency destroyer known as spectatoring. George, for example, had a good sexual relationship with his wife for many years. He worked hard, and looked forward to the time he and his wife would retire, do some traveling and enjoy themselves without a lot of responsibilities. Unfortunately, shortly before George was scheduled to retire, his wife became ill and died. Understandably, the loss of his life partner threw George into a deep depression.

Gradually, over a period of months, the 62-year-old man recovered. He slowly picked up the pieces of his life and began to make new plans. Now single, this attractive and vigorous man began receiving lots of invitations. George began dating, and after a while, he limited his attractions to just one woman, Claire, a 55-year-old real estate agent. It was with her that George first experienced an erection problem. "I was just unable to get a total erection," he says, still uncomfortable at the memory. "Claire obviously felt it was my problem, not hers."

At first, George attributed his erection difficulty to the loss of his wife, an interpretation his doctor agreed with. But as it persisted, he noticed a change in himself. Beset with anxiety about his ability to perform—would it work this time or not?—he watched himself as though he were someone else. He monitored his body's reactions instead of enjoying them. This *spectatoring* caused more potency problems, more anxiety for George. A vicious cycle of potency problems, depression and stress was launched.

In George's case, he had been diabetic for years, but it had never caused him erection problems (see chapter

4 for more on diabetes). The death of his wife was an enormous shock and caused him great stress and depression. By themselves, depression and other mental conditions can cause erection difficulties. In combination with other factors, they can be even more formidable. It seems likely that George's first as-a-widower experience with erection problems was due to a combination of diabetes, some depression and perhaps anxiety over being with a new partner. Some empathetic professional counseling and information about diabetes and impotence, perhaps along with physical treatment, might have prevented the cycle from continuing.

Unrealistic Expectations

Unrealistic expectations are another huge block to a fulfilling and enjoyable sexual relationship. Let's return to our friend William. He expects himself to respond on demand despite what is going on in other areas of his life. (This reminds us of the movie hero who is able to sneak in some lovemaking in the midst of truly life-threatening activities.) William doesn't realize that exhaustion, job stress, long hours and medication affect his potency. This middle-aged man thinks his mind and body should be able to ignore these very real pressures and stresses, and function like he was a well-rested 18- or 19-year-old.

Unrealistic expectations may result from lack of knowledge about what is normal. William probably wouldn't expect himself to have the same quick reaction time in his tennis game he had when he was in his teens, but he can make up in skill, perhaps, for this change. If William knew that getting an erection at age 43 normally requires more stimulation from his partner than at age 20, he might save himself needless anguish. He could relax, enjoy foreplay and "go with the flow" instead of panicking because his penis doesn't become hard immediately.

Sharon's knowledge and participation are also crucial. She can actively involve herself in lovemaking, instead of being a passive (and insecure) partner.

Make Sex a Priority

Lack of time is another major factor in this scenario. Although William clearly views sex as something of great importance, he often plans it as literally the last thing to do on a busy, event-filled day. He doesn't give his sexual relationship time when he is well rested, free of tension, relaxed. If William had decided to wait until Saturday morning instead of late Friday night, he would have been more relaxed, more rested and possibly found that he had no problem.

It's important to take time out for sex. Sex therapists tell people to allocate one hour per day to sensually caressing, massaging and relating to one's partner. But you don't have to pay a therapist to benefit from this advice and to reap the pleasurable results.

Sensual Pleasures

William has problems making love with his wife because he focuses on making his penis do what he wants rather than enjoying being close to Sharon. *Forced erection* is a false notion. Although he caresses and cuddles her, he doesn't concentrate on her touch, the smell of her hair, the taste of her lips and the sight of her body. Instead, he is preoccupied with whether his penis will "work." That's like eating dinner and being involved with the knife and fork, rather than the gourmet feast before you. What a waste.

Trouble at Home

An *unhappy relationship* coupled with a demanding partner is another possible source of erection problems. In this case, as in others, separating the erection problem from the relationship is often counterproductive. Marion and Walter, for example, had been married for more than 20 years. It was not a happy relationship. Walter did not turn out to be the ambitious, energetic man Marion had wanted. Faced with conflict, he withdrew. Over the years, Marion had built up a lot of anger over her husband's "failure," his lack of responsibility, his unwillingness to participate in family events. But she did not deal with the issues openly. Instead, she took the battles into the bedroom. She compared her husband's sexual skills with those of her best friend's spouse, with the expected disastrous results. "Mary's husband doesn't have erection problems. But you do!"

The predictable result was that Walter's erection problems increased, and Marion had something else to be angry about.

This was a no-win situation for both partners, but the erection problem was only a part of a very troubled and unfulfilling marriage. Some people might see Walter's lack of erection as a way of punishing his wife, or as a logical response to a hostile situation. Feeling under attack, he and his penis withdrew.

No More Casanova

Of course, psychologically caused erection problems aren't confined to basically unhappy relationships. Sometimes a good relationship can get sidetracked by the man becoming too concerned with his abilities as a lover. He gets so involved with giving his partner an orgasm that he doesn't feel his own pleasure. And he can lose his erection as a result of this preoccupation.

Henry, for example, always took great pride in his ability to satisfy a woman and "give" her an orgasm. As Henry got into his 40's, he noticed that on occasion, his erections took longer to appear. This is a normal result of aging, but Henry didn't look at it that way. He saw it as a personal defeat, as a sign that his powers were waning. His new wife, Anne, didn't have orgasms every time they made love, but she told Henry she didn't feel deprived by this, saying "I don't keep score." But Henry took his wife's occasional lack of orgasm as yet another sign that his skills as a lover were on the decline. He agonized over this state of affairs. One night, Henry lost his erection while making love. He became terribly upset and decided he needed medical attention. As it turned out, Henry didn't have an erection problem until he created one in his mind; his overconcern about his adroitness as a lover was the initial stress, and his anxiety about his "failure" was the fuel that kept it going.

It's important to check out all physical causes of potency problems before attributing the situation to psychological factors. At the same time, we think it's essential not to ignore the psychological impact that physically caused erection problems can have, especially if they are allowed to continue untreated for a long time. Simon, for example, became severely depressed when he could no longer get an erection. His condition was due to a problem with his blood-flow system. After a complete workup and evaluation, Simon decided to have a penile implant. Several weeks after the surgery, he recovered his potency and his wife was very pleased. Simon, however, remained somewhat depressed, although he insisted that he was satisfied with the implant. But the memory of his lack of erection seemed to dog him. "He doesn't realize that he's not impotent anymore," his wife remarked. For this middle-aged man, the lack of erection signified a great loss of self; after his problem was corrected, he remained unhappy for several months. It took a long time for him to let go of his feelings of loss and resume normal living.

Stress

Getting back to William, it is clear that stress is a major force in his life right now. It wouldn't surprise him if someone pointed out that his high-pressured existence could affect his sleep, his eating patterns, his digestion and the way he does his job. But his sex life? Never. Despite the breakneck pace he keeps, he expects his body to "perform" as usual.

William, a man under stress, feels he cannot relax. He is preoccupied with the source of his tension. He is not enjoying life one moment at a time. Instead, he worries about what happened before and what is coming next. Consequently, he will find it difficult or impossible to relax and enjoy his senses in a sexual encounter. If, still in this frame of mind, he does succeed in having intercourse, he may not experience real pleasure. Often, such distress may lead to erection problems, which in turn can cause further stress and self-doubt. A vicious cycle can develop. To counteract this, a man in this situation needs to find time to enjoy himself and feel alive. He needs to say no to outside pressures and yes to his own pleasures.

Clearly, William needs to make some adjustments in his life, to help him handle some of his increased stress. He might find a daily swim, regular deep breathing exercises or taking a stress management class would put him in the here and now and help him live more fully.

Drugs Can Sabotage Your Sex Life

Drugs and medications are relevant to William's situation. Indeed, it wasn't until after William began taking a prescription drug for high blood pressure that his first problem with erection occurred. Yet William doesn't link the medication with the potency problem. Sadly, this is all too typical. Drugs are a major cause of potency problems, and it's likely that William's medication caused his initial problem. Often, simply stopping the medication or changing the dose—on the advice of your doctor—will clear up the problem. But first you and your doctor must decide whether your problem is due to drugs.

> ### Cast a Critical Eye on Medications
>
> It sounds incredible, but doctors have identified a common prescription eye medication, timolol maleate eye drops (Timoptic), as the possible culprit in some erection problems. A very small percentage of men using this drug experience erection problems and lack of sexual desire.
>
> How many men may have had such problems and not reported it? Nobody knows. But the lesson is clear: If you develop an erection problem after taking *any* medication—pills, shots, ointment, eye drops—don't keep it a secret. Tell your doctor, and find out if changing the dosage or the drug could restore potency.

Here are some important things to keep in mind when it comes to drugs and erection problems:

- Many different drugs can cause erection problems (see the chart, pages 52-59), including drugs too new to have been identified as problem causers yet.
- Different men have different degrees of sensitivity. A certain drug may not affect Joe but will leave Bill puzzled because he can't get an erection.
- Drugs interact with each other. You can take drug A alone with no erection problem. You can take drug B alone with no erection problem. But if you take A and B together you may find yourself unable to get an erection.
- A man's tolerance for a certain medication may change over a period of time. Sometimes a man will take a drug for years, with no side effects. Then, suddenly, the drug will ruin his sex life. Drugs can be sneaky this way.

Always ask your doctor or pharmacist if a medication can cause potency problems—even if the problem occurs after you've been taking the drug for a while. And remember to ask about how drugs interact with each other and with alcohol. Doctors differ in their approach to the drug/erection problem. Some believe that volunteering the information that a medication may cause impotence just sets the patient up for performance anxiety. Others strongly assert that a well-informed patient is in a much better position to report any difficulties, and that patients can be saved needless anxiety by knowing what might happen. We favor the second approach. In any case, you can protect yourself by always asking if a medication can affect your potency. If you ask directly for the information, the physician should provide it.

Many patients do not connect medications with potency, and neither do their wives. Think how differently William and Sharon would have felt if, when the first erection problem occurred, William said, "Well, it might be the blood pressure pills. I'll call the doctor in the morning. Maybe he can switch me to a different medication, or change the dosage." A lot of pain and anguish might have been avoided.

Recreational drugs, like marijuana, amphetamines and narcotics can also cause erection problems. As with medications, responses to these drugs vary: Some men find that even small doses leave them unable to get an erection, or maintain one, while others have a higher tolerance.

Problem Drugs

Many drugs can interfere with erection. On the following pages is a list of the more common troublemakers. In some cases doctors aren't sure if the drug is really causing the problems; with almost all of these drugs, some men may experience potency problems while others remain unaffected. If you think one of them may be contributing to your erection problem, consider switching to another drug or type of treatment. But be sure to talk over any change with your doctor first. Stopping a drug treatment on your own can be dangerous.

Problem Drugs (continued)

Fortunately, the negative effects of drugs on potency are almost always reversible, though it may take some time for your system to get back in gear after you quit taking the drug.

Generic Name	Brand Name
Blood pressure medicines and diuretics	
acebutolol	Sectral
acetazolamide	Dazamide, Diamox
alseroxylon	Rautensin, Rauwiloid
amiloride	Midamor, Moduretic, Hydro-Ride
bendroflumethiazide	Naturetin, Corizide, Rauzide
benzthiazide	Aquatag, Exna, Hydrex, Maurazide, Proaqua
bethanidine	
chlorthalidone	Hygroton, Hylidone, Thalitone, Combipres, Tenoretic
clonidine	Catapres
cyclothiazide	Anhydron, Fluidil
enalapril	Vasotec, Vaseretic
ethacrynic acid	Edecrin
flumethiazide	Rautrax
furosemide	Laxix, Apo-Furosemide
guanadrel	Hylorel
guanethidine	Ismelin
hydralazine*	Apresoline
hydroflumethiazide	Diucardin, Saluron, Hydro-Fluserpine, Salutrensin
indapamide	Lozol
labetalol	Normodyne, Trandate
mecamylamine	Inversine

* Least likely to cause potency problems.

BIOPOTENCY

Problem Drugs (continued)

Generic Name	Brand Name
methyclothiazide	Aquatensin, Enduron, Ethon, Diutensin-R, Enduronyl, Eutron
methyldopa	Aldomet
metoprolol	Lopressor
minoxidil*	Loniten
nadolol	Corgard, Corzide
phenoxybenzamine	Dibenzaline
phentolamine	Regitine
prazosin*	Minipress
propranolol	Inderal
rescinnamine	Cinnasil, Moderil
reserpine	Serpasil, Sandril
spironolactone	Aldactone
thiazides	Diuril, Esidrix, Hygroton and others
trichlormethiazide	Aquazide, Diurese, Naqua and others

Antianxiety medications

buspirone	Buspar
chlordiazepoxide	Librium
clorazepate	Tranxene
diazepam	Valium
meprobamate	Miltown, Equanil
oxazepam	Serax
tybamate	Tybatran

Antidepressants

amitriptyline	Elavil
desipramine	Norpramine
doxepin	Sinequan
imipramine	Tofranil
isocarboxazide	Marplan

* Least likely to cause potency problems.

How *Not* to Get an Erection

Problem Drugs (continued)

Generic Name	Brand Name
lithium carbonate	
maprotiline	Ludiomil
nortriptyline	Aventyl
pargylene	Eutonyl
phenelzine	Nardil
protriptyline	Vivactil
tranylcypromine	Parnate
trazadone	Desyrel
trimipramine	Surmontil

Major tranquilizers

chlorpromazine	Thorazine
chlorprothixine	Taractan
droperidol	Innovar
fluphenazine	Prolixin
haloperidol	Haldol
mesoridazine	Serentil
pimozide	Orap
prochlorperazine	Compazine
promazine	Sparine
thioridazine	Mellaril
thiothixene	Navane
trifluoperazine	Stelazine

Drugs for bladder or bowel spasms

anisotropine	Valpin
atropine (usually used in combination with other drugs)	
clinidium	Quarzan, Librax, Chlordinium Sealets, Clindex, Clipoxide, Lidox
glycopyrrolate	Robinul
hexocyclium	Tral

Problem Drugs (continued)

Generic Name	Brand Name
isopropamide	Darbid, Chlor-Iso TR, Combagen, Combid and others
mepenzolate	Cantil
methantheline	Banthine
oxybutynin	Ditropan
propantheline bromide	Pro-Banthine
tridihexethyl	Pathilon, Hexabamate and others

Drugs for Parkinson's disease

benztropine	Cogentin
biperidin	Akineton
cycrimine	Pagitane
levodopa	Larodopa, Sinemet
procyclidine	Kemadrin
trihexyphenidyl	Artane

Drugs for allergies and motion sickness (antihistamines)

dimenhydrinate	Dramamine
diphenhydramine	Benadryl
hydroxyzine	Vistaril
meclizine	Antivert, Bonine
promethazine	Phenergan

Muscle relaxants

baclofen	Lioresal
cyclobenzaprine	Flexeril
dantrolene	Dantrium
orphenadrine	Norflex

Problem Drugs (continued)

Generic Name	Brand Name
Drugs for irregular heartbeats	
disopyramide	Norpace
flecainide	Tambocor
mexiletine	Mexitil
Miscellaneous drugs	
carbamazepine	Epitol, Tegretol (antiseizures)
cimetidine	Tagamet (antiulcers)
clofibrate	Altromid-S (antihyperlipidemic, anticholesterol)
cyproterone acetate	(a hormone used to treat certain types of cancer)
deserpidine	Harmonyl, Oreticyl, Enduronyl (antihypertensive, antipsychotic)
diethylpropion	Depletite, Tenuate, Tepanil, Dietic, Nobesine, Propion, Regibon (diet pill)
digoxin	Lanoxin (for heart problems)
disulfiram	Antabuse (antialcohol)
epsilon aminocaproic acid	Amicar (for abnormal bleeding)
estrogens	(female hormones used to treat prostate cancer)
ethionamide	Trecator (antituberculosis)
ethylestrenol	Maxibolin (anabolic steroid)

Problem Drugs (continued)

Generic Name	Brand Name
fenfluramine	Pondimin (diet pill)
furazolidone	Furoxone (antibacterial)
glucocorticoids	(hormones used to treat severe allergies, asthma and other breathing problems; arthritis, lupus and other diseases)
immunosuppressive agents	(sometimes used to treat arthritis, lupus and transplant rejection)
indomethacin	Indocin (mainly for arthritis)
isotretinoin	Accutane (antiacne)
ketoconazole	Nizoral (antifugus)
ketoprofen	Orudis (anti-inflammatory, arthritis)
leuprolide	Lupron (prostate cancer)
mazindol	Mazanor, Sanorex, Teronac (diet pill)
methadone	Dolophine (narcotic analgesic)
methandrostenolone	Methandroid (anabolic steroid)
methysergide	Sansert (headache)
metoclopramide	Clopra-"Yellow," Maxolon, Reglan (gastric stimulant)
metronidazole	Flagyl (infections)
nicotine	Nicorette (gum used to quit smoking)
oxymetholone	Androl-50 (anabolic) steroid)
phendimetrazine	Adipost, Anorex, and others (diet pill)

Problem Drugs (continued)

Generic Name	Brand Name
phenmetrazine	Preludin (diet pill)
phentermine	Adipex-P, Obephen, and others (diet pill)
phenytoin	Dilantin (antiseizures)
probucol	Lorelco (antihyperlipidemic, anticholesterol)
procarbazine	Matulane (used to treat Hodgkins disease)
progestins	(female hormones used to treat certain types of cancer)
rantidine	Zantac (antiulcer)
stanzolol	Winstrol (anabolic steroid)
timolol	Blocadren, Timoptic (antiglaucoma)
verapamil	Calan, Isoptin (antianginal, calcium channel blocker)

Commonly abused drugs

- alcohol
- amphetamines
- barbiturates
- cocaine
- marijuana
- narcotics (such as heroin and morphine)
- nicotine
- opiates

Sources: *Drugs and Male Sexual Dysfunction.* American Urological Association Update Series, (Houston: American Urological Association, 1984). Lieberman, M. Laurence, *The Sexual Pharmacy: The Complete Guide to Drugs with Sexual Side Effects,* (New York: New American Library, 1988).

Alcohol: Loaded with Problems

"It provokes the desire, but it takes away the performance. Therefore much drink may be said to be an equivocator with lechery." (*Macbeth,* 2.3.28.)

If only William knew what Will Shakespeare knew: Alcohol can cause erection problems. Alcohol is a drug. In very small quantities it may stimulate arousal, but that's not the same thing as promoting erection. Far from it. Ultimately, alcohol is a depressant. It slows down reflexes and decreases all sensation, including sexual pleasure. Researchers have confirmed Shakespeare's assertion that liquor can cause temporary loss of potency. It can also reduce pleasure and, in some men, result in even less intense orgasms.

While a rare binge will not permanently affect potency, long-term abuse of alcohol can wreak havoc on a man's ability to get and maintain an erection, even when he is not drinking. And in some cases this physical loss can be permanent if it's allowed to go untreated.

Often, alcoholics don't come for treatment of impotence until they're on the wagon. Once on the road to recovery, the alcoholic man may find that his potency has not returned. Roger, for example, a 50-year-old accountant, visited a clinic complaining of a potency problem. A widower for many years, Roger was now living with a woman he hoped to marry. He wanted his new relationship to work, but his sexual problems were causing a strain.

Many alcoholic patients don't volunteer information about their drinking habits, but Roger was rather direct about his past habits, his medical history and the details of his erection problems. He had been drinking very heavily for more than a decade and he had been a recovering alcoholic and "dry" for two years. Over the last decade, he noticed his erections getting softer. Sometimes he was incapable of getting an erection, no matter how aroused he felt.

Roger had expected that his potency would return to normal once he finally stopped drinking. Instead, although he remained on the wagon, his erections remained quite soft. And even more distressing to him and to his housemate, in recent months there were times he couldn't get an erection at all, even though he felt intense desire for his partner.

A complete physical examination and several tests turned up just one physical abnormality which could be responsible for Roger's condition: His blood showed low levels of testosterone, probably a result of his previous alcohol abuse. Such heavy drinking can permanently decrease the testicles' ability to produce testosterone, and liver damage can change the way the body uses testosterone. This can mean less sexual desire and decreased ability to get an erection.

Roger was given a series of testosterone shots, administered every three weeks, in the hope that the additional hormone would be properly used by his body. It sounds logical. But in the case of alcoholics with low testosterone, injections of the hormone don't always work. In fact, some alcoholic men may develop some feminine characteristics, such as enlarged breasts, because their damaged metabolism converts the male hormone to a female hormone. Some men find that the same hormonal abnormalities caused by excessive drinking make their testicles actually shrink in size. Roger was lucky. He didn't have any of the most severe symptoms and his system was still partially functioning. So the shots did help. He was able to get erections more frequently, and his erections were more firm. He was happy with the noticeable improvement. (If testosterone injections don't work, other methods of treatment, discussed in chapter 8, can help.) The bottom line on heavy drinking is that too much alcohol can ruin erections. If a man stops heavy drinking soon enough, he may be unaffected. But every individual is different. Play it safe—if you drink, do so only moderately.

Combining Alcohol and Medication

Coming back to our friend William, it's important to note that he was combining alcohol with his high blood pressure medication. It's possible that either alcohol or the drug alone would not cause erection problems. But the combination is powerful and may have been too much for his system to take.

In general, any time you combine alcohol and medication you're setting yourself up for a potential health problem—which may or may not affect your sexual potency. Before you add hard liquor, wine or beer to your body chemistry, ask your doctor or pharmacist: What are the possible side effects if I drink while taking this medication? Could the combination of alcohol with this drug affect potency?

Where There's Smoke, There's No Fire

Cigarettes have long been part of the mystique of romance and sexuality—look at Bogart and Bacall curling gray smoke from their lips as they speak seductively to one another—but in reality smoking can make sex go up in smoke.

There is much scientific evidence that smoking can lead to hardening of the arteries—including arteries that are vital to erection because they let blood flow to the penis. When these arteries harden or narrow they are unable to expand enough to allow blood flow sufficient for erection.

This doesn't mean that smoking cigarettes will automatically lead to impotence; there are too many potent 25-year-old smokers who disprove that notion. What is true is that, over time, smoking can increase your risk of narrowed arteries—and thus impotence. Indeed, research indicates that in some highly sensitive individuals cigarette smoking may cause impotence even without permanently narrowing the arteries, just by preventing the arteries from dilating enough to allow erection. Stopping smoking "cures" this problem.

And smoking is linked to erection difficulties in another way: It can cause bladder cancer that requires surgery, which in turn causes impotence. Patients who have radiation therapy for the cancer instead of surgery also may become impotent, because radiation in the pelvic area may damage nerves or blood vessels essential for erection. (We discuss this in more detail in chapter 4.)

The problem is so obvious that one urologist tells his patients to choose between sex or cigarettes. Faced with such a choice, most opt for sex, he reports. While kicking the habit may not be sufficient treatment for most people, it can help many men with erection problems get back to normal.

Diet

High-fat diets have received a lot of bad press lately, much of it well deserved. A high-fat diet helps clog up your arteries and can cause blockages, harming arteries that are essential for erection.

High-calorie diets can lead to overweight, as William is discovering. In a person susceptible to diabetes, overweight can make the illness appear. And diabetes can lead to potency problems.

To help keep your arteries clear, your heart healthy and your circulatory system fit, we advise you to eat a low-fat diet, and keep your body at a healthy weight. William is fond of heavy meals, but a menu of frequent he-man dinners—with the main ingredient a large, juicy, fat-marbled steak—can eventually lead to potency problems.

Exercise

Exercise is a wonderful stress-reducer, and William has just been adding to his tension by eliminating his noontime squash games. And exercise is certainly a help in keeping weight normal. The more calories you burn, the less likely you are to be fat. Fat can lead to health problems which can then result in erection problems. (More about how your lifestyle can help you prolong potency is found in chapter 11.)

Setting the Stage for Sexuality

Taking *all* these factors into account, let's look at how another man more successfully handles a situation similar to William's.

Jeff, 44, works for the state government in a middle-management position. He has a certain number of hassles to deal with every day on the job. He runs his department with efficiency, but budget cutbacks have left him short-staffed, and everyone is feeling crunched by the amount of work they must do.

Recently promoted, Jeff has to listen to his staff's complaints about the poor working conditions, and he finds this one of the most difficult parts of his job. His work day starts early but he usually tries to leave by five o'clock. Once a week he plays soccer with a neighborhood team, and at least twice a week he and a co-worker shed their business suits and jog out of the office during lunchtime.

Jeff has been married to Sara for 15 years. They have two children, Susie, 4, and Jeff, Jr., 10. Recent months have been filled with stressful events: the death of Sara's father; the serious illness of another grandparent; Jeff's recent promotion, which hasn't worked out as well as they had hoped; and tight finances, partly because Sara's employer reduced her hours at work.

Jeff has never had any erection problems until recently. One Friday night, he found himself unable to become erect, despite the fact he was very aroused. But he didn't panic. "I knew it was the beer I'd been drinking," he says, smiling as he recalls the incident.

Because he knew the cause of his difficulty, Jeff did not experience performance anxiety. And he didn't feel threatened as a man, but just took it in stride. His self-awareness was crucial in his response to the situation.

How *Not* to Get an Erection 65

Jeff told his wife he thought the culprit was the six-pack and she agreed. Sara didn't attribute any deep meaning to the problem, probably because she felt secure in her relationship with her husband.

And Jeff didn't withdraw from his wife. Instead, he cuddled with her for a while, before they each drifted off to sleep.

Let's suppose that a week later, the same problem recurs, but this time, alcohol isn't in the picture. Jeff's response to the problem is crucial. He doesn't immediately assume the worst. In his mind, he goes over recent changes in his life. He did just start taking a prescription drug. Feeling that it's something of a long shot, he calls his physician. After consulting a reference book, the doctor somewhat apologetically confirms that impotence can be a side effect of the medication. Reducing the dosage solves the problem.

Even without such a simple explanation, Jeff's *attitude* remains a crucial element in how successful he is in solving his problem. In general, Jeff has a positive attitude towards sex, despite "zero" formal sex education. "I never took a class in high school or college where the physiology of erection was explained or even discussed." Now, having read a lot on his own, he feels more knowledgeable.

Jeff's attitude towards lovemaking and his marriage is positive. "I have a certain philosophy about making love," says this soft-spoken man. "When you don't make love, you've lost the time, and it can't ever be regained. So it's nice to enjoy it often." Unlike William, who takes his stresses and pressures to bed with him, Jeff is careful to leave the rest of the world behind when he wants to make love. "I shut off the office when I close the bedroom door," he says. That's such good advice, we might all do well to use it as a motto.

Jeff's and William's stories are good examples of sexual success and failure. The moral of both is that the way to sexual success is to understand the factors behind erection problems and to deal with them in a logical, constructive way.

4

Keep Illness from Undermining Potency

While self-sabotage and bad health habits play a key role in impotence, erection problems may have many other origins. And what at first looks like the sole cause of impotence is often only one factor among several. Still, there are a few common health problems that by themselves frequently cause loss of potency. Consider these troublemakers if you experience impotence. Be sure your doctor also takes them into account.

Diabetes

Diabetes is a common disease in which a person's body doesn't control blood sugar properly. There are two basic types of diabetes. Type I, sometimes called juvenile onset diabetes, usually starts early in life. It is typically more severe and more likely to require the person to give himself shots of insulin, the hormone that controls blood sugar. On the other hand, Type II, sometimes known as adult-onset diabetes, is usually not as drastic (it can often be controlled with dietary changes and exercise) and is frequently associated with lifestyle factors like obesity. Both types tend to run in families, so your chances of getting diabetes are greater if you have close relatives with the disease. Classic symptoms of diabetes include excessive thirst, a frequent need to urinate and unexpected weight loss. Sometimes, however, adult-onset diabetes can be "silent," with none of these symptoms. Using certain blood tests, diabetes is fairly easy to diagnose.

In general, diabetic men experience more erection problems than their nondiabetic counterparts. And these problems develop at a younger age than they do in healthy nondiabetic men—erection problems usually show up about 10 to 15 years earlier than in men without the disease. In some cases, even relatively young men who have had diabetes for fewer than 10 years may find getting or maintaining an erection a problem. It is estimated that in the U.S. alone, diabetes is responsible for about one-fifth of all potency problems. This means that there are about 2 million American men who can hold diabetes partially, or even completely, responsible for their impotence. That's not to say that a diagnosis of diabetes sentences you to impotence, because diabetes does not always lead to erection difficulties. Some researchers claim that only about 1 in 4 diabetic men will eventually develop erection problems, while others estimate that the odds are 6 in 10.

Diabetics are more at risk because they often develop blocked arteries (arteriosclerosis) at an earlier age than nondiabetics. And these blockages can occur in those crucial arteries that supply the penis with blood during an erection.

Nerve damage is another potency troublemaker for diabetics. Diabetes can cause a man to lose sensation or trigger a "tingling" in his arms and legs. And this same damage can affect the part of the nervous system that controls erection.

It's not uncommon for a man diagnosed as diabetic to go for many years without any erection problems. Then difficulties may develop, sometimes slowly, sometimes more quickly. Daniel, for example, is in his mid-30's and has been diabetic since he was 13. The diagnosis came as a shock, but he took to heart the advice his doctor gave him. "He told me to live life as fully as possible."

An attractive man who is successful in his work, Dan takes obvious pride in his appearance and keeps himself in shape by lifting weights at a health club. But despite his seemingly carefree demeanor he has a lot of experience dealing with and adjusting to his diabetes. In the last few years, for instance, he's had some problems with numbness in his legs.

Daniel didn't have any problems with erections until about three years ago. But then, in less than a year, he went from having no problems to losing his ability to become erect. "First, I had semierections. Then, no erections. I knew diabetes could be a factor. I knew that was probably why this happened." Daniel made the connection between his illness and the potency problems, and, in so doing, suffered less anxiety. His doctor confirmed that diabetes was indeed the culprit, and offered Daniel a choice of treatments.

Impotence: The First Symptom of Diabetes?

Sometimes potency problems are the first sign that a man has diabetes. New York researchers studied three groups of men who were thought not to be diabetic. The men in the first group were impotent, the men in the second group complained of premature ejaculation and the men in the third group had normal sexual function.

Blood tests to diagnose diabetes showed that about one in eight of the men complaining of impotence were diabetic. These men had no other diabetic symptoms. None of the men in the other two groups were found to be diabetic. The lesson: When potency problems develop, it's important to check for diabetes.

In Daniel's case, the "downhill slide," as he called it, happened fairly fast, once the problem surfaced. But other men find the problem develops much more gradually, over a period of several years. Bert, a manufacturer's representative, was diagnosed as diabetic when he was 31. Even after the diagnosis he didn't always take proper care of himself, he admits, and after several years he developed circulation problems in his feet as well as other complications. But it took about five years for him to notice a change in his erections, and even then it was several years before he considered problems with erections a chronic condition. "I just gradually got to the point where I couldn't have sex," he says.

For Bert, the problem wasn't only damage to the nerves and arteries—when Bert's diabetes got out of control, his erections got worse. The strain on Bert's body made erections impossible. When his diabetes was under better control, his erections improved. Bert, however, is a case study of how *not* to deal with diabetes. For some people, restoring normal blood sugar will restore normal potency. The key is not to ignore the problem until it's too late.

Maintaining a proper diet, using prescribed medication and following a doctor's recommendations for exercise and weight control are essential for the diabetic man who wants to put all the potency odds in his favor. This way, you're more likely to avoid other complications of this disease: nerve damage, blood-flow blockages and blindness. A diabetic man without these unpleasant conditions runs less chance of developing erection problems than a man who has such problems.

Also, alcohol may present a special erection threat to diabetic men. Researchers have found that the more alcohol a diabetic man drinks, the more he increases his chances of losing potency.

Cigarettes have a similar effect. Diabetic men may be particularly susceptible to the negative effects of smoking on erection. One study evaluated 30 diabetic men, all with erection problems. Ten smokers were instructed only not to smoke. Ten smokers were given medication to improve blood flow, and also told to cut out smoking. And 10 nonsmokers took medication.

Those who quit smoking and took their medication

did the best. Almost half of the men treated this way, when retested for sleep erections, were found to be normal.

And three out of ten diabetic men who did nothing but quit smoking found themselves with adequate erections.

It is important to realize that, without proper tests and evaluation, you cannot assume that your disease is the cause of the problem. Certainly for some diabetic men erection problems are not linked to their disease, as was demonstrated by a study done at Loyola University's Sexual Dysfunction Clinic. Out of 27 diabetic men with erection problems who underwent sex therapy with their wives, 22 were able to have intercourse just a few weeks after beginning treatment. (Some experienced this welcome change in just the first two weeks.) While it is true that this particular group of diabetic men may have been in better control of their disease than some others, clearly the study director, Domeena C. Renshaw, M.D., is correct in stating that "diabetic impotence is *not* always due to diabetes." If a man convinces himself that he will develop sexual problems, he may talk himself into having them, physical factors or no. For many patients, sex therapy can be very helpful whether they have a physical condition to blame or not (see chapter 9). And men who get partial erections due to physical problems can learn how to get the most out of what they have.

While there are no magic potions to cure diabetes-caused potency problems, there are some treatments that are frequently effective. Penile implants, penile shots, medications, and sex therapy (all discussed in later chapters) have been used with good success. And in the future, some medicines may be able to improve the way damaged nerves work and possibly help some diabetic men. Currently under investigation, these drugs are not commercially available. Trials at several major medical centers are underway to test just how effective they are.

Blood Vessel Disease

Consider this scenario. Barry, a 65-year-old retired salesman, has a heart attack. Suffering from excruciating pain in his chest and left arm, Barry manages to call for help. He gets to the hospital quickly and receives immediate medical attention. After some time in the hospital, Barry is ready to go home. His doctor tells him he must make some changes in his life, especially in his diet, but assures him that he can otherwise resume normal activities—including sex. After several weeks, Barry is feeling close to his old self, but he still worries about his heart. He is concerned that the exertion caused by sex will bring on another heart attack. And finally, when he does try to have sex with his wife, he finds that he can't get an erection.

There may be physical causes for Barry's lack of erection. But his problem may be due only to anxiety —unnecessary anxiety. The exertion required by intercourse is roughly equivalent to that of climbing two flights of stairs, walking several blocks, or taking a heart stress test in the doctor's office. Researchers estimate that if a patient can do these activities without chest pain, palpitations or abnormal shortness of breath, there is only about a 1 in 10,000 chance that intercourse will bring on sudden death from a heart attack.

Heart-attack patients do not have to live in fear of having intercourse. If you've had a heart attack, ask your doctor to monitor your heart on the electrocardiogram (ECG) machine while you have a stress test. If you pass the test, you don't have to worry. Some men may want a portable ECG to monitor their heart at home, but for most this is not necessary.

Okay, you're probably not going to die during sex. But what if you get over the anxiety and *still* can't get an erection? What's happening?

Two studies concluded that 50 to 70 percent of men who were impotent after their heart attacks had experienced erection problems prior to their attacks, meaning that their erection problems were probably a sign of the same artery-blocking process that can lead to a heart attack. A heart attack happens when one or more arteries to the heart close up, and such an attack can be just the culmination of a long process of narrowing of the arteries. When the same narrowing occurs in one or more of the arteries supplying blood to his penis, a man is unable to get an erection.

In fact, it's estimated that a million and a half American men can blame their erection problems on arteries and veins that don't work properly. In one autopsy study, all men over age 38 had some narrowing of the arteries to the penis. Fortunately, however, that can largely be prevented with a healthy diet, proper exercise and general good health habits. (A small number of arterial-blockage cases occur when a man suffers a major trauma, such as an accident.) Some relatively rare diseases, like lupus, which affect the arterial system as well as other parts of the body, can also short-circuit erections by interfering with the blood-flow system.

Despite what you may have heard, even young men can have arterial disease, although it may take years before the damage presents itself in the form of erection problems or heart attacks. If you do develop blockage in the arteries supplying the penis, help is available. Usually, an implant will be the treatment of choice, but some patients can benefit from having a surgical bypass of the penile arteries (see chapter 8).

Arteries, though, are only half the story—the way the blood enters the penis. But the blood has to stay there for you to be potent. For that you need healthy *veins*.

For years, doctors thought only malfunctioning arteries deserved the blame for blood-flow problems in the penis, but now doctors have found that many men suffering erection problems can place the blame on their veins. Why?

Keep Illness from Undermining Potency

When a man's penis is flaccid, the veins keep the blood flowing out of the organ as part of the normal blood circulation. But during erection, the veins, squeezed by the blood-filled sinuses, must shut down partially to keep blood in the penis so it will stay firm and erect. If the veins don't shut down as they're supposed to, a man will experience a disheartening situation. He may get no erection at all; he may find himself with an erection which just never gets really firm or he may get an erection that disappears before he and his partner have a chance to enjoy it. What causes this discouraging condition? Apparently, some men are born with leaky veins; their veins never or almost never function properly.

Jason, a 60-year-old, first noticed a problem with erections when he was in his teens. When he was with a woman, he could not maintain an erection, although he felt very aroused. And even when he masturbated, his erection would disappear before he could ejaculate.

Jason went to numerous doctors, seeking help. Although his testosterone level was normal, Jason was given shots of the hormone—but there was no improvement in his erections. Jason got married after a doctor said it would solve his problem, but that didn't help either. Only very rarely could he maintain an erection for enough time to allow him to have intercourse. His wife was frustrated, depressed and hurt by the situation, and so was Jason.

The couple went to more doctors, seeking help. One psychiatrist tried to persuade Jason that he could live without sex, saying that companionship was all that really mattered. But the suggestion didn't go over very well with Jason and his wife. They wanted to enjoy sex.

Other doctors, unable to identify a physical cause for Jason's problem, told him he had a psychological problem. "Everyone told me it was psychosomatic," says this soft-spoken, well-dressed man, who looks younger than he is. But although no one could find a physical cause, Jason was reluctant to believe that his problem was indeed "all in my mind." Over many years, Jason paid a high price for his leaky veins—and the lack of medical knowledge about erections that existed during most of his life. He felt his self-esteem and confidence slipping away, and believes this contributed to problems at work. He was often depressed and withdrew from social activities to spend more and more time alone. After several years, Jason and his wife stopped having any type of sexual relationship. They were too frustrated.

But recently, new tests (discussed in chapter 7) found that leaky veins were the source of Jason's impotence. He had surgery to correct his malfunctioning veins, and for the first time in many, many years, Jason reports that he wakes up in the morning with an erection. (More about the surgical treatments for vein problems is found in chapter 8.) After some adjustment to their new physical relationship, Jason and his wife are able to enjoy intercourse.

Researchers believe that only a small number of men are actually born with leaky veins. But they theorize that there's another, more widespread cause of vein problems—arterial disease. It works—or rather doesn't work—like this. Normally, when a man becomes erect, the veins are squeezed shut as the sinuses in the penis fill with blood. Consequently, the veins become narrower and the blood flow through the veins out of the penis decreases. But if the blood flow into the penis is significantly reduced due to blockage of the diseased arteries, there's less pressure on the veins. This type of blood-flow problem develops gradually and can be caused or aggravated by smoking, a high-fat diet and diseases such as diabetes.

One sign of mild vein problems is that erections improve when the man stands up. Why? Because when even the most well-endowed man stands, his heart is higher than his erect penis. Consequently, the blood has to flow uphill to get back to the heart. The result is that the penis stays full of blood longer.

Very sophisticated tests like cavernosography (discussed in chapter 7) help detect vein problems. Once correctly diagnosed, vein problems can be treated, either by tying off the offending veins, or, if arterial disease is also severe, with a penile prosthesis (see chapter 8.)

Kidney Disease

Severe kidney disease can destroy a man's potency as it destroys his health. There are lots of reasons for this. Kidney disease can lower testosterone production and raise the level of another hormone, prolactin, which can cause erection problems. Recently, some doctors have successfully used a prescription medicine, bromocriptine, to lower prolactin levels. With this treatment, men with kidney disease have improved their erectile ability. Patients with kidney disease may suffer damage to nerves that are essential for erection. And even dialysis, the mechanical blood-cleaning process that can save patients with kidney disease, can cause impotence. Some doctors have found that dialysis may remove zinc from the body, and too little zinc can cause erection problems. Giving patients extra zinc to make up for this loss may help with potency. But the results are not clear; different researchers have come up with different results, some finding that zinc supplementation doesn't help.

(We hasten to point out that in healthy individuals in the U.S., zinc deficiency is quite rare. Extra zinc is *not* a cure for impotence.)

Hormone Imbalances

The Pituitary Gland

We all know that what we *think* can affect us sexually, but what goes on *physically* inside a man's brain can also have an enormous impact on his erections—specifically, what goes on inside his pituitary gland.

Just a little bigger than a peanut without its shell, and located in a recess at the base of the brain, the pituitary gland produces a hormone (luteinizing hormone) that tells the testicles to produce yet another hormone—testosterone—which is necessary for potency.

So necessary, in fact, that pituitary disease may not be all that uncommon among men who have erection problems. In different studies, researchers have found that 7 to 19 percent of patients with erection problems referred to medical clinics had pituitary disease that interfered with the proper functioning of their testicles.

The pituitary gland can be involved in another hormonal short-circuit: the *overproduction* of prolactin, a substance that in large enough quantities can reduce the production of testosterone and render ineffective the little that is manufactured. Prolactin excess is serious business—the extra hormone is produced by a pituitary tumor. Fortunately, the tumor is treatable by surgery or medication. And, in a sense, impotence here is a gift—it's a warning sign that a pituitary tumor may be developing. In fact, about 70 to 90 percent of men with such tumors do develop potency problems. These men can also experience a reduced sex drive, less facial and body hair, and their testicles may actually shrink in size. Sometimes they develop swelling of the breasts, but this quite obvious clue is uncommon, showing up in only about 10 percent of all patients. As we mentioned, erection problems caused by prolactin tumors can be successfully treated by surgically removing the tumor, or by blocking the effect of the excess hormone with medication. Once this is done, potency returns. Such erection problems are not permanent.

The Adrenal and Thyroid Glands

Adrenal or thyroid glands which go into overdrive, or shut down almost completely, can sabotage erections quite effectively—by reducing sexual desire and by making the man feel terrible. In many cases, such disorders are fairly easy to spot because the symptoms are obvious to a trained medical eye—sometimes they're so dramatic that anyone would realize something was wrong. A man with an overactive thyroid, for example, may have a fine tremor in his hands, bulging eyes, thinning of his skin and a very fast heart rate, as well as a decreased desire for sex and poor erections. In fact, in most cases, patients with such problems do get treated, because the unpleasant and uncomfortable symptoms send them to their doctors. There are some cases on record, however, in which the only symptoms were erection problems. Blood tests can identify these less obvious cases.

The two adrenal glands, which are located just above the kidneys, can also wreck potency if they produce too much or too little of cortisone-like substances. Once this condition is corrected by surgery or medication, adrenal patients will find their potency restored. No permanent damage to potency takes place.

Testicular Problems

Testicles that don't work properly can ruin a man's ability to get or maintain an erection, because the testicles produce testosterone, the male hormone vital to erection and sexual desire.

Men commonly develop testicular problems after the testicles have functioned normally for many years. Many things can hamper the testicles' ability to do their hormone-producing job: infections (such as mumps), chemotherapy, radiation treatments and prolonged alcoholism.

Occasionally, a man's testicles never function properly. If the testicles don't get in gear in time for puberty, a boy may never mature into a man. He will grow into normal size, but he won't develop the large muscles, body hair, beard and enlargement of the penis typically found in adult males. But if the boy who suffers from such damage or defects is treated with testosterone, he will develop normally.

> ### Klinefelter's Syndrome
>
> Named for the physician who discovered it, Klinefelter's Syndrome strikes about two men in every thousand. The degree to which this condition affects the man varies quite a bit, but typically these men have very small, jelly-bean-like testicles. There may be no other physical symptoms.
>
> Men with Klinefelter's are born with two female (X) chromosomes, instead of the usual one. The result: Their testicles don't produce normal amounts of testosterone. Not all of these men suffer from erection problems, but it's generally believed that all are infertile. Adding testosterone usually clears up the potency difficulty, but the infertility cannot be reversed.

Another cause of testosterone problems is age: The body's ability to use this hormone decreases with age. But this is typically such a gradual decrease that any effects usually don't show up until a man is quite elderly.

How do you know if you have low testosterone? Your body has warning signals: low energy, listlessness, a lack of sex drive and erection problems. But the only sure way to know if testosterone is lacking is to get a blood test. However, because a man's testosterone level is not constant, but spurts, pooling of several samples to get an accurate measure may be necessary for accurate results.

The effect of hormones on erections is still something of a mystery. Some men with low testosterone experience dramatic improvement when they get extra amounts to bring them up to normal. What's confusing is that not all men with low testosterone suffer from the effects of it—some are able to get normal erections without difficulty. A man with normal levels of testosterone will not get better erections if he takes unneeded supplements of the hormone, but his desire may increase—and he may endanger his health.

The fact that we can't say absolutely what is normal for any particular man makes the treatment of men with borderline low testosterone somewhat of a judgment call.

Injury to the Testicles

Nature has done a fairly good job of protecting the testicles despite their somewhat vulnerable location. Simply getting bumped or bruised in the groin will not usually cause any permanent damage to these sexually vital organs—although it can be excruciatingly painful. But severe injury to the testicles, which results in significant swelling, bleeding and bruising, can permanently damage these organs and impair their ability to manufacture testosterone. Luckily, nature has given men some protection by providing testicles in pairs; if just one testicle is injured, the other will almost always produce enough testosterone to keep the body running properly. For potency to be affected, both testicles must be impaired.

Testosterone: Pills or Shots?

Your doctor can prescribe testosterone in pill form, or give you injections. Because the pills aren't absorbed efficiently in the body, and may cause liver damage, we favor taking any needed testosterone by shot. The slight inconvenience of the needle seems outweighed by the increased effectiveness and safety of the drug. (Usually, the shots must be given about every three weeks.)

Nerve Diseases

Any disease or injury that damages the nervous system can cause erection problems. Multiple sclerosis, spinal cord injuries and other back problems, epilepsy, stroke and Parkinson's disease are among the most common causes of nervous system-linked potency problems, a few of which are discussed below.

Multiple Sclerosis (MS)

This disease, which seems to favor younger people as its victims, makes the nervous system degenerate. Small lesions attack the spinal cord and the brain and other parts of the nervous system which are essential to erection. Some male MS patients completely lose the ability to get an erection. Sometimes, men with MS can get erections, but they disappear before they can be enjoyed. Also, men with MS may find they can't ejaculate, and for some, sexual desire also decreases or disappears. In some men, the disease causes numbness in the penis. Some researchers think that only one in four male MS patients develops erection problems from the disease; others think almost half of them do.

Sometimes, erection problems go hand-in-hand with other signs of the disease; at other times impotence is the first sign that something is wrong. For example, Brian, an engineer, was 43 years old when he first noticed a change. "I was unable to get an erection, even with candlelight, wine, a romantic setting, the whole bit. Sometimes it just wasn't there." Over a period of three years this distressing condition went from being an occasional problem to a chronic one.

At first, Brian couldn't figure out what was wrong. He was filled with fear. "I just got very paranoid and embarrassed. I was afraid there was something wrong with me. I couldn't tell anyone about it, except my wife. But mostly we avoided the subject. And I avoided being intimate with her. She knew that failure would just depress me more."

After several months, Brian noticed he had problems walking. "I got very weak and collapsed. Finally I went to a doctor who suspected MS and confirmed the diagnosis. Actually, I felt relief at just knowing what was wrong."

Brian was faced with the enormous challenge of coping and adjusting to the debilitating changes that go along with MS. But, although Brian made it plain to his doctors for several years that he also wanted help with his erection problem, he didn't receive any. The doctors he consulted did not seem eager to deal with the issue. "Their attitude seemed to be 'Sorry about that, Jack, the impotence is just a side effect of MS.'"

Luckily, Brian found out about penile implants and was able to have the operation. (Penile shots—see chapter 8—are also used to treat MS patients.) Although the MS has taken its toll, Brian is glad that once again, at least sometimes, he can make love with his wife.

Spinal Cord Injuries

As far as the ability to get and maintain an erection is concerned, the location of the spinal cord injury is crucial. If the nerves which connect to the penis are injured in the place in the lower back where they leave the spinal cord, a man probably will not be able to get an erection because the nerves controlling the erection are injured. (Occasionally, patients with such injuries report that they can get an erection from being mentally aroused, but not from physical stimulation.) If the injury is higher and actually inside the spinal cord, a man may be able to get reflex erections from local stimulation even though he doesn't feel it. Such erections may not be well maintained, and they may disappear quickly. In some men, however, the erections work well and they are pleased they can satisfy their partner.

For Eddie, 28 years old, making his wife happy is important. An automobile accident two years ago left him permanently paralyzed from the waist down. Eddie's nerves were damaged so severely that now he can't feel anything below his waist, and he is completely unable to get an erection. But Eddie's brain was unaffected by the accident, and he still has quite powerful sexual desires for his wife, Carla. At first, Eddie and Carla went to see a urologist because they wanted to have another child. They found it easier to talk about fertility than about sexuality. But after some discussion, it was clear to them and the doctor that having a satisfactory sex life was also a great concern.

It's a terrible fact that Eddie will never recover from the devastating damage done to his nervous system. But he and his wife don't have to live the rest of their lives without being able to enjoy intercourse. Penile shots helped Eddie and Carla have sex for the first time in two years. This made them both very happy.

Back Problems

Back problems can cause erection difficulties. If a disc between the vertebrae slips and compresses the nerves coming out of the spinal cord, the pressure on the nerves can short-circuit the process necessary for erection. (And certainly the pain from a slipped disc can make sex the farthest thing from a man's mind.) Sometimes, surgery on the disc corrects the problem and restores potency; in other cases, the back pain disappears but the lack of erection remains. Such cases can be helped with penile shots or implants.

Diseases of the Penis

Priapism

Priapism is when a man gets an erection that won't go away. While this may sound like everyone's fantasy, priapism is actually dangerous and serious. Not only is it usually extremely painful, but priapism, left untreated, can cause permanent impotence.

What causes an erection that won't disappear? There are many known causes of priapism and then there are also some cases which defy explanation. The culprits are the blood vessels not doing their job properly. Rather than draining blood out of the penis on cue, the veins remain shut down and the arteries continue trying to pump blood into the penis. This state of affairs can be caused by sickle cell anemia, trauma to the penis, tumors in the penis or pelvic area or even, in some cases, by blood-thinning medications taken by men to keep their blood from clotting too readily. Some other drugs, such as certain tranquilizers and antidepressants, can also bring on priapism, probably because they affect the nervous system's control of the blood vessels.

If you find yourself with an erection that will not disappear, go to the nearest emergency room. Priapism needs to be treated within four to six hours after it develops—sooner, if at all possible.

Peyronie's Disease

Peyronie's disease, named for the doctor who discovered it, can also cause erection problems. Most often, this condition occurs in middle-aged men, who usually show up in the doctor's office complaining of a penis that curves to one side when erect. Sometimes this curvature makes intercourse difficult. Sometimes there is also pain that disappears when the erection does. And some patients can actually feel a lump in their penis. (They usually think they have cancer, but growths caused by Peyronie's disease are not cancerous.)

Not all men with Peyronie's disease become impotent, but some do. Sometimes the disease appears to be caused by injury to the penis, and even, according to some experts, by medications. And there appears to be a genetic component, since it sometimes runs in families.

For reasons doctors don't fully understand, the disease causes scarring in the corpora cavernosa, those all-important cylinders in the penis which must fill up with blood for erections to occur. This scarring can create the lumps, bending and pain which are the hallmarks of the illness.

A whole variety of treatments have been tried to stop the progress of the disease, including medication, radiation, injection of steroids into the penis and surgical removal of the lumps, but none have been proven particularly effective. About half of all patients get better over time (usually after about a year), so it's important to take the most conservative approach you can live with. If you do decide to try any type of treatment, be sure you're well informed about all the possible consequences. You may want to get a second (or third) opinion before proceeding. If severe bending with erection persists, an operation to straighten the penis may offer a permanent solution. In some cases, a penile implant may be necessary.

Surgery Can Cause Erection Problems

Any operation involving a part of the body necessary for erection can cause potency problems if it disturbs crucial arteries and nerves. The following operations have the greatest potential for causing erection problems.

Prostate Surgery

The prostate is strategically located—it's surrounded by nerves that control the penis, and arteries necessary for erection are close by. That's why surgical removal of the gland can cause potency problems. The prostate is removed for two reasons: a noncancerous (benign) enlargement of the gland that causes unpleasant side effects, or prostate cancer. Each condition requires a different type of surgery, and the resulting effects on potency can be dramatically different.

Surgery for Benign Enlargement of the Prostate A noncancerous enlargement of the prostate can go for years without causing any problems. Sometimes, however, it can cause serious, even life-threatening situations by causing urine backup and kidney damage.

More often, the prostate enlargement results in irritating but minor difficulties: difficult or slow urination, having to go to the bathroom very frequently and feeling the need to go almost all the time, even when there's not much urine in the bladder.

The solution to these unpleasant symptoms is the partial removal of the inner prostate, an operation called transurethral prostatectomy (TURP for short). This procedure doesn't require any incision, since the surgeon inserts his instruments through the end of the penis. And the shell (the exterior) of the gland is left intact. About 10 percent of men over the age of 50 have this surgery.

What does the operation do to potency? The short answer is: It doesn't hurt, but it doesn't help. If a man has normal erections before surgery, usually he won't have any problems after the operation. Fortunately, nature placed the nerves crucial to erection along the outside of the prostate, an area left untouched by the surgeon. If a man does have erection problems prior to surgery, however, typically they won't get better, and may become worse. Why? It may be because the nerves near the outer layer of the prostate are mildly damaged during surgery, or because of scarring that occurs during healing.

Surgery for Cancer of the Prostate The second type of prostate operation is done when a man has cancer of the prostate. Called a radical prostatectomy, this procedure involves the removal of the entire prostate and the seminal vesicles, always through an incision in the body. It's much more common for crucial nerves to be injured during this type of procedure. Because surgeons have now identified the exact location of these nerves, however, new methods have been developed to save them, and the odds that potency will be maintained are much better. Using these new techniques, popularized by Patrick C. Walsh, M.D., Chairman of the Department of Urology at Johns Hopkins University, the surgeon can preserve the nerves next to the prostate that control erection. The results are striking: One year after having their prostates removed, 86 percent of men who were potent before surgery retained their ability to get an erection. Previously, the vast majority of men who had such surgery were physically incapable of getting an erection. It does take some time to regain potency following prostate surgery; less than a third of the men were potent after just three months, but after nine months about 60 percent had regained potency. Younger patients were faster to recover their erectile abilities, and the smaller the cancer, the better the odds for preserving the nerves and the ability to get an erection. The nerve-sparing technique is now widely known, and any man contemplating prostate surgery should discuss the methods to be used with his doctor.

Dry Ejaculation It's important to know that after either type of prostate surgery, a man will retain his ability to feel an orgasm, but he won't ejaculate any fluid. Because the prostate produces part of the fluid a man ejaculates, after surgery he has less fluid to discharge; what does come out goes back into the bladder. This isn't harmful, and the ejaculated fluid simply mixes with urine and is discharged when the man voids.

Some research suggests that just knowing what to expect after prostate surgery can help a man keep his potency. So here's our advice for prostate patients.
- Be sure you understand why the doctor is recommending prostate surgery.
- Specifically, ask how it will affect your sexual functioning. Make sure you get a clear and comprehensive answer.
- If you're having a radical prostatectomy, make sure your doctor is familiar with the new nerve-sparing

methods. Some large tumors cannot be treated this way; if your physician advises against the new techniques, be sure you understand the reasons. Make sure you understand the pros and cons of any alternative treatment.
- Make sure your wife understands the procedure and the amount of time it will take you to recover. Encourage her to discuss with you and the doctor any concerns she may have.

For those patients who do lose potency after prostate surgery, penile prostheses or penile shots (discussed in chapters 7 and 8) can enable a man to get and maintain an erection.

Radiation-Associated Impotence Patients with prostate cancer may be given the option to have radiation therapy instead of surgery. On the face of it, you might expect that radiation therapy would be less damaging to potency than surgery. But recent research, reported by Dr. Irwin Goldstein and colleagues at Boston University, contradicts this assumption. Dr. Goldstein's research, all done on prostate cancer patients, found that pelvic radiation often causes the arteries to the penis to significantly narrow, thus impeding the blood flow necessary to maintain an erection. The researchers studied 23 patients. After pelvic radiation, 16 men who were potent before treatment lost their ability to get an erection.

Smoking and high blood pressure increased the odds that lack of erection would follow pelvic radiation. The men who didn't smoke and didn't have high blood pressure stood a better chance of remaining unaffected by the radiation treatment.

Radiation can also be given by placing radioactive "seeds" in the prostate. This procedure will often spare potency. Unfortunately, early results of this method indicate it may not be as good as other methods of treating cancer.

Bladder Surgery

Surgery for advanced bladder cancer requires removal of the bladder and the prostate. New nerve-sparing techniques can help prevent erection problems. Early tumors can also be treated by limited surgery performed through the urethra. This surgery will not affect potency.

Rectal Surgery

Rectal surgery for cancer is similar to radical prostate surgery in that crucial nerves may be injured. Unfortunately the nerves essential for erection are just too close to the rectum to allow for nerve-sparing techniques. Surgery on the rectum for nonmalignant disease, however, can be modified so that the nerves are preserved and the ability to get an erection is maintained.

Penile Surgery

The good news about surgery on the penis is that it's rare. It's usually performed when a patient has cancer of the penis (a disease which strikes very few men) or for a very severe case of Peyronie's disease, discussed earlier. It is not true that all penile surgery inevitably leads to lack of erection. Crucial blood vessels or nerves must be damaged for this to happen.

Testicular Surgery

Removing one testicle will have absolutely no effect on a man's physical ability to get and maintain an erection. The remaining testicle will produce enough of the male hormone, testosterone, to keep the man's erections just as normal as before the operation. Why would a man ever need to have both testicles removed? For two conditions: advanced prostate cancer and cancer in both testicles (an extremely rare condition).

Just as the healthy prostate depends on testosterone to keep functioning normally, prostate cancer needs testosterone to keep growing. In very advanced cases, the surgeon may recommend removing both testicles in order to get rid of the cancer's source of growth, testosterone. (This is another incentive to have annual rectal examinations if you are over 40 years of age; the sooner prostate cancer is detected, the better it can be treated. Early detection and treatment almost always leaves a man with both testicles.)

It's extremely rare for a man to develop testicular cancer in both testicles, but it does happen on occasion. Unfortunately, removing the testicles (the major source of testosterone production) also takes away much of a man's sexual desire. In this case, however, testosterone does not promote growth of the testicular tumors, so the hormone can be replaced with shots.

All of these potency-sapping medical problems are serious, and no man should try to diagnose and treat them on his own.

5

It Takes Two to Tango

If you're like many men, your initial response to an erection problem will be to leave your wife or lover alone—physically and emotionally. You'll feel you have enough trouble dealing with the problem yourself without confronting her with it. But your partner is greatly affected by your problem.

In fact, if you are married or seriously involved, the woman in your life can be extremely important—sometimes even essential—to helping you regain your potency and enjoy your sex life. Understanding and honest communication between partners can be the key to sexual success.

Isolation, neglect and misunderstanding will often only exacerbate the problem. Relationships are sometimes wrecked more by the couple's reaction to the potency problem than by the problem itself.

Jeff knows how important communication is. From the first time he had sex as a teenager, Jeff had a problem maintaining his erection. He could become easily aroused, but couldn't stay erect during intercourse. Doctors were never able to help him, and the problem caused him untold distress. When he was in his mid-20's, Jeff met the woman of his dreams, Ellen, and fell head over heels in love. Despite his erection troubles, he decided to get married. In fact, his doctor encouraged him to get hitched, thinking that the change in his lifestyle would cure the problem.

It didn't. Although Ellen had known about his lack of potency before they got married, and was understanding, she too had harbored hope that marriage would take care of the problem. Obviously she was disappointed, though she didn't make an issue of it.

They lived with the problem for many years, and it exacted a considerable toll. "We would try to make love," Ellen remembers. "And it wouldn't work. Jeff would become depressed within 24 hours. He felt inadequate, that he wasn't a man. It tore me up to hear him say such terrible things about himself."

The lack of intercourse was a serious problem for both of them, but they still reacted to each other with love and commitment. "It was very frustrating, but we had to get on with our lives. Impotence would not break up our marriage," Ellen says with certainty.

Their determination and good relationship paid off in the end. Although no one was able to determine the exact cause of Jeff's problem, he was treated with a penile implant. Now, two years after the surgery, Ellen and Jeff happily make love.

Jeff and Ellen's story may be more the exception than the rule. Let's face it, in this age of "sexual liberation," most of us still find talking about sex extremely difficult—especially if we're talking to the person who's nearest and dearest to us. Often, we're afraid of how our lover will respond. For people who have trouble expressing their feelings, sex talk may be completely off limits. But even people who are more emotionally open may find sex the one area they prefer to keep under the covers.

Such noncommunicative behavior can set in motion a chain of misery and pain. It can also make people a little crazy. For an illustration of just how crazy, let's look at another sensitive topic that has many parallels to potency: money.

Joe and Mary have been married for more than ten years, and each contributes to the family income. In their budget, each partner is allocated a certain amount of personal spending money. The rest of the money goes for joint expenses, like food, house payments and savings.

Suddenly, Joe is demoted at work, and his hours are cut. His paycheck suffers a huge reduction. Although the change at work isn't Joe's fault, and lots of other employees are similarly affected, Joe's sense of self-worth is shot full of holes. He feels like less of a man.

Joe doesn't tell his wife about the change in his situation and how bad it makes him feel. Without a word, he just cuts back on the amount he contributes to the family budget. He feels embarrassed, ashamed and guilty about his reduced participation, and he withdraws as much as possible. He doesn't talk much to Mary. He refuses social invitations. He becomes quite depressed.

Naturally Mary reacts by worrying about the reduced household budget. Although she is filled with questions—Is Joe spending his money on someone else? Did he lose his job, or get reduced hours at work? Does he feel less love for her, and thus want to contribute less?—she is afraid to ask them.

Joe deals with Mary's silence with his own set of unspoken questions. How is she coping with less money? Doesn't she mind? Is she making up the difference by getting more money from someone else?

If this tension and anxiety increase and the situation is allowed to continue, it will develop a life of its own, with each partner attributing negative motives and feelings to the other. The once-positive relationship Joe and Mary enjoyed will be poisoned by their imaginations. But this does not have to happen. Simple questions and answers spoken early on, coupled with warmth and support, can break this communications deadlock. Joe and Mary can decide what they want to do about the change in their finances—together. The same applies to potency problems.

Why Men Can't Talk about Potency

It may seem farfetched that a couple could go for years without discussing so vital a matter as a major change in finances. But many couples react in just this way when it comes to vital sexual matters. Erection problems may be particularly difficult to talk about, because in our culture, many men equate erectile ability with being a man. Even a man who is basically secure may find himself questioning his professional and personal competence when he faces an erection problem. He may suffer reduced confidence, lack of self-esteem and depression.

The importance of erections to many men's self-image is clear when we look at the comments of some men who used to have erection problems, but are now potent. For some, the significance of erectile ability goes far beyond sex.

One elderly man says that even though intercourse, because of ill health, is no longer a priority with him and his wife, he feels that restoration of potency was important. "It relieved some stress on my mind," he explains. "The idea of being able to perform helps me a lot."

Another man attributes his newly returned ability to get erections to a dramatic change in his whole attitude: "Now I feel that I can continue to function as a man. I fly an airplane and travel. I feel very special. I now move about in my social circles with confidence and pride. I am able to cope with life without embarrassment or doubts, and I enjoy every day as it occurs."

The fact that erection is crucial to many men is supported by interviews with the wives and girlfriends of some men with potency problems. Many of these women are very specific about their partners' changes in behavior and attitude. Typically, they found their husbands became depressed and very pessimistic when they couldn't get or keep an erection. Some say this negative attitude extended to work and even to such things as trying out new restaurants. Sometimes, out of desperation, a man would tell his wife to get a boyfriend. And sometimes just the opposite happened. Some men became extremely jealous when their wives had innocent social contact with other men, even though such extreme possessiveness had never before been a problem in the relationship. It was very common for the man to withdraw, physically and emotionally. And some women report—with pain—that their man rejected them pointblank when they tried to hug, kiss or just touch him.

This behavior is an unnecessary tragedy. A man who sees his self-worth measured in his penis is selling himself short. He's setting himself up for emotional trouble, because the odds are that sooner or later his erection will not come up to his expectations. For some this will be a momentary problem; for others it will develop into a chronic condition requiring professional treatment.

Not all men, of course, fall victim to such a restricted self-image that ties their penis to their self-worth. One man explains that he saw his erection problems as just another difficulty to be resolved, and he matter-of-factly compares his implant to the eye-

---

Breaking the Ice

You and your partner *can* talk about erection problems, even if the subject has been completely off limits up until now. In fact, you must talk. Here are some tips to make your first discussion a little easier:
- Pick a time when you are both relaxed.
- Make sure you have plenty of privacy.
- Start by telling your partner how much you value your relationship.

You may want to bring up the questions below. The goal is to use this time to *listen* to your partner. Don't try to change the way she feels, just try to understand. Questions to consider:
- Does the potency problem change the way you feel about me?
- What can I do to help the situation—and you?
- How has my behavior changed since the problem started?
- How does this change make you feel?
- What should we do about the problem?

glasses he wears. With this positive attitude, he accomplished his goal with much less anguish than many other men experience.

How Women React

Women have many of the same fears as men. And a wife or lover may be afraid that by talking about the problem she'll find out that *she* is the problem—that she's doing something that turns him off. And she may fear finding out that her husband does fine with other women. She also may be afraid that his health is the problem; she may resist talking about the difficulty, hoping it will "cure" itself, so she'll know he is physically okay. And some women want to protect their husband's feelings. Sensing their partner's reluctance to talk, they avoid the topic. They don't want to, as one woman says, "make him feel any worse than he already does."

Our research indicates that women react to erection problems in a wide variety of ways. In many cases we looked at, the way a woman responded appeared to be greatly influenced by the way she and her husband normally communicated. The more reassurance and love that was available on both sides, and the more both were involved in solving the problem, the more manageable the sexual difficulty was. When there was less communication there was more opportunity for hurt feelings, self-doubt, blame and anger to fester—and erupt.

Some women, especially those in relationships where potency had been a long-standing unresolved problem, felt cheated. Some saw erection as proof that they were truly desired by their husbands, and to them, the absence of erection meant rejection. As a child, Jenny, now 47, had learned rigid ideas about what constituted "normal" sexual behavior, and had never critically examined them. She never masturbated until she was well into her adult years, and then only allowed herself this pleasure after a doctor assured her it was acceptable. Unfortunately, because of her husband's long-standing erection problem, she was able to have successful intercourse with him only a few times during their 25-year marriage. "I've been deprived my whole life," says Jenny. "I haven't worked with him as well as I could. I think if I knew we *could* have intercourse, then other kinds of sex would be all right—it's almost a matter of principle." Fortunately, Jenny's husband was able to benefit from recent research into blood-flow problems, and since having surgery, he's been able to get and maintain nearly normal erections.

A woman who sees an erection as a type of lie detector which reveals the man's true feelings may be so concerned about her own self-worth that she may ignore her partner's explanations and his pain. "I tried to explain my situation to one woman I cared for," recalls Andy, a 34-year-old insurance agent whose potency problem is caused by his diabetes. "But she couldn't accept what was happening."

Good Talkers Make Great Lovers

The couples that seem to come through the experience of erection problems best are the ones who keep the lines of communication open. Sometimes it takes a great effort on the part of both the husband and wife. Potency problems are potentially more destructive players in a relationship than other health problems. When the partners maintain open communication, are supportive of each other and take the attitude that "we're going to work this thing through," a relationship can even be strengthened by the problem. Jay and Hilda have been married three decades and have had more than their share of troubles, including financial setbacks and some serious health problems for both of them. "We've been through a lot together," says Hilda, reflecting on their shared years. "The two of us, and our two sons. But we're a special, good family. In a way I think our troubles have made us especially close.

Even now we will sit around the kitchen table and just talk things out."

Jay is a plain spoken man who had to quit school at an early age to go to work to support his family. Now nearly ready to retire, he regrets his lack of education and the fact that he's labored at factory jobs all of his life. But he takes great pride in the fact that he's always supported his family and managed to help put his two sons through college. Jay is also a man who always had a strong sex drive, and he and Hilda count sex as one of the great pleasures in their lives.

"My goal has always been to satisfy my wife," he says. "Our communication is excellent. After all, what's good for her is good for me."

"We always had a good sex life," Hilda concurs.

Several years ago, Jay suffered a series of health problems. He had major surgery several times, including a prostate operation. Unfortunately, Jay's doctor gave him little advice or information about the possible changes the surgery and the major stress on his system from the different operations could bring. As far as sex goes, "He just said use it or lose it," recalls Hilda.

Once Jay recovered from his health problems, he was eager to resume relations with his wife. But he couldn't keep an erection. "I had a lot of stress in my life, still," he says. "I had two kids in college, and Hilda has a chronic illness which sometimes flares up." So, at first, Jay attributed his erection problems to these very real pressures.

But when the problem persisted, it began to take its toll. "The way it happened, my husband decided he wasn't interested in sex. This was a big change! He was always the one to initiate sex," Hilda says. "But he couldn't maintain an erection. We talked about it. Jay was very concerned, and said, 'Every time we start I know I won't keep an erection, or I won't get one.' I kept reassuring him. I didn't want him to worry."

Jay was frustrated, and tried to use up his sexual energy on more physical activities. He took up athletics with a vengeance. He felt better after a good sweat, but the erection problem persisted. Yet, unlike some couples, Jay and Hilda did not stop communicating. All through this difficult period, they remained emotionally close. The skills that had enabled them to weather financial and health problems kept them going through this very difficult time. Bolstered by the fact that they had such a strong relationship, Hilda didn't feel personally threatened by her husband's problem. And she made sure she was completely involved in seeking a solution. "I went with him to the doctor all the time! In fact, I insisted on being there. One doctor kept trying to get me to leave, but I told him, you're not going to show me anything I haven't seen before!"

Finally, after a confusing and frustrating period of time, a specialist diagnosed Jay's problem: Peyronie's disease. Although some patients get better with nonsurgical treatment, the physician thought Jay's condition was unlikely to reverse itself. If Jay wanted to have erections, his treatment would have to be a penile implant.

As with every other aspect of the problem, the couple discussed the proposed solution in some detail. Jay decided to have the operation, and Hilda agreed and supported his choice.

It's now been almost 18 months since Jay had the surgery, and he and his wife are quite happy with the results. "We had coped with so much that this wasn't all that much to deal with. We work together," says Hilda.

In this case, Jay and Hilda functioned as a team throughout Jay's potency problem the same way they had dealt with other stresses. And although Jay's physicians apparently didn't take full advantage of the fact that Hilda was an available source of important information about her husband's spirits, concerns and general well-being, she and her husband made sure that she remained involved.

Jay and Hilda had a lot going for them including many years of practice in talking openly to each other and a history of good sexual relations. But even couples who get off on the wrong foot can reroute themselves before it's too late.

Fixing a Communication Breakdown

Gary manages a furniture store and he met Cynthia, his second wife, when she began working at a nearby business. Gary and Cynthia dated for almost a year before they married.

Cynthia was burdened by a painful history when she married Gary. She had previously been married to a man who constantly criticized her and belittled her appearance and her sexuality. For a long time, she believed that she was incapable of enjoying sex or of pleasing a man sexually. But being with Gary changed all that. "It opened up a whole world to me, it was wonderful," says this petite, shy woman. Then, after a couple of years of marriage, Gary developed erection problems. "It came on gradually. There was absolutely no problem when we first married," says Cynthia.

Gary and Cynthia didn't talk about the change in their sex life and their painful silence continued for three long years. "I kept thinking it was an isolated problem. But it was driving me up the wall and the last year I finally had to accept the fact it just was not working, and I tried to talk to Gary about it," says Cynthia. She prepared herself for this discussion by reading a book on sexual responsiveness. But just mentioning the topic upset Gary tremendously. Concerned that she had caused him such pain, Cynthia dropped the matter. "We went for two weeks without talking about it—at all. Then he said, 'Okay we really should do something.' So we tried to follow some of the recommendations in the book—sort of doing sex therapy at home. And it helped some. But I got impatient. I short-circuited the whole thing."

Gary finally sought medical help several months later, but he didn't tell his wife until after he went to the doctor. She was greatly relieved when she learned that he had finally taken this first step. "I didn't want to bring up the subject again because I felt guilty. I mean, on some level, when a failure occurs, when he can't get an erection, I feel he must hate me. It feels like rejection."

Gary went through several tests, and much to the surprise of his physician, was found to have extremely low levels of testosterone. In addition to causing Gary's erection problems, this abnormality could even have contributed to his lack of motivation to correct the situation, since low testosterone can reduce desire. Gary was placed on shots of the hormone, and several weeks later reported that his erections were normal. And he and Cynthia were able to make love again.

"It's been reasonably successful," says Cynthia of the treatment. "But Gary still doesn't talk about the cause. We don't talk about it." Tears well up in her eyes. Although her husband has a demonstrable physical cause for his potency problem, she still feels rejected. And his silence hasn't helped her.

Cynthia's experience illustrates some important points. A woman can see her partner's erection as proof of her own desirability. If she's insecure about her sexuality, an erection problem, even in a good marriage, can trigger a lot of painful emotions. And she may react as Cynthia did, by feeling rejected and not wanting to deal with the issue directly. Gary's potency problem was easy to treat. The communication problem might have been more easily solved if Gary and his wife had gone to the doctor together. Cynthia could have learned about the many causes of erection problems and understood the reasons for the tests; and perhaps a private discussion with the physician would have laid to rest many of her fears.

For Gary and Cynthia, the story has a happy ending. Cynthia told a close friend about her fears, and was encouraged to take the initiative and ask Gary more questions about his condition. That got the communication ball rolling, and Gary not only answered her questions, he also began volunteering information and reassuring his wife that she was in no way to blame.

For Gary and Cynthia, the communications logjam

was gradually broken, and their marriage did not suffer permanent damage. But what happened illustrates another important principle:

If you and your partner don't discuss what is going on, there will be an information gap. And each of you will fill in this void by imagining what is happening to the other, and why. This will only lead to further problems.

For example, a man may wonder why his wife isn't making their lack of intercourse an issue—doesn't she enjoy sex with him? He may guess that she thinks him "less of a man." He may become jealous, even if he's never been jealous before. "In the back of his mind he questioned if I would be faithful," remembers Terri, whose marriage of more than 20 years never had been troubled before by such doubts. "I felt this insecurity, and he mentioned it. This bothered me." Fortunately, talking about the problem removed her husband's fears that she would leave him.

And it's common, in the absence of other information, for a woman to assume that an erection problem is somehow her fault. While a woman who is very secure in her own self-image and in her relationship may not feel this way, many women take erection problems as a sign that something is wrong with them. Like Cynthia, they may feel they have done something wrong. Or they may see an erection as a sign that they are sexually attractive and capable, and see the lack as an indication of their own failure. The cure for such lack of communication: involvement, information and reassurance.

Waiting Can Be Hazardous to Your Relationship

It's important not to let the situation fester for a long time without talking about it. Be honest and up-front about how difficult it is for you to discuss it—and then start talking. The longer you wait, the more opportunity there will be for bad feelings to develop.

This happened to Walt, a field supervisor for a large

private utility, and Becky, his wife of 20 years, who ran her own crafts business. They were a happy couple with three children in high school. Walt, a muscular, physically-fit man spent his free time on family activities and kept his small farm running smoothly. Sex was very important to him, and he took pride in the fact that he and his wife had an active, satisfying sexual relationship.

Walt was the kind of man who never was sick, but after his 42nd birthday he developed a severe infection in his bladder. Excruciating pain forced him to go to the doctor, but the infection proved stubborn and remarkably resistant to treatment. In rare cases, such a condition can infect a testicle, and that's what happened to Walt. Although he was given an antibiotic that ultimately cleared up the bladder infection, the infected testicle could not be saved and had to be surgically removed.

Now, as we've explained in previous chapters, the removal of just one testicle does not affect a man's ability to have an erection, or reduce his chances of fathering a child. The other testicle simply picks up the testosterone-producing and sperm-manufacturing functions of the missing organ.

But for Walt, who took such pride in the appearance of his body, losing one testicle was an enormous shock. Physically, he recovered from the operation, but he was beset with anxiety and fear. Walt felt that a vital and essential part of himself was missing. For the first time in his life, this man began to have trouble maintaining an erection. When Walt started to have intercourse, his erection would disappear.

Becky was totally unprepared for this turn of events. Sometimes she became very disappointed when Walt lost his erection while she was sexually aroused. She didn't understand the reasons for the sudden change in her husband (neither did he), and sometimes she became angry.

Even now, several years later, Walt becomes upset when he remembers what happened. "My erections went away overnight." He became more and more troubled and increasingly fearful of trying to have intercourse.

This was an enormous and painful change for Walt and Becky, who considered sex a major and important part of their relationship. But even though the problem continued, they didn't talk about it. Instead, Walt put his energies into avoiding sex—and his wife. He put in long hours at work, and when he was home became extremely creative in finding reasons to stay away from Becky. "I didn't want to start anything I couldn't finish," he says.

It seems clear from Walt's story that his erection problem was psychological, not physical. When his anxieties about the loss of his testicle first surfaced, he could have been helped by some intensive, short-term counseling aimed at reassuring him that he was just as capable of having an erection as he ever had been. Perhaps Walt needed to mourn the loss of a part of his body that was important to him. He also could have had his missing testicle replaced by a lifelike artificial one which would have given him the appearance he valued so highly.

But, unfortunately, Walt did not seek out and did not receive help. And neither did Becky. In fact, they went for three years without consulting anyone. That's a long time to go without sex, and Becky and Walt were living together without physical affection of any kind, without much warmth or tenderness and with limited communication.

Going into the fourth year of the problem, Walt finally mentioned it to his family doctor. By then, however, the damage to the marriage was irreparable. Although Walt ultimately was able to regain his potency, he and Becky separated.

Even now it is difficult for Walt to talk about his experience. "My wife is a good woman," he says with apparent pain. "But she couldn't put up with my problems. If I had to do it over again, I'd get help sooner." That's good advice from someone who knows.

Putting the Cart before the Horse

Sometimes a couple may decide to work on their relationship before they try to fix the man's potency. If your doctor suggests that you go to a counselor, he might be giving good advice. If you fix the erection problem, but because of emotional difficulties in the relationship, your partner isn't happy with the result, you might have taken the wrong approach. Howard did.

Howard, a 55-year-old successful businessman and former professional athlete, arrived at the doctor's office with his fiancée, Christina, a slightly plump, attractive widow of 45. Howard and Christina looked like a happy couple about to embark on a second marriage after knowing each other for several years. But their facade crumbled within a very short period of time.

Howard explained with some hostility that he had come to see the doctor only at his fiancée's insistence. She thought he had a problem. The short blonde woman smiled, but she refused to participate in the conversation, and all the doctor's attempts to involve her yielded nothing. Finally, Christina excused herself.

Once his partner was out of the room, Howard reiterated that Christina was the problem, not him. He was perfectly satisfied with his ability to get and maintain an erection. Furthermore, he explained that he took great pains to sexually satisfy his fiancée. He appeared quite knowledgeable about male and female physiology and talked about many different ways to achieve sexual pleasure.

At this point, the confused physician decided he would talk with Christina alone. She was somewhat reluctant, but she agreed. First Christina double-checked the door to the doctor's office to make sure it was securely shut. Then she sat down, looked the physician straight in the eye, and declared, "He doesn't get a good erection. He thinks he does, but he doesn't!" Christina's shy, somewhat timid manner disappeared:

She insisted that Howard was fooling himself about his ability to function; she was sure that her partner's erections were not satisfactory.

The doctor decided that a complete physical examination of Howard was in order. Howard turned out to be in excellent physical condition. He had no chronic diseases which could cause erection problems; he had normal blood pressure, and wasn't taking any medications which were known to cause potency difficulties.

To test Howard's ability to get an erection, the doctor gave him a penile shot (see chapter 7). Within a short period of time, Howard obtained a full, firm erection, demonstrating that his essential-to-erection blood-flow system was in good working order. "This is just like the erections I normally get," Howard declared with obvious satisfaction.

The doctor was curious to see if Christina would agree with Howard's assessment. But although she came into the room, Christina refused to look at the erection.

What was going on here? How could Howard and Christina differ so radically about what happened between them? The doctor was puzzled, but he was sure of one thing: Howard and Christina were not communicating, and that problem needed to be solved before any possible erection difficulty was addressed.

The doctor pointed out that since Howard and Christina had strong differences in perception they might benefit from some counseling. Somewhat to the physician's surprise, they agreed this was a good idea. On the doctor's recommendation, they made an appointment with a psychologist who was also a well-trained, experienced sex therapist.

The therapist saw Howard and Christina together, and separately. She also gave them some tests to determine their attitudes towards sex and gauge their sexual experience.

All the results pointed to much unresolved conflict between Howard and Christina that was due to problems other than sex. She was very upset at her fiancée, but she was unable to express it directly. Instead, even with the evidence of his erection, she denied that he was able to function sexually as he thought he did—something which was of great importance to him.

In this case, the physician was able to determine in fairly short order that Howard's erections were not the major problem, but were just singled out as the target. If the doctor had concentrated his efforts on "fixing" Howard's erections (which didn't even seem to be "broken"), the communication problem would have remained unresolved, leaving Howard and Christina unhappy and at odds with each other. Instead, the couple agreed to see a professional counselor who would help them deal more directly with their anger.

Don't Leave Her in the Dark

Sometimes, the desire for a "quick fix" to an erection problem backfires because the woman's needs, and the whole structure of the relationship, are ignored. It's important that both partners agree on the therapy.

Martin's experience illustrates just how crucial the involvement of the partner can be. This quiet man had been married for some 30 years and was nearing the age of retirement. He'd suffered from erection problems for the last 10 years, but didn't think anything could change that. While in the hospital for a minor surgical procedure, however, Martin began talking with the nurses and doctors, and found out about penile implants. Martin decided this was the solution he was looking for.

A few weeks later, Martin showed up at the clinic. He was very direct about the problem and the solution. Tests showed that blood-flow problems were the culprit in his inability to get an erection, and a penile implant was suggested as a solution. First, however, the doctor wanted to explain the procedure to Martin's wife. "My wife thinks the implant is the greatest thing since sliced bread," Martin declared, and explained that she had been called out of town on pressing business. He assured the doctor, however, that he had explained the entire procedure to her, that she had no questions and that she was totally in favor of the operation.

The urologist, taking Martin at his word, performed the surgery without talking to or meeting Martin's wife. Everything went without a hitch, and, after several days in the hospital, a happy Martin was sent home to recover, with instructions not to use the implant until the doctor said it was all right (usually, several weeks after surgery).

Martin had done extremely well in the hospital, with few complaints of pain. But after he returned home, he was very uncomfortable. Several office visits failed to establish any cause for the unusual amount of pain, and in fact Martin was healing very well. No one could find anything wrong with him, but he was clearly unhappy.

Finally, just three weeks after the surgery, Martin returned once again to the clinic, this time demanding that the implant be removed. "Take it out or I'll cut it out myself," he yelled.

Martin refused to discuss the matter in any detail. He was adamant that the "thing" be removed, and would not answer any questions about his wife's feelings about his operation.

Faced with this situation, the clinic doctors decided they had no choice but to schedule surgery to remove the implant. But the staff was troubled by Martin's dramatic change in attitude. Finally, a staff member, attempting to reach Martin at home, found himself talking with Martin's heretofore elusive, always out-of-town-on-business wife. She was extremely angry. "How dare you put this thing in my husband? It was those young nurses in the hospital who convinced him to have this done! I won't let him back in the house until you remove it," she said.

Martin's wife said further that she had told him from the very beginning that she did not want him to have the surgery. She was through with sex, and she wanted things to remain as they had been.

As it turned out, Martin had never consulted his wife about having his potency problem treated. Like many couples, Martin and his wife had lived with the erection problem for ten years, and in many respects had adjusted to that situation. To change it suddenly without the clear and informed involvement of both partners was a disaster.

The surgeon, resolving to never again put an implant in a married man without first interviewing the wife, removed the prosthesis from Martin. He recovered without difficulty, and returned home.

Cases like this just reinforce the fact that the woman should be involved in treatment to boost potency.

The Woman's Needs

Many women have told us that although they took pains to make sure they remained involved in their husband's diagnosis and treatment, they felt ignored by the doctor. One woman said the doctor treated her like a piece of furniture. "I was there the whole time. None of the doctors ever talked to me. Nobody asked me what I was going through, how I felt. I would have found that helpful, yes," says Andrea, who's been married to her husband for ten years.

Andrea learned the hard way that some doctors must be pushed to involve the woman in therapy. One way to guarantee the woman's participation is to make it plain that you and your wife function as a team. If your doctor doesn't agree, and you aren't satisfied with the explanation, consider seeing someone else. After all, you're paying for the service, and you have a right to have your needs met.

The physician may want to interview and examine you alone, but you can explain that you want your wife included at the end of each visit, to hear for herself what's happened and what the next step is. The idea is to make sure that you and your wife have ample opportunity to voice any concerns and questions.

6

Self-Help: A 12-Week Potency Program You Can Try at Home

Self-help is sometimes the best way to solve a potency problem, because when it works, self-help can save time, anxiety, and money and give you a real understanding of your body. The key to making self-help work is informed analysis. You've got to know what you are doing. You've got to take a good hard look at your habits, stresses and feelings and then decide just how they might affect your potency.

The best time to try self-help is at the beginning of your problem, before your potency difficulties have had a chance to become part of the pattern of your life. You'll also be in better shape emotionally to help yourself—and your lover—than you would be after months or years of frustration and disappointment.

We think it's extremely important that you decide up front how much time you will spend on self-help before turning to professional help. We recommend that you try self-help for no more than 12 weeks after the erection problem starts—after that, you should see a specialist. Since it can take that much time to get an appointment with some experts, you may want to schedule a visit and then use the waiting time productively on self-help.

So that you won't jump blindly into a self-help program that might do more harm than good, we've designed a safe, effective plan for you. Here's what you should do.

(A note of caution before we begin describing the program. Sometimes a self-help program is *not* the proper first step. If your erection problem has persisted more than 12 weeks, you should see your physician first, to make sure impotence is not your body's way of signaling an illness. And of course, if you have any symptoms other than the erection problem, you should see your physician without delay.)

The 12-Week Self-Help Program

Weeks 1 through 3: Stopping Self-Sabotage

These first three weeks are the time to examine your lifestyle for common erection saboteurs. Sometimes your problem can be solved just by getting rid of these problems. The first thing you must do is quit smoking. Amazing as it sounds, some men find that if they stop smoking, their erections return in short order. Smoking sabotages potency by constricting the blood vessels, including those in the penis that are essential to erections. The result: Not enough blood gets into the penis to produce or maintain an erection. Some men find that soon after giving up cigarettes their blood vessels return to normal, and their ability to have intercourse returns. Right now, there's no way to predict which men will reap sexual rewards from quitting and which won't. So every man should quit. (By the way, tobacco is the culprit, not just cigarettes, pipes and cigars. This means that chewing tobacco, nicotine gum and other, similar products may also mess up your erections.)

If the thought of quitting tobacco forever depresses you, try quitting for at least three weeks. That much time without nicotine should be enough to let you know if eliminating tobacco will solve or help your problem.

For example, Ralph, a 47-year-old auto parts salesman, had suffered erection problems sporadically, for a long time. But then they became common, and even when he was able to become erect, he often could not stay that way long enough to enjoy intercourse.

Ralph started smoking cigarettes in high school, and over the next three decades his habit increased to three packs a day. Apart from that threat to his health, he took good care of himself: He was not overweight, he exercised regularly and he drank only occasionally, and then with moderation. He had no chronic illnesses which could explain his erection problem.

Ralph went in for a complete examination and history. The physician was curious to see if Ralph was physically capable of getting and maintaining an erection. So he gave him a penile shot, a diagnostic test explained in chapter 7.

The result was less than spectacular: Ralph's erection was at half mast, and quite soft. Within a few minutes it had completely disappeared. Clearly, his physical system was not working normally.

Ralph was scheduled to have some additional tests in three weeks, but in the interim, the doctor advised him to cut out all smoking. Although the physician was privately skeptical that it would actually make a difference, he figured it was worth a try before Ralph underwent complicated and expensive tests.

Ralph quickly went from three packs to three cigarettes a day. Three weeks later, he returned to the clinic, eager to report that his erections had returned. He was able to sustain them and have intercourse.

There is research to back up Ralph's experience. As part of one study, 20 men—longtime smokers who went through at least one pack each day—were told to stop smoking. None of the men had sleep erections at the beginning of the research, all of them were suspected of having blood-flow problems and half were known to be diabetic. After six weeks without tobacco, 7 fortunate individuals found that they could get erections again.

Along with giving up tobacco, you should drink only moderately—especially if you are a heavy or regular drinker. Heavy consumption of alcohol can ruin potency in the short term. And in the long run, too much alcohol can shrink a man's testicles, reduce or remove sexual desire and render him impotent.

If you drink only occasionally, analyze your habits. If your erection fails on the days that you drink, try eliminating all alcohol on the days when you know you want to enjoy sex.

Individual tolerance varies quite a bit. One man may be able to drink four stiff ones without being affected, while another may find that just two drinks wreck his potency. And when alcohol is combined with other drugs, it can have an even greater effect on your potency—and endanger your general health.

It's a popular belief that alcohol reduces inhibitions and thus makes it easier for the drinker to become aroused. But research tells a somewhat different story. If a man is relaxed, not distracted, and able to concentrate on sex, alcohol may help him respond sexually. However, if he has worries and concerns about sex and other matters (and who doesn't?) alcoholic drinks may just make it more difficult for him to respond.

So we suggest that you try remedying your erection problems by cutting down your alcohol intake. (If you need help, ask your doctor, or find a self-help group.)

These first three weeks involve cutting a lot of things out of your life, and here's one more thing you should examine: medicine. Make a list of all medications you are taking—both prescription and over-the-counter. You may suspect that a drug deserves the blame for your sexual problems, and you could be right (see the drug chart in chapter 3). In many cases, changing the medication, the dosage or the time you take it will help solve the problem.

In the interest of your health, never reduce, eliminate or change the way you take a prescribed drug without first checking with your physician. (A man who suddenly stops taking his high blood pressure medicine, for example, may find that a stroke is the first—and, possibly, last—sign that he has made a mistake. Obviously, such "mistakes" should be avoided.)

Recreational drugs can also wreck potency. It's not uncommon for a man on street drugs to lose his sexual desire. Sometimes it's a physical response. Other times the drugs just may become more important to the man than his sex life.

So if you want to regain your erections, try quitting these drugs—even if you indulge only occasionally. If you need help to quit, get it—quickly.

Hopefully, your potency will be restored after the third week of watching your medication and cutting out tobacco, alcohol and drugs. But if it isn't, or if you didn't smoke, drink or take drugs in the first place, you'll want to move on to the next stage in the self-help program, which encompasses weeks 4 through 12.

The Next Level: Reducing Stress, Boosting Confidence

Sometimes, particularly in the case of a young, healthy man, it's possible to rule out most of the physical causes of the erection problems just with some simple self-evaluation.

If *everything* below is true, your erection problem probably doesn't have a physical cause:
- You are in good health.
- You don't abuse alcohol or drugs, and haven't in the past.
- You're not currently taking *any* medications.
- You've suffered no injury or trauma to your pelvic area or nervous system.
- You have normal morning erections—most of the time, you awake with an erection.
- When you masturbate, you can get a full, firm erection—and sustain it.
- Your desire for sex is about the same as it was before the problem started.

If these are true, chances are your problem is the result of stress, tension or emotional pressures. Some men can link the onset of their erection problem to pressures on the job, at home or in their relationship with their wife or lover. And stress can be heightened when a man's behavior changes as a result of a potency problem. Some men distance themselves from their wives, avoiding physical intimacy like hugging, kissing and cuddling because they are afraid to start something they can't finish.

Men who don't have a regular partner should consider the effect impotence has on their social life and dating habits. Some men blame their erection difficulties for their loneliness when actually they've withdrawn and pushed others away.

If you fit any of these profiles, stress and anxiety may play a major role in your erection problem. If so, you should try to give yourself a break and take a breather from concentrating on your erection problem. Sometimes the best way is to stop trying to have intercourse for a short period of time—say, a few weeks. Of course, you should share this decision with your partner.

Your partner may welcome a time to cuddle and be close, a vacation from the pressures of solving the erection difficulty. An intimacy break without intercourse may help—and might even solve your problem.

Also, you should realize that if you are withdrawing from your partner, the harm done to a relationship is often far worse than the damage caused by lack of intercourse itself. So, relax and remain affectionate.

Thomas learned the importance of this, but it took a while. This tall, thin, 55-year-old businessman first developed an erection problem as a side effect of some medication he was taking. Thomas's doctor changed his prescription, thinking that would be the end of the problem. But it wasn't. Thomas still could not become erect. He was furious. He was convinced that the medicine had permanently damaged his sexual ability. His physician's assurances that Thomas was, in fact, "the same man" did nothing to change his belief, quiet his rage or cure his erection problem.

A few weeks later, Thomas showed up at another

clinic, extremely tense and nervous. He had difficulty talking about his problem, but gradually, with a lot of encouragement, his story emerged.

He explained that after the "failure" of his first doctor he quickly became disgusted with traditional health care. Instead, he sought out an "herb" doctor, who prescribed a potion. (Analysis of this "drug" later revealed that it contained human placenta, ginseng and ground-up animal testicles among other things.) Although Thomas had been taking this mixture faithfully every day, as instructed, he had seen no improvement. And he would have noticed any change: He was attempting intercourse compulsively at least once a day, so he would know exactly how he was doing. To bolster his efforts, he stole some time from his business to go to peep shows to see if what he watched would produce an erection. Still, no luck. The failure of the herb medicine finally drove him to seek medical help once again.

Clearly, Thomas was a rather high-strung guy, and just sharing his story seemed to defuse some of his anxiety. He confided that a major source of stress in his life was a small bakery he and his wife owned. Competition from larger outlets was fierce and the couple worked 14-hour days just to keep their business afloat.

Despite all of Thomas's very real pressures, he had several important things in his favor: He'd only been without erections for a few weeks, so the potency problem, while painful, had not yet become ingrained in his life. He still had a good relationship with his wife, although she did not appreciate her husband's obsessive daily attempts to have intercourse. What she didn't like the most, Thomas confided, was watching him berate himself after each "failure."

Thomas was a good candidate for self-help: He was healthy, eager to solve his problem and open to a new approach. And fortunately, he could count on his wife's cooperation.

So his doctor prescribed a self-help program—one that was far removed from Thomas's rigid and self-defeating program of daily performance tests and peep-show tours. Instead, the self-help program called for Thomas to take the pressure off. The doctor told him not to attempt sexual intercourse at all for two weeks. He was encouraged to enjoy sexual pleasure in other ways, but intercourse was off limits. And he was to share this plan with his wife, and enlist her support.

A few days later, relieved of his pressure to perform, Thomas's erections returned. At his next clinic visit, he reported that he and his wife were again enjoying intercourse.

It was fortunate that Thomas had not shut himself off from his wife when his problem began. Some men withdraw physically and emotionally from friends, family and work because they feel somehow less than "a whole man." If you react like this, get professional help for your potency problem, and for the stress you and your loved ones are feeling.

Some men aren't aware that they suffer from stress and performance anxiety. Jimmy, a 24-year-old graduate student at a large university, visited a urologist, complaining that he was unable to get an erection. Like many students, Jimmy was juggling a lot of demands. He had a part-time job, a heavy class load and still made time for personal relationships. He was attractive and charming, so he had little trouble meeting women. The problem, he said, was that his relationships did not last. Occasionally, in a new relationship, Jimmy would become erect, but he usually lost potency before he could have intercourse.

A crucial piece of information came to light when Jimmy revealed that he could get satisfactory erections when he masturbated. He had no trouble sustaining an erection when he was alone. And he frequently awoke with an erection. He had no chronic illnesses, and a complete physical examination showed only that he was a very healthy man.

Jimmy wanted to believe that he had some physical problem to blame for his impotence—something that could quickly and easily be "fixed." But in his case, anxiety was the culprit. He needed to learn to relax, to

Support Groups

A well-organized support group, made up of men and women who have experienced erection problems, can help you and your partner keep the lines of communication open and find the best treatments. Two of the best-known groups are Impotents Anonymous (IA) and Recovery of Male Potency (ROMP). Both organizations have local chapters in many areas.

At meetings, you can meet other men and women who've experienced the same stresses and frustrations, and learn how they have resolved them successfully. You can also get consumer information about treatment, insurance coverage and professionals in your area who are qualified to deal with erection problems.

Perhaps the most valuable help such groups offer is a nonthreatening, supportive environment where men and women discover that they are not alone with their problem. "There was no one to talk to," one man remembers of the period when he first developed potency problems. "I wouldn't talk to anyone then except my doctor. And since I started going to Impotents Anonymous, I've seen guys who are totally frustrated, filled with anger; some are even suicidal. One young man had to have several drinks before he could come to an IA meeting." But people at Impotents Anonymous meetings understand these feelings. Everyone there is in the same boat, and the embarrassment can give way to a problem-solving approach.

Support groups can also help partners communicate. Just hearing other men and women openly discussing the issue can make a couple more comfortable. Typically, partners are encouraged to attend and participate, and some groups offer them separate meetings.

To find out if there is a group in your area, check with a urologist specializing in potency problems or with your family doctor. Or contact one of the following groups directly.

> **Support Groups (continued)**
>
> Impotents Anonymous (IA) and I-ANON (for partners) have chapters all over the country. Call 615-983-6064, or write (enclosing a stamped, self-addressed envelope) Impotents Anonymous (IA) I-ANON, 119 South Ruth St., Maryville, TN 37801-5746.
>
> Recovery of Male Potency (ROMP) also has chapters in many states. Outside Michigan, call 1-800-tel-ROMP (Michigan residents, call 313-927-3219), or write ROMP, Cindy Meredith, M.S.N., R.N., Dept. of Nursing, Grace Hospital, 18700 Meyers Rd., Detroit, MI 48235.
>
> Potency Restored is another self-help group. Write Giulio Scarzella, M.D., 8630 Fenton St., Suite 218, Silver Spring, MD 20910.

give himself permission not to have intercourse until he was ready, to feel comfortable with his partner and not withdraw from her emotionally in the event of a "failure." Perhaps most of all, he needed to stop looking at intercourse as a test which he would either pass or fail. To do this he had to learn to be comfortable—physically and emotionally—when close to a woman.

Jimmy found a sex therapist to help him. You might find that on your own you're able to pinpoint the factors that make you stressed, and overcome them.

Weeks 4 through 6: Don't Attempt Intercourse

Continue with the program as outlined in weeks 1 through 3, and follow these suggestions to remove the stress of "trying." Instead, explore different, nongenital ways of pleasing yourself and your partner. Breast touching is off limits, too. The idea is to relax and enjoy the pleasure of being close without any expectation that intercourse will take place.

Make time for this as often as you can, at least 30 minutes, five times a week. Don't try to squeeze this into your busy day; actually schedule time for this, make it a priority. To make sure you and your partner both enjoy these sessions, alternate being in charge, so that each of you acts as the "leader" and neither feels left out.

Obviously, it's important that you discuss the program with your lover so this change doesn't come out of nowhere.

Weeks 7 through 9:
Continue with the Previous Suggestions

Feel free, however, to add genital and breast touching. Continue to avoid intercourse. Just enjoy yourself. If you don't get an erection, don't worry. Explore your partner's body and let her make new discoveries about yours. If you get an erection and ejaculate quickly, try the stop-start or squeeze techniques, described later in this chapter.

Weeks 10 through 12:
Continue with the Program

If your erections have returned, at this point you may enjoy intercourse. If you lose your erections quickly or find impotence still a problem, go back and repeat the instructions, beginning with weeks 4 to 6.

Some important advice: Don't expect immediate success. Don't let a "failure" (or several) stop you. If the program works for you, great! If it doesn't, professional sex therapy may help. Some couples find it difficult to follow a program without a professional's direction and support.

Here are some other self-help techniques that can improve potency.

Preventing Premature Ejaculation

One common "erection problem" isn't really a potency problem at all. Sometimes a man has trouble maintaining an erection simply because he ejaculates too quickly. He may ejaculate before entering the vagina, or just seconds later.

If this sounds like you, it's important to realize that you probably don't have an erection problem. Since you can get an erection, your physical system is probably working just fine—just a bit too quickly for your taste.

If you're a little confused by the term "premature ejaculation," you're not alone. Premature according to whom? Therapists don't agree on a single definition of premature ejaculation.

Premature ejaculation can occur when a man is anxious, distracted or simply hasn't had intercourse for a while and so is extremely sensitive to the sexual stimulation. For our purposes, let's say that the problem is however you and your partner define it.

It is sometimes true that when premature ejaculation persists, a man will develop an erection problem caused by anxiety. The scenario goes like this: Jeff has a problem with early ejaculation. He tries to ignore his problem, but it persists. After a while Jeff is convinced he will always ejaculate too soon, and he develops anxiety about having sex. This performance anxiety can actually result in impotence. This scenario is avoidable, and persistent premature ejaculation can be successfully treated.

Sex therapy can work wonders with early ejaculation; success rates of 50 to 100 percent have been reported. At least one study suggests that couples can teach themselves to avoid premature ejaculation without much more than written instructions and telephone conversations with their therapists. There are exercises to prevent premature ejaculation: the stop-start method, developed by Dr. James Semans, and the squeeze technique of Masters and Johnson.

The Stop-Start Method

The stop-start method aims at giving the man a sense of control over his ejaculations. It starts with masturbation. In a quiet, private, secure place where he can relax, the man stimulates himself up and down the length of his penis, so that what he feels is similar to what he would enjoy during intercourse. While doing this, he needs to concentrate on how he feels, especially in his penis. When he senses he is going to ejaculate, he stops and waits until this feeling completely passes. Then, he begins self-pleasuring all over again. He may continue in this manner until the fourth time of wanting to ejaculate, when he allows himself to do so. He continues these exercises over a period of time, until he can control his ejaculation to his satisfaction.

Now, if there's a partner, she can become involved by caressing her lover in the way described above. He can control her hands and stop her when necessary. Sexual fantasies can be an important part of this process.

Once a man can delay his ejaculation with masturbation and with his lover's manual stimulation, he's ready to try intercourse. It's best to start with the woman on top, because in this position the man has less general body tension and his partner is free to stop moving when he signals her to do so. When the couple first begins intercourse, the man and woman may lie still for a while or may enjoy caressing each other in nongenital areas. Once thrusting begins, he can use the stop-start technique to avoid early ejaculation. He may want to hold on to her hips to control the movement and the stimulation he feels.

The next-to-the-last step in the process is for the woman to be able to thrust herself while on top, without the man being in control. However, he may stop her if he feels he will ejaculate too soon.

Reaping the benefits of this technique takes time. You should expect premature ejaculation to continue for a while as you're becoming familiar with the method. Once you have mastered each phase (a week for each period would be expected), you can try other positions during intercourse.

The Squeeze Technique

The other way to treat early ejaculation is with the squeeze technique. A man starts this method with masturbation, and then, when successful, progresses to intercourse.

The squeeze technique is similar to the stop-start method, with one important difference: When a man senses he is going to ejaculate, he puts his first and second fingers on the top of the head of the penis and places the thumb just below this area (see illustration). He squeezes for several seconds, until the feeling of imminent ejaculation goes away. (If the man has begun to ejaculate, it's important to stop squeezing, because to continue to do so can cause the semen to build up too much pressure in the urethra. Not only is this uncomfortable, but it can occasionally cause bleeding.) Obviously, the squeezing can be done by the partner, and some lovers prefer this. The couple can resume making love when the man feels in control again.

Some people don't like the squeeze technique because if the couple is having intercourse, the man must take his penis out of the vagina in order to squeeze or be squeezed. An alternative is to squeeze the *base* of the penis for roughly 15 seconds. The advantage of this method is that the penis may remain inside the woman while it is squeezed, if she is on top.

It's important to realize that ejaculation does not mean you and your partner can't continue to caress and be close without further intercourse.

Regardless of the method you try, the following suggestions are helpful.

- Use as many squeezes or stops as you need—as you practice, you'll need fewer and fewer.
- Apply pressure slowly and firmly, but don't squeeze so hard that it hurts.
- Don't become concerned about occasionally ejaculating too soon.

Self-Help: A 12-Week Potency Program   123

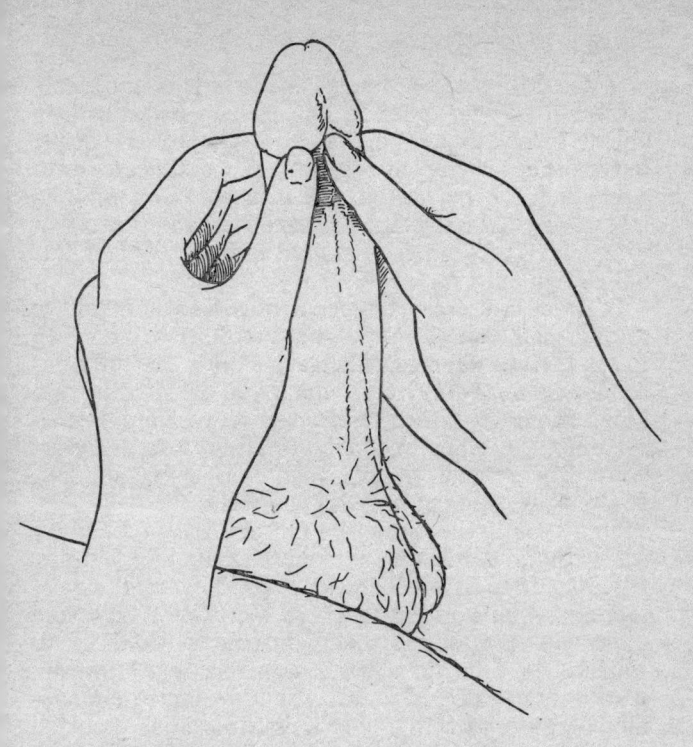

- Keep communication open and clear with your partner. If she gets a little frustrated by the exercise, explore ways of satisfying her that don't include intercourse, like oral sex.

This is a good place to lay to rest the popular belief that the way to last longer is to think of something else when you're having sex. Some men count backwards from a thousand or think of baseball scores or other unromantic topics. Not only does this method inhibit your enjoyment, it also prevents you from identifying the point of ejaculatory inevitability—a sense you need to have if you're going to delay ejaculation. If a man wants to gain control over his ejaculations, he needs to concentrate on the sensations he is feeling.

Build Those Muscles

You know from previous chapters that the penis itself contains no muscles, but exercise still might be able to help your sex life. We're not sure exercise helps, but some sex therapists suggest that Kegel exercises to strengthen the pelvic muscles may help you prolong intercourse. (Kegel exercises have for years been recommended to women who want to increase their sexual enjoyment.)

In order to exercise the pelvic muscles you first have to find them. There are two ways to do this, according to sex therapist Bernie Zilbergeld, Ph.D., the author of *Male Sexuality.* You can pretend you are holding in a bowel movement; the muscles you squeeze are the pelvic ones. Or, when you are urinating, stop and start your flow several times; when you stop the flow, you're squeezing the muscles you want.

Once you know where the muscles are, you can try squeezing and relaxing the muscles 10 to 15 times, twice a day. Dr. Zilbergeld suggests you gradually increase your workout to 60 or 70, twice a day. And once you've mastered that, you can try holding the squeeze for a bit longer and then relaxing. However, it's important not to overdo it and to increase gradually, because, as with any exercise, too much too soon can make you sore.

Some therapists say that strengthening these muscles can help you last longer and control your ejaculations more easily. If you tighten these muscles just before you ejaculate, you're doing a kind of internal squeeze technique.

Be Careful with Sexual Aids

There are lots of self-help sexual aids on the market, many of which are sold with the claim of fantastic powers. While some of them do work for some men, you should *never* use any of these devices without first consulting your physician. You need to find out if your potency problem is caused by a medical condition, which in itself requires treatment. Consulting a doctor before you buy anything might also save you a lot of money, disappointment and even harm to your health.

Cock Rings

One common aid used to boost potency is the cock ring—and it does work for some men. After a man has attained the best erection he can, the cock ring will hold the blood in the penis to keep it erect. These rings may be helpful for men who can get an erection but have difficulty maintaining it. But used improperly, they can cause pain and even permanent damage. A man who cannot become erect at all usually will not find them helpful.

Cock rings are sold in sex shops and by mail order houses. They are often made of thick rubberlike material, which stretches easily so the ring can be slipped around the base of the penis once an erection is present. The rings come in different types of designs; some even have bumpy areas to stimulate the woman's clitoris.

If, after consulting your physician, you decide to try a cock ring, it is essential that you observe precautions. You should use the ring only for short periods of time —never over 30 minutes. This is very important, because otherwise the penis can swell and make removal difficult and painful. Think of how your finger swells if a too-tight ring is left on.

So, clearly, being able to get the ring off easily is of prime importance. Some rings stretch easily for removal, others have snaps which you have to unfasten. *Only use rings which can easily and quickly be removed or cut off.* If you can't get a ring off, it can cut off the blood supply, which can cause gangrene and possibly require amputation of the penis. Therefore, plastic, wood or metal rings, or thin elastic or rubber bands which can be lost in the skin and difficult to remove, are *absolutely not recommended.* One man kept a metal cock ring around his penis for several days. When this unfortunate fellow finally came into a hospital emergency room, the ring was literally cutting into his penis, causing profuse bleeding. It took a special saw to cut the metal and remove the ring.

If you have pain, your penis feels tender or you see any type of discoloration on the organ, remove the ring immediately. And if any of the symptoms or discomfort persist after removal, see your physician without delay.

And we hasten to add that a man with poor sensation in his penis should never use a cock ring, because he won't feel the warning signs that tell when a ring is causing damage.

All the potential problems aside, in the right circumstances, a cock ring can provide a workable solution for an erection problem. Jack is a man who knows the cause of his erection problem and chooses to use a cock ring as a temporary and effective measure. A 32-year-old businessman, Jack has been a diabetic for all of his adult life. But it's only been in the last few years that he's had difficulty with erections. Fortunately, he still has normal feeling in his penis, but can only attain a partial erection.

Jack made it a point to be extremely well-educated about the possible side effects of diabetes, and about all the treatment options available to him. A permanent solution to his problem would be an implant, but Jack wasn't ready for this surgery. After all, he pointed out, who knows what treatment or cures medical science might develop in the years to come? He simply did not want to take such a final step—especially because some of the time, he still enjoyed a "half-mast" erection.

So Jack bought a cock ring that made it possible for him to have intercourse, although his erections remained somewhat soft. Jack was prudent: He showed the ring to his doctor and listened carefully to the physician's advice. And he was very careful to use the ring only for short periods of time—never more than 30 minutes.

For Jack, an easily-removable cock ring is a good solution—for now. What makes Jack different from many other users is his awareness of the cause of his problem, his knowledge of the alternative solutions and his careful and complete discussions with his doctor. Jack understands how the ring works, the potential dangers and how to avoid them. So should you.

Pencils, Swizzle Sticks and Other Dangerous Ideas

Sometimes a man who's desperate will insert some long, hard object into his penis, in the hopes that the organ will become erect around it. But there's no such luck. Instead, in short order, the man is in great pain, in danger of developing an infection, and possessed of a great and immediate interest in getting the object out. However, he usually finds it's impossible to remove the object on his own. Emergency room doctors can recount tales about the variety of objects they have removed from men's penises: pens, pencils, eyedroppers, swizzle sticks and even animal penises are some of the items doctors have extracted from this sensitive area.

Inserting a foreign object into your penis will not produce an erection, but we can almost guarantee it will produce pain and soreness. Sometimes the object prevents a man from urinating, which can be a very dangerous situation. And for some unfortunate individuals, permanent injury to the penis results from infection or damage caused when the object is finally removed.

"Miracle" Vitamins and "Love" Potions

There are a lot of over-the-counter substances advertised as cures for impotence—miracle drugs which will supposedly turn a normal man into a superstud. The ad copy is often accompanied by photographs of happy, smug-looking men and exhausted, satiated women. Most of these so-called miracle drugs are nothing more than vitamin pills, which you can get from your local drugstore for a great deal less money. There is no medical evidence that adding vitamins to an already healthy diet will do anything to improve potency in a healthy man. (That goes for vitamin E and zinc, too.) If you think that you are deficient in some vitamin or mineral, you should see your doctor before self-prescribing. In very large quantities, vitamins can actually harm you.

There is no scientific medical evidence that ginseng, sometimes advocated for men with erection problems, will cure or improve potency difficulties. And Spanish fly, made from a type of beetle, can effectively irritate your urinary system and your penis, but it won't help an erection problem. In large enough doses, it can cause serious harm or even kill you. Our advice is to stay away from all of these substances, and stick to the safe self-help program we recommend in this chapter.

We hope that self-help works for you, but if it doesn't, your next step is to find a qualified professional who can diagnose the cause of the difficulty, and successfully treat it.

7

Who to See and What to Expect

Once you decide that you need help with your sex life, you'll have to choose among an array of doctors and other health professionals—an array that might seem confusing and even contradictory. There are urologists, endocrinologists, general practitioners, psychiatrists and numerous other therapists who may claim to have the answer to your problem.

And to add to the confusion, there are widely varying levels of competency within each specialty when it comes to dealing with impotence. Not all physicians are well informed about erection problems. And some doctors just aren't comfortable discussing potency. Professionals can be vulnerable to the same distorted ideas, hangups and myths that plague the rest of us.

You need to find a health professional who is sensitive, well informed, capable, knowledgeable and interested in sexuality. He should also feel free to admit his ignorance where it exists, and should not be afraid to refer you to another specialist if it's in your best interest. Finding a doctor like this is about as likely as finding an empty cab in a rainstorm, right? Wrong. There are real pros out there to help you. And it is your right to be treated by the best of them. You don't have to settle for someone who doesn't meet your standards. In the long run, your time and effort will pay off in sexual success. After all, 90 percent of men with potency problems can be successfully treated. You might as well take advantage of these odds by getting help from the best.

Attitude Counts

Knowledge alone isn't enough. The attitude of your doctor is critical to your sexual success. Some people, doctors included, can talk about anything—except sex and death. But a doctor who's embarrassed discussing sexuality won't do you much good, no matter how much he knows about the subject. Your doctor should be at ease when talking about potency.

And the reverse is true. A doctor who's easygoing, intent, respectful, talkative and kind but doesn't know much about what does and doesn't make a man potent won't be of much use to you. Because the erection process is complicated, and currently the subject of much exciting research, it's essential that you find an expert who treats potency problems frequently and keeps up with the latest findings. Many physicians have received little or no formal training in this area, and the information they do have may be out-of-date. For example, when a patient told one young physician about the usefulness of penile shots, the doctor initially thought it was a joke. But there are physicians, psychologists, sex therapists and other professionals who are well trained and equipped to help you.

We recommend that you start with a urologist who specializes in treating impotence. Or, if you meet *all* the criteria for psychologically caused impotence we gave in chapter 6, you may want to start with a trained, qualified sex therapist. But even if you suspect your problem may be psychologically caused, we recommend that you have a urologist do a thorough physical evaluation. Many of the physical causes of erection difficulties are subtle and easy to miss.

The only way to find a good urologist who specializes in potency is to ask around. Here are some places to start:

- Ask your family doctor for a referral.

- Call the urology department of the nearest university medical school and ask them for advice.
- Contact your local medical society for a list of doctors who treat potency problems.
- Contact support groups such as Impotents Anonymous (see chapter 6).

Once you find a doctor who might be good, it's time to ask some serious questions. Don't be afraid to quiz your doctor. Remember, you deserve the best. If a doctor "doesn't have the time to be bothered" with your questions, you should consider looking for someone else.

Here are some questions to ask:
- What training have you received specifically related to erection problems?
- How do you keep current on the subject? For example, do you attend continuing education courses on impotence, do research into the problem or routinely review medical journals for the latest findings?
- How much of your practice is devoted to treating problems like mine?
- Do you regularly consult other experts?

You should be able to tell from the answers how experienced the doctor is in treating erection problems.

Another important tip is to steer clear of anyone who's a proponent of just one particular treatment for all potency problems. Unless he's already seen a complete physical workup of you and thoroughly understands how the problem is affecting you, the doctor should not assume on your first visit that he knows the solution to your problem.

Jason learned a painful lesson about the importance of choosing the right doctor. It had taken this reserved and very private man a long time to finally decide to seek help for his persistent erection problem. He was too uncomfortable to really ask any questions when he made an appointment with a doctor he had picked out of his local telephone directory. Jason was a 48-year-old man, but he was quite nervous as he was ushered into the doctor's office. He explained his problem with great difficulty and turned to the doctor for an answer.

Suddenly the urologist took a penile prosthesis out of a drawer, slammed it down on his desk and announced triumphantly to his stunned patient, "We'll just stick this in you!"

Not surprisingly, Jason left the office and never returned. Fortunately, he later found help from a doctor who wanted to listen to his story, do a complete workup and then explain in detail the choices for treatment.

Jason's experience also illustrates the importance of sensitivity. You're going to be discussing some very intimate experiences, and it's essential that the doctor be at ease—and help you to feel the same way.

It's also important that the physician welcome—not just tolerate—the involvement of your wife or lover. Some doctors actively seek the participation of the partner; others just leave it up to the patient to decide whether she should be involved. Ideally, the physician should direct some of his attention to your partner and should try to make her feel comfortable and part of the process (see chapter 5).

Warning Signs

Sometimes the best way to tell if you've found a professional who may be able to help is by what he or she does *not* do. The following are some warning signs. We suggest that you look elsewhere for your care if your doctor does any of the following things:

- He refuses or is unwilling to have your partner involved in diagnosis and treatment.
- He ignores your sexual problem or tries to change the subject every time you bring it up.
- He tells you to adjust to life without sex, or tells you that sex isn't important.
- He fails to take a complete medical history specifically aimed at diagnosing impotence.
- He makes any automatic, unfounded assumptions about the cause of your problem. If your doctor tells

you without giving you a thorough evaluation that your erection problems are caused by psychological difficulties or that you have a problem just because you've been working too hard, run, don't walk, out of that office. Generally speaking, *no one can assume the cause of your problem without a thorough evaluation* specifically focused on your potency problem. Don't let a well-meaning but ignorant professional dissuade you from seeking all the help you need.

- He can't tell you the success rates and the dangers of various treatments.
- He is quick to tell you, "If this treatment doesn't work, nothing will!" If you hear this, bolt for the door! No knowledgeable professional will put you under such wholly uncalled-for stress. There are almost always alternative treatments that will help. If you decide on a particular course of action, find out about alternatives if your first attempt at a solution (preferably the least expensive and least complicated treatment) doesn't work.

What to Expect at the Doctor's Office

In general, the doctor will start by taking your history and giving you a physical examination aimed at detecting the cause of your condition. Part of this evaluation for impotence should include checking to see if you have any underlying medical conditions which could be responsible for the problem, including diabetes, kidney disease, liver disease and blood-flow problems. It's important to check for the risk factors of heart and blood vessel disease, because erection problems can be your body's way of signaling that your blood vessels aren't working properly.

A workup for impotence should include:
- A complete history of your problem.
- A thorough physical examination, with special attention given to your reflexes, sensations and pulses in the leg and pelvic areas, and a good exami-

nation of your penis and testicles to check for any abnormalities.
- Blood tests to determine your testosterone (male hormone) levels.
- A complete discussion of all medications you use.
- A thorough look at your use of alcohol, cigarettes and recreational drugs.
- Sleep erection and/or penile shot tests (explained later in this chapter) to determine your physical ability to get and maintain an erection.

Depending on the results, further sophisticated nerve, blood-flow and psychological tests may be given.

Why Test at All?

Sometimes men wonder why they should bother having any tests and histories done. Since there are so many effective treatments like penile implants, penile shots and sex therapy available, why not just fix the erection instead of spending time and money on complicated tests?

For one thing, the tests are useful for detecting any undiagnosed ailments. Your erection problems might be a symptom of another disease that could cause you a great deal of trouble. And only with the tests will the doctor be able to determine the simplest and best treatment for your particular situation. Also, if your doctor finds a physical cause for your impotence, your insurance policy is more likely to cover your medical expenses.

Here are some questions to ask before you have any test:
- Why do you think I should have this test?
- How accurate are the test results?
- How will the results help you give me better treatment?
- Are there any tests that cost less or are less painful, that will provide the same information?
- What complications or side effects could result from this test?

> ### All about Blood Tests
>
> Blood tests are a crucial part of a workup for erection problems. Here's what your blood is being tested for, and why:
> - Testosterone and prolactin. Testosterone is necessary for sexual desire, and, apparently, also for erection. Prolactin is a hormone from the pituitary gland which, in excess, can sneakily sabotage erections. If your body makes too much prolactin, low sexual desire, decreased testosterone and impotence may result.
> - Fasting blood sugar and glucose tolerance. To see if diabetes may be contributing to your problem.
> - Thyroid function. Too much or too little thyroid hormone may be connected with potency problems. (It's an easily treated condition.)
> - Liver function. Because liver disease can affect potency.
> - Kidney function. Kidney function can also affect potency.
>
> Not all of these tests may be required in each case. In the absence of any suspicious evidence of disease, the last three tests may be omitted. Discuss this with your doctor.

Taking Your History

Your doctor should ask a lot of detailed questions about your general health habits, like how much you smoke or drink now, or if you were a heavy consumer in the past. It's important for you to be as accurate with your answers as possible. Don't underestimate your past consumption just because you want to "look good" to the physician.

Some physicians ask their patients to fill out a questionnaire. Your answers help your doctor determine what issues are particularly important. Something essential and unique to your situation may not be covered in detail on the questionnaire, so if you have concerns that aren't addressed, write them down or tell the doctor directly.

You should always let your doctor know about any present or past medical illness, even if it's not bothering you right now; any surgery you've had; and any injuries you've suffered, especially to the back or pelvic area.

You should expect to be asked in great detail about the specifics of your problem. This information can be crucial to making a correct diagnosis and providing the best treatment for you. That's why it's vital that you feel comfortable talking with the doctor you select.

Your wife can also provide valuable information, and some doctors now ask or even insist that married patients bring their spouses. Your wife may recall certain details you forget, and she has a different perspective to offer. Making up a list of questions to ask the doctor can be a joint project that will help keep the lines of communication open between you and your wife.

If there is information you prefer not to share with your wife (for example, if you're able to have an erection with another woman, you might not want your wife to know), make sure you do tell your doctor over the telephone or when you are alone with him. "My doctor knows things about me nobody else does," one man told us.

Your doctor should ask detailed questions about the specifics of your problem. He'll want to know when your problem started, how long it's been going on, if it's always present or sometimes not. He may ask you to photograph your erection, so he can get an idea of how it looks. He'll want to know if you get erections when you masturbate or when you wake up, and if so, what the erections are like.

It's relatively rare, but sometimes a man finds himself with a penis in which one part is erect and another is not. The shaft of the penis may be erect, but the tip is flaccid. The penis may also curve to one side when erect. Such specific descriptions will help your doctor focus on the possible causes of your potency problem.

Be sure to tell the doctor about *any* circumstances in which you can obtain a full, firm erection. A man with the "pelvic steal" syndrome may be able to maintain an erection if he lies on his back and is less active during intercourse than if he is on top of his partner. A man with this syndrome has diseased arteries. When he's very active, the muscles in his legs and buttocks rob the blood from his penis, leaving it flaccid.

How you feel emotionally is also an essential part of your story. How is the situation affecting your life? How do you feel about yourself?

How your partner is handling the situation is another crucial piece of information. A supportive, involved partner can be immeasurably helpful in treatment and make a successful outcome more likely—and pleasurable. On the other hand, a hostile partner can make successful treatment difficult or impossible. Remember that many women feel they are somehow to blame for the situation, and need a lot of reassurance and support. You can help your partner and yourself by keeping her involved and informed whenever possible.

If your relationship is on the rocks and you can't seem to get back on the right track, we recommend you and your partner seek help either before you resolve your potency problem or at the same time you are undergoing treatment. Simply curing your potency difficulty will not, by itself, heal a damaged relationship (see chapter 5).

Physical Examination

After taking your history, the doctor will probably give you a complete physical examination. This is an essential part of the medical detective work involved in diagnosing and treating erection problems. Your doctor is looking for signs of unsuspected diseases which could cause or contribute to your difficulty.

The physician should pay special attention to your pulses and arteries to check for signs of arterial disease which could make blood flow to the penis difficult or impossible. He'll feel the arteries in your groin, behind your knee and in your feet. This may seem strange, but a sign of blockage in these arteries can be a tip-off that you have similar problems in the arteries to the penis. While your doctor may also try to feel arteries in the penis, they are very small and often escape detection. So, the state of your other arteries may be the best clue to the state of your blood-flow system.

The nervous system also deserves special attention. Testing the "knee jerk" reflex in your legs and ankles is one indicator of the health of your nervous system. And the doctor may pinch your penis near the tip. He's looking to see if your anal sphincter contracts, and checking the same response in the bulbocavernosus muscle, the one that encircles the urethra and propels semen. When these reflexes are present, it indicates that the nerves from the penis to the spinal cord and back to the penis are healthy. The absence of this reflex does not necessarily indicate a problem, but it may steer the doctor to further tests.

The doctor may test for a similar reflex by pricking (lightly!) the anal sphincter with a pin. The sphincter should contract. If it doesn't, you may have nerve damage. The same type of pinpricks can be used to test sensations around the penis and the rectum. Brushing with a soft cotton ball also works—and feels better. The doctor may also test your ability to feel vibrations by putting a tuning fork or a special instrument on your penis. The whole point is to see if nerves in these crucial areas are functioning properly.

And, of course, a close inspection of the penis is in order. The doctor should feel your penis carefully. He's checking for hard, lumpy scars that can be a symptom of Peyronie's disease, which can cause impotence.

> ### Physically Caused Erection Problems Can Mimic Psychological Difficulties
>
> A report from the sex therapy clinic of Masters and Johnson illustrates how physical problems can mimic psychological ones. Eight out of 136 male patients at the clinic were found to have blood levels of the hormone prolactin that were high enough to cause erection problems. The 8 men were found to have pituitary tumors, a common cause of high prolactin levels. Usually, surgically removing the tumors or giving medications can restore potency to men with this condition.
>
> What's significant is that the abnormal hormone levels were not discovered until *after* the patients went through two weeks of intensive sex therapy, which, according to the authors, resulted in "some degree of improvement of sexual function." However, "full restoration" of their sex drive didn't occur until the hormone imbalance was treated.
>
> Once the physical problems were corrected, the men's erections were firmer and occurred more quickly. And the men's sex drive and sexual activity increased.
>
> The lesson to be learned from all this is that these men were at the clinic to be treated for psychological impotence. None of their previous doctors had diagnosed hormonal problems. While sex therapy can help some patients with physically caused impotence get back in the swing of things, it's no substitute for proper diagnosis and treatment of underlying medical problems.

A rectal examination is a universally unpopular part of the process, but it's necessary. And the payoff can be twofold. The doctor checks the state of the anal sphincter to gauge the health of your nervous system and at the same time he's making sure you don't have prostate disease. You'll remember from previous chapters that the prostate itself is not necessary for

> ### Getting Insurance to Pay
>
> Insurance coverage for impotence varies widely. Some plans pay for only physically caused potency problems, while other policies are more liberal. Some insurers pay for only certain types of implants. And some plans require specific documentation, such as test results, to show that the problem is indeed physically caused.
>
> You should check your policy to see if sexual dysfunction is included. Even if it isn't, you may be able to obtain coverage if your problem is due to a medical condition which is itself covered. Then get prior approval for payment. Ask your doctor to write the insurance provider and give them the specific facts of your case. One insurance expert recommends that the physician attach a medical journal article discussing the particular condition you have and the treatment proposed. And it doesn't hurt for the physician to note that a speedy reply is necessary, since treatment has been scheduled by a certain date.
>
> If you're having implant surgery, the manufacturer of the prosthesis may be able to help with insurance problems. Your doctor will know how to contact the company.
>
> If, after all this, the coverage is denied, appeal the decision. Be sure the medical director or another high-ranking executive reviews your case. And if the denial remains firm, you may want to consider complaining to your state insurance commissioner's office.

erections, but when it becomes cancerous it can require surgery which might reduce your potency.

Of course, another essential part of the physical exam is feeling your testicles to make sure they are of normal size and consistency. The doctor is also looking for any lumps or bumps, because some rare types of tumors in the testicles produce hormones which can reduce sexual desire and cause potency problems.

Checking the System

All the desire in the world won't give you an erection if your physical system is on the fritz. That's why there are tests to see whether or not you can have an erection.

The Nocturnal Penile Tumescence (NPT) Test

This test determines if a man has erections when asleep. Remember, it's normal for a man to have several erections during a good night's sleep. NPT tests can be done in a sleep laboratory or at home. The lab version is more accurate than the home test, but both types give important information. The laboratory version, of course, is a lot more expensive, but some health insurance plans cover this cost.

Some experts consider the laboratory NPT the best test to measure a man's physical ability to get an erection, because if you don't get good erections at night and you're sleeping normally, chances are that you have a physical problem.

A laboratory NPT means you'll probably spend two or three consecutive nights sleeping in the lab. Your only companions will be the machinery you're hooked up to and the technician. Your wife or lover stays home. Sleep erections are a product of dreams, not the result of lying next to a woman.

Before you go to bed, you'll be hooked up to electrodes that tell the researchers when, and if, you go into the rapid eye movement (REM) stage of sleep. It's during the REM stage that erections occur. Tubes that look a little like rubber bands are placed around your penis to measure the erections. If you do have an erection in the night, the technician will measure its rigidity. Although it can feel strange to be hooked up to all this gear, you'll feel no pain.

Not everyone needs to sleep in the lab for several nights. But often patients have trouble going to sleep in such unfamiliar and unusual circumstances, so more nights are necessary to get an accurate reading. If you have a good sleep and normal erections the first test night, you probably won't need to repeat the experience.

The NPT test is very reliable, but it is not 100 percent foolproof. Even in a well-equipped sleep laboratory operated by trained personnel, the NPT test can give misleading results on occasion. For example, a man with the pelvic steal syndrome or damaged nerves may register normal on the NPT test but still have a physical cause for his potency problem.

And it's important to recognize that when doctors use the NPT test, they're assuming that a sleeping man isn't affected by psychological factors. Well, that's generally true, but not always. Researchers at Columbia University studied two severely depressed men who had abnormal NPTs. After they were successfully treated for their depression, the NPTs were normal—and both men were able to have intercourse with their partners. This finding isn't surprising, since depression can cause sleep disturbances, which can affect sleep erections.

The Home Erection Test

Because of the considerable expense and inconvenience of sleep lab tests, cheaper at-home versions of the NPT test have been developed. These take-home varieties can actually measure how many erections you have during the night, and how long each one lasts. Usually, you just carry home a little suitcase containing equipment similar to that used in the sleep lab. The device is safe and quite accurate when used properly. Be sure you get an in-office demonstration so you understand just how to use the device before you take it home.

Some of the take-home tests have a beeper that goes off when an erection registers, so the man or his partner can check the firmness. One home NPT test monitors the rigidity itself. But many of these tests do not test firmness, which is certainly an important factor.

Other at-home tests, while useful, can only measure one erection per night. There are essentially two types: the Snap-Gauge and the stamp test. The Snap-Gauge is a piece of Velcro which is placed around the penis. As the penis expands and becomes rigid, little plastic bands on the gauge will break, indicating that a firm erection has taken place. However, it can't measure how long the erection lasts. Like all other types of NPT tests, this one doesn't hurt. And it is easy to use.

Another alternative is the use of commercially available stamps, called PotenTest, made specifically to test erection capability. Like the other methods, you place the stamps around your penis and go to sleep. The stamps break along the perforation when you have an erection.

Both the Snap-Gauge and the stamps have drawbacks. They don't measure the length or the frequency of erections. Most men normally would have several erections during the course of a single night, and this information is not collected by these methods. Furthermore, if you roll over or are a very active sleeper, both the stamps and the gauge may falsely indicate an erection.

There's one method that requires no equipment at all—you just need a willing partner who will observe you while you sleep to see if you have any erections. If you do, she can feel the penis to determine rigidity. For this test to be accurate, your partner has to stay awake all night. You have to lie on your back or side—this won't work for stomach sleepers! Trying this once should be enough. If it doesn't work, you can use another technique to get the same information. Not all partners want or are able to stay up all night, but finding out that you have just one normal erection is an important piece of information to share with your doctor.

Penile Shots

A new method to test for erection may sound unappealing. And that's completely understandable. What man wants a shot in his penis? Well, rest assured that the needle used is very small—less than an inch long—and that the patients who've had the shot report that it causes only minor pain which goes away when the needle is removed.

It may seem surprising that a shot in the penis can produce an erection, and this is indeed a new diagnostic and treatment method. Because it is so new, many specialists may not know much about it and may not have much experience with it. It works because the drugs that are injected increase the blood flow into the penis, causing an erection.

This method often provides valuable diagnostic clues, since if a man can get an erection from the shot, it's a good indication that his arteries and veins are working well. A poor erection can mean arterial blockage, leaky veins or just a nervous reaction that causes the arteries to constrict. Because the drugs used mimic the action of the nerves, patients with nerve damage may still get erections from these shots, even though they are physically damaged.

The drugs most commonly used for the shot are papaverine, papaverine in combination with phentolamine, and prostaglandin E-1. The shot causes the arteries and sinuses to relax and allows increased blood flow into the penis. In some men, in fact, the blood flow produced by these shots may be somewhat greater than that which occurs during usual erections. Consequently, men whose nerves and blood vessels don't work properly may be able to get an erection from a shot. After the shot, a small amount of pressure on the injection site is necessary to prevent bleeding.

If the shot works, results can be dramatic. In just a few minutes, a man who has had potency problems for years may find himself fully erect—and very happy.

Jerry, a 50-year-old construction worker, had been unable to get an erection for ten years, ever since he fell on the job and suffered a painful and serious back injury. Jerry considered himself lucky to have recovered enough from the accident to be able to walk, but his potency did not return.

Jerry came to see a urologist, hoping that something new would be able to help his sex life. He had never heard about the shots, but was eager to try them. The first shot produced an erection—which surprised and pleased Jerry and his wife. The shots confirmed the doctor's belief that Jerry's erection problems were caused by nerves damaged in the fall. The shot, in effect, opened up the arteries and did the job the nerves were supposed to do. Subsequent shots resulted in the same reaction. After a decade without intercourse, this couple's dry spell was over. Jerry ended up using the shots for regular treatment (see chapter 8).

The shot is not without possible complications. Occasionally, a man will have some bleeding and a bruise where the medicine has been injected. But usually this clears up by itself and causes little or no pain. A more serious problem occurs when the artificially induced erection won't go away. This can be a serious situation which, if left untreated, can cause permanent damage, when the blood clots and injures delicate tissues in the penis. If the erection won't go down, the doctor will have to insert a larger needle into the shaft of the penis and suck the blood out with a syringe. Or he may need to inject another drug to counteract the effect of the first shot.

When you first have a shot, your erection should be gone before you go home. If the erection isn't gone within four hours, or sometimes sooner, the doctor should remove the blood without delay.

Although these shots represent a real breakthrough in diagnosing impotence, they are not without risk. Clearly, patients who have such injections require expert supervision and care by physicians (usually urologists) who are able to handle the possible complications. Be sure you understand the procedure thoroughly before you agree to it.

Some experts think that the penile shots will become a commonly used diagnostic tool, and some researchers even believe the technique may eventually replace the NPT test in many cases.

Checking Blood Flow

Think of the arteries which carry blood into the penis as expressways. Two of these arteries are the most crucial to erection—they supply the corpora cavernosa, which must fill up with blood in order for a man to become erect. A traffic jam in this finely tuned system —even a minor one—can prevent a man from getting an erection, or make it impossible to maintain one.

Unfortunately, nature did not design a man's body to give a clear signal—like a rash or a high fever— when such a tie-up occurs. The signs are much more subtle, and sometimes quite difficult to decipher. One way to know if there's a blockage in the arteries supplying the penis is to check the blood pressure in the penis. Low penile blood pressure means the arteries aren't doing their job.

Taking the blood pressure in your penis is a painless test, much like the one done to measure pressure in your arm. The equipment used is different, however. The cuff wrapped around the penis is smaller and a special stethoscope is used to allow the doctor to hear the pulse in the very tiny blood vessels in the penis. Usually the doctor will listen to your penile arteries in different places to get an accurate reading.

Your top number penile blood pressure should be at least 70 percent of the top number of your normal, measured-in-the-arm blood pressure. Let's suppose your regular blood pressure is a normal 120/80. Your penile blood pressure should be at least 70 percent of 120, or 84.

If your pressure is lower than this measurement, it

means that not enough blood can get into the penis to produce a good erection. Higher than 70 percent is a good sign that your arterial expressways may be carrying the right amount of traffic.

The arteries in the penis are quite tiny, and zeroing in on them to take the pressure can be difficult. If the wrong arteries get measured, the results will be inaccurate. That's why recently many doctors are using the more sophisticated duplex Doppler.

Using the radar-like duplex Doppler, doctors can actually measure the increase in blood flow that a man is able to generate to get an erection. This sophisticated and nearly painless test can let the doctor actually see the arteries in the penis, and figure out how well they're doing their job.

For years, doctors have used the duplex Doppler to look at other parts of the body. Tom F. Lue, M.D., and colleagues at the University of California Medical School in San Francisco, developed a new way to use it. We can now measure the increase in blood flow to the penis and the change in diameter of the blood vessels during an erection. This crucial information shows if the arteries are sufficiently healthy to deliver enough blood to the penis to sustain an erection.

Usually, these measurements are taken before and after a penile shot which will, of course, usually produce an erection. By checking the change in blood flow between a man's erect and nonerect state, the doctor knows if the arterial expressways are doing their job.

Sometimes a man with blocked arteries may be advised to have surgery to reroute blood around the defective arteries. If you're considering this, you'll need to have an arteriogram which can actually pinpoint the arteries at fault. First, dye is injected into the arteries which supply the penis, and then an X-ray is taken.

Another artery test, thermography, measures the heat in the penis. The temperature is an indication of the amount of blood flow. But thermography has recently fallen out of favor with many urologists, since more accurate measurements of blood flow are now available.

The Pelvic Steal Test

Pelvic steal is a disheartening syndrome that works like this: A man gets a full erection, but when he starts to have intercourse, his arteries sabotage him. The buttocks and leg muscles used in intercourse demand oxygen from the blood to nourish their movement, so they steal blood away from the penis. In a man without arterial problems, the blood flow would just increase to meet the demand. But with pelvic steal disease, the penis is robbed of the blood it needs to maintain an erection and the man loses his potency.

Wally was a typical pelvic steal patient. This 73-year-old retired seaman complained of poorly sustained erections. He was able to get good erections, but as soon as he started to thrust, they would disappear. Of course, both Wally and his wife were upset by this turn of events. The problem had come on gradually, and Wally and his wife didn't understand what was happening.

First, the doctor took Wally's penile blood pressure. Then he had him exercise vigorously for about five minutes by going up and down a small staircase, without stopping. After this brief exertion, it was time to measure Wally's penile blood pressure again.

Sure enough, in Wally's case, his pressure was noticeably lower after the brief exercise. Often the problem may be solved simply by having the woman on top, and Wally and his wife found this suggestion solved their problem satisfactorily. If this change doesn't work, surgery to remove the obstruction, to bypass the affected area or to dilate the offending pelvic arteries may resolve the difficulty.

Checking Out the Veins

Until very recently, most doctors thought that veins, which carry blood out of the penis, weren't important culprits in erection problems. Doctors thought that the amount of blood leaving the penis didn't change much, whether a man was erect or not. The arteries were the main concern. The fact that some veins in the penis could be abnormal and sabotage erection all by themselves wasn't recognized.

That view has undergone a radical shift in just the last few years. New research has demonstrated that abnormal veins in the penis *can* sabotage erection. They do this by letting blood flow too rapidly out of the penis, thus preventing a man from getting or maintaining an erection. Normally, when a man becomes erect, the veins partially shut down, restricting the blood flow. Leaky veins, however, don't get the message, and keep the blood flowing out of the penis.

In fact, some experts now think that a significant percentage of men with physically caused erection problems may have leaky veins. Doctors are continuing to study the problem and new research should soon tell us even more.

Tests for Leaky Veins

To diagnose leaky veins you often need to have a cavernosogram. This test has been around for a while, but recently it's become more widely used to check out vein problems. It can provide important information which just isn't available any other way.

The cavernosogram test takes about 20 minutes, and while it involves sticking a small needle in your penis, it is an otherwise painless procedure. You are given an artificial erection with a penile shot. The doctor then injects some dye into the penis which makes any leaky veins show up on an X-ray. If everything is normal, the dye should just stay in the erect penis. But if a man has leaky veins, the dye will leave the penis and show up in the veins. With this test, your doctor can determine the size and location of the leak.

Another test, the xenon wash-out, gives some of the same information but unfortunately can't pinpoint the location of the leak. Because the cavernosogram gives more information, it's usually preferred.

The crucial thing about vein abnormalities is that they can be exceedingly difficult to diagnose. If a doctor doesn't look for them, vein problems are easy to miss. Any leak in the system may be a lifelong problem, or it may develop after years of satisfactory erections.

Eric, a 40-year-old fisherman, had always enjoyed sex very much. He never had problems with erections. A large and very strong man, he prided himself on his health and the effort he put into keeping physically fit. But two years ago, Eric developed a problem maintaining his erections. He didn't know what was wrong and neither did his steady girlfriend, Margie. As time went on, Eric's difficulty increased. He went to several doctors, but no one could find anything wrong with him. Finally, Eric was referred to a urologist who specialized in potency problems.

Sure enough, Eric checked out fine on every test— but one. That test showed that he could blame his veins for the change in his potency. At this point, we don't know just what makes some veins fail after functioning well for years. Fortunately, Eric didn't have to resign himself to the situation. He had a choice between having the veins repaired, or having a penile prosthesis (see chapter 8).

Testing the Nerves

Men with spinal cord injuries, diabetes or a history of back injuries may have nerve damage to blame for their sexual difficulties. Specialized tests for nerve damage are not routinely necessary, but when the physical exam raises a question about nerves it's important to investigate.

A urodynamic test (or cystometrogram) tests the function of the bladder and, indirectly, the nerves which control erection. To do this test, the doctor must place a catheter in your bladder. (Often a topical anesthetic will be used to make you more comfortable.) The test takes a few minutes, and is performed in the doctor's office.

In order to measure the amount of sensation you can feel in your penis, the doctor may use a vibrating instrument called a biothesiometer. The smaller vibration you can feel, the more sensitive your penis. Surprising as it sounds, a man may have reduced sensation in his penis and yet not be aware of this condition.

There are some men who actually are partially numb in their genital areas. Up until recently it was difficult to document this kind of problem. Now, a new test, developed by Boston University doctors, measures how well the nerves send messages from the penis to the brain, thus allowing a man to feel pleasure.

Currently, nerve damage isn't something we're able to cure. But the impotence can be treated with a penile implant or injections. The importance of doing these tests varies according to each patient. But if it's important to know whether impotence has a physical cause, and if nerve damage is suspected, these tests can provide answers.

Psychological Tests

There are many different psychological tests that have been used to try to differentiate organic from psychological impotence. But right now, there's no one psychological test that can actually do this with any degree of reliability.

Still, psychological tests can help the professional understand you better, including your feelings about sexuality. They can be a valuable tool in determining the best treatment for you.

Remember, before you take any test, ask your doctor any questions that are on your mind. If you've taken the time to find a good physician, you're likely to get good answers. And chances are that your therapy will pay off in good sex.

8

Medical Solutions for Physical Problems

Sometimes potency responds best to treatments only a doctor can give. Often these treatments are administered by your doctor in his office, with additional instructions that you follow at home. Other times surgery is necessary. Either way, medical treatments have restored potency to a lot of men—permanently. And there are a lot of treatments to choose from. Here's the latest.

Penile Shots

It seems frightening, but it works wonders: the penile shot. Sticking a needle in your penis to get an erection might not be as romantic as a candlelit dinner and a snapping fire, but some men with potency problems are finding that the shots boost their sex lives. Once they learn the technique, they can use the injections at home when they want to make love.

Your reaction to even the thought of an injection in your penis is probably to shrink back. But really, there's not very much to worry about. Men report that the injection doesn't hurt any more than any other type of shot—and the pain doesn't last.

The needle is so small—about three quarters of an inch long and quite skinny—that the initial jab itself isn't very painful. The needle is inserted into the side of the penis, about midway along the length of the organ. There is a slight burning sensation when the medicine is injected, but it quickly disappears.

The drug injected may be a combination of phentolamine and papaverine, a solution containing prostaglandin E-1 (also called PGE-1), or papaverine alone. These medications dilate the arteries in the penis, thereby increasing the blood flow to the organ. They also dilate the sinuses within the penis where the blood is trapped during an erection. Dilation of the sinuses compresses the veins so there's less blood leaving the penis.

The drugs are not without side effects, however. For about 10 percent of the men who use PGE-1, the drug causes an ache in the penis, sometimes severe enough to require the man to discontinue treatment. Papaverine may cause scarring in the penis. Scarring can cause bumps and other potentially serious problems. Recently, the manufacturer of papaverine has stated it should not be used for penile injection therapy.

And a man with an erection from a penile shot may not lose his erection when he ejaculates, because the drug will keep working. The man will still feel pleasure and may be able to ejaculate again, although the ejaculation might seem less intense. The erection may subside only as the medicine gradually leaves the penis and disperses throughout the body.

As a treatment, the shots are quite new. (They are more commonly used as a diagnostic tool, as we discussed in chapter 7.) Many specialists are using this method because of positive reports from clinical researchers. However, because this is still a somewhat experimental treatment, some physicians will not want to use it. It is important to stress that these shots should never be used without a doctor's prescription and instructions.

Penile shots can salvage the sex lives of men who have nerve damage, whether it's caused by traumatic injuries to the spinal cord, diabetes or surgery. Men with significantly advanced artery disease or extremely leaky veins probably will not be helped by this method, although patients suffering milder forms of these blood-flow problems may find the shots work for them.

And this treatment isn't safe to use all the time: As a general rule, the injections should not be given more than two times a week, because sticking needles in the penis can eventually lead to some scarring. Over time, a buildup of scar tissue could cause the penis to bend or even make it impossible for the organ to become erect.

It's important to determine just how much medicine you need, so you should receive several shots at different times, in the doctor's office. These test runs can tell you if the shots will work for you, and if there are any complications. Sometimes, a man with leaky veins will spill the medicine out of his penis into his bloodstream too quickly, and become dizzy as a result. In rare cases, his heart rate may slow down. This unwanted side effect can be counteracted by medications.

A more serious situation can occur when a shot produces a full, firm erection which will not subside. As we've explained, an erection that won't go down can cause permanent physical damage which could prevent you from ever getting another erection. *If an erection ever lasts longer than four hours, contact your doctor immediately. Do not wait until the next day!*

The doctor will probably insert another needle, drain out the medication and release the trapped blood. When this relatively rare complication occurs, future doses need to be drastically reduced, and, in some cases, penile shots must be avoided entirely.

Once you determine your dose, make sure the doctor shows you exactly how to position the needle so you inject the drug without injuring any of the vital nerves which run along the top of the penis. After the injection, you need to apply some pressure to stop the bleeding. And doctors recommend that you massage the penis gently to distribute the medicine.

An Unexpected Bonus

Sometimes the shots give an added bonus. After three or four injections in the doctor's office, some men find that their erections actually return to normal and they don't need the shots anymore. Others still need the shots, but not on such a regular basis. Right now, researchers don't understand why some men are fortunate enough to be affected this way. One study found that men with blood-flow and psychologically caused problems were the most likely to get erections on their own after a few shots, while those with nerve damage were most likely to need a shot each time they had sex.

Sidney, 62 years old, is a good example of a patient for whom the shots worked well. He had been married for almost 30 years, and first noticed problems with his erections 5 years before he visited a clinic. He was distraught that he was now completely unable to get any erection. Sidney had read a lot about the new advances in treatment for erection problems, and he announced his decision before he even sat down: He wanted a penile implant.

It wasn't clear just what was causing Sidney's problem, and the doctor decided that a penile shot could give important diagnostic information. Sidney responded to his first injection with a very poor erection, and he was clearly disappointed. Other tests showed that Sidney had a lower-than-normal flow of blood to his penis, a condition probably caused by important arteries being partially blocked. Sidney's hormone levels were fine, and he didn't suffer from any chronic diseases which could cause such a potency problem.

Sometimes men with mild artery problems respond well to the penile injections, so the doctor suggested the method was worth another shot. On a subsequent visit, Sidney received a second shot, and his erection was noticeably improved. He was extremely pleased by this turn of events, and eager to continue the shots.

On his third visit, Sidney happily reported that for the first time in many years, he had been getting erections at home. Apparently, because of factors doctors don't yet understand, Sidney was one of those fortunate men in whom the shots spur the erectile system into action. And when he got his third injection, the results were quite satisfying: In just a few minutes, he obtained an almost normal state of physical arousal.

As time goes on, Sidney may find that he needs to have an occasional shot to keep his system functioning. But as of the third visit, he considered himself cured. He decided that he didn't need a penile implant.

Still, most men who get good results with the shots will need to keep using them. For these patients, self-injection at home is obviously preferable to having to visit the doctor to get an erection.

Lionel, for example, a 54-year-old, could not get an erection after he had surgery to correct severe back pain, because the operation damaged some crucial nerves. Lionel had a very strong relationship with his wife, Terry, and the couple adapted to this situation by expressing warmth and closeness in other ways. But they still felt something was lacking. For seven long years Lionel and Terry lived this way. Doctors told them it was very unlikely that Lionel's body would heal itself. If Lionel wanted to have intercourse, he had two choices: a penile implant, or the shots.

After some discussion with his wife, Lionel decided to give the shots a try. After all, if the injections didn't work, he could still have implant surgery. What did he have to lose?

Like some other patients with nerve damage, Lionel was extremely sensitive to the medication. The first injection of only a small dose of the drug brought him a very satisfactory erection—and brought a big smile to Terry's face.

It took several office visits to determine the best amount of medication for Lionel, and to make sure he didn't suffer any side effects. Then he and Terry were ready to try the shots at home. Terry was eager to learn the technique, so both of them learned how to give the injections. In fact, the couple later reported that giving the shot had become Terry's job.

As long as Lionel keeps his regular checkup appointments to make sure the shots are working well for him and not causing any problems, he should be able to continue the shots for an indefinite period of time. But because the injections are so new, at this point we don't know the possible long-term side effects and complications.

Will the shots provide a permanent solution for patients like Lionel? Right now, it's just too soon to make such a prediction. As we pointed out earlier, repeated injections can cause scarring in the penis, and scar tissue will not expand like normal tissue. So it's conceivable that scarring from long-term use of the shots could actually prevent a man from being able to get an erection.

Suction Devices

Suction or vacuum devices work by creating a vacuum around the penis that sucks blood into it. There are basically two types. After obtaining an erection with one type, the Erecaid System, available only with a doctor's prescription, a man slips a constricting band similar to a cock ring on the base of the penis to hold the blood in the organ, and removes the suction device.

(Some men have reasoned that they'll save money and use their vacuum cleaners to produce erections—with absolutely disastrous results. Vacuum cleaners are designed to clean floors and furniture, not to make your penis erect. These machines can literally strip the skin off your penis and cause permanent and serious injury. So don't even consider using a vacuum cleaner.)

Because the suction devices work by pulling blood into the penis and then trapping it there, a man who can't get an erection using a cock ring alone may find the suction apparatus does work for him. However, some men do find these devices uncomfortable to use.

You've got to be careful with these devices. If you pump one up too energetically, you can bruise your penis, in much the same way that you can give yourself a "hickey" by sucking on your arm. The biggest danger is leaving the constricting ring on too long and constricting the blood flow to the penis, because gangrene can result.

Again, as with a cock ring, it's extremely important that a user not leave the ring on longer than 30 minutes.

After using such an apparatus, some men may find it somewhat uncomfortable to ejaculate. This is because the ring constricts the penis, making it difficult for semen to get out.

The device is not tiny, so you can't put it in your wallet before a hot date. And it's unlikely that your partner won't notice it, so we suggest you not spring it on her unannounced. A suction device does have some benefits, however. There's no surgery involved, and if you don't like it, you can just stop using it. If you use it properly, it won't cause injuries and won't prevent you from proceeding with other treatments in the future. In one study of 1,517 men using the device, 92 percent reported that it allowed them to have intercourse.

Discuss the device with your doctor in detail before using it. Ask him if any of his other patients have ever used such devices and what the possible side effects are in your particular case. If you and your physician decide it's worth a try, be sure that the doctor shows you how to use the device—do a test run in the office. Follow all instructions exactly; never use the device for a longer period of time than recommended by your doctor and the manufacturer. Err on the side of caution.

The second type of suction device, the Correctaid, looks like a very thick condom. It is placed on the penis and kept on during intercourse. To produce an erection, suction is applied to a small tube attached to the condom. Because this type of device is quite new, it's too early to say how it will be received. It is available without a prescription, but as with any other sexual aid, we think it's essential that you talk with your doctor before you try it.

Surgical Solutions

Surgical methods to improve potency have undergone major advances in recent years. Blocked arteries that prevent blood from traveling to the penis can now be reopened or bypassed. Leaky veins that sabotage erection can be tied off, restoring potency. And penile prostheses, or implants, can restore potency to men who otherwise would have to resign themselves to a life without intercourse.

Of all these options, penile implants have received the most publicity—good and bad, informed and fabricated. It's hard for the consumer to sort through the myths and misinformation to find the truth. Well, here are the facts.

There are three basic types of penile implants, made either of plastic or silicone. Each will provide an erection. Each makes it possible for a man to have intercourse. Each must be surgically inserted.

In most cases, the implant will leave your ability to have an orgasm and ejaculate unchanged. If you can ejaculate before you have the surgery, you'll be able to afterwards; if you can't, you won't.

Implant surgery is a final commitment, because once you have the operation, your chances of ever having a natural erection are almost certainly lost. That's because the surgery usually damages the sinuses within the corpora cavernosa that normally fill with blood during an erection. A man who gets partial erections or occasionally gets a full erection must realize that if he gets an implant his natural capability will in all likelihood be gone and he will be dependent on the prosthesis. That's one of the important reasons why all prospective implant patients should explore other solutions before deciding on surgery. And they should decide exactly why they want an implant. Some people want them for the wrong reasons.

Just as important as knowing what an implant can do is knowing what it cannot do.

Not a Cure-All

An implant will not change your personality. It will not make you the most popular guy on the block. It can't be counted on to save a failing marriage.

Having an implant does not, by itself, make you feel aroused. What causes you to feel desire before surgery should have the same effect after the operation. By the same token, if you rarely feel sexual desire before getting an implant, that's unlikely to change.

Implants are not magic problem-solvers. The prosthesis will not change lifelong sexual patterns. If you rarely had sex before your erection problem developed, the operation will not turn you into a sexual superman. By itself, an implant will not increase your sexual appetite or desire. *The prosthesis doesn't change behavior; it just enables you to have an erection and makes intercourse possible.*

Implants produce a simulated erection which, although close in appearance to a natural erection, is not identical. The implants are placed in the corpora cavernosa (those two cylinders which run parallel along the length of the penis, and, in a natural erection, fill up with blood). The head of the penis, which is part of a separate and much more delicate area called the corpus spongiosum, does not become erect with any of the implants. And it's not likely that a model with such a feature will be developed, because of this area's small size, irregular shape and closeness to the urethra.

The implant erection usually is not quite as wide or as long as a naturally produced erection. An implant won't increase the size of a man's penis.

Making the Choice

Deciding if a penile implant is right for you is a complicated personal and medical decision. Of course, your feelings are crucial. But so are your partner's. Both of you need to have realistic expectations of what the surgery will and won't do. The more your partner participates, voices her concerns, asks questions and gets answers, the more comfortable she is likely to be with the process—and the more satisfied with the outcome.

When doctors talk about a "good" candidate for implant surgery, they're referring to someone who is likely to be satisfied and happy with the results, can withstand the physical and emotional stress any surgery can bring and can effectively deal with the recovery process.

Gary, for example, a 46-year-old, lost his erections to a combination of diabetes and high blood pressure medication. Unfortunately, he couldn't change his medication and he had trouble managing his diabetes as well as he might have. A series of job and financial setbacks compounded the stress on his body and his emotions. On those rare occasions when he was able to become erect, he quickly lost potency. Five years after he first noticed any sexual problem, Gary was completely unable to have intercourse. He was, understandably, very frustrated by the situation. And he was depressed. The potency problem nagged at him, eroding his self-confidence.

Throughout this difficult period, however, he tried to remain close to his wife, Dottie. They remained physically affectionate, touching often, and continued to have sexual contact. And Gary and Dottie did several things that helped them during this stressful time: They did not blame each other for Gary's lack of erection, and they discussed the difficulty, but they didn't make it a point of argument. "We were very supportive of each other; we had a good relationship," Dottie explains.

A Wise Choice

Answering these questions will help you decide why you want a prosthesis, and if you're willing to undergo the discomfort of surgery.

- Do I want the implant to make me and my partner happy, or because I think I *should* be having intercourse?
- Can I be happy with other ways of having sex besides intercourse? Can my partner?
- Am I going to think of the prosthesis as just a part of me, or am I going to be concerned that it is "unnatural"? How does my partner feel about this?
- Will I be satisfied with an erection that's not exactly natural in appearance?
- Do I make love frequently now, even without intercourse?
- Am I willing to undergo surgery, and am I prepared for the recovery period?
- Is it worth the risk of the complications?
- Have I discussed this matter thoroughly with my partner?

Gary had a very clear reason for getting an implant: Plain and simple, he wanted to have intercourse with Dottie. She was concerned that the operation might pose a risk to her husband's health, but she also was eager to get their sex life back on the track.

Gary and Dottie made several visits to the doctor, and discussed the options in detail. In the end, Gary chose the inflatable implant (discussed later), partly because it was more natural in appearance and he belonged to an athletic club. "I didn't want anyone to know I'd been impotent and had an implant."

Now, about a year later, Gary and Dottie are quite happy with the results of his surgery. Gary is enthusiastic: "Satisfied! I could not even begin to describe it. If it broke, I'd be at the hospital tomorrow. I would get it replaced even if I had to get it done weekly!"

In a separate conversation, Dottie echoes her husband's pleasure. "Yes, I'm pleased. Very pleased. Sex is as good as—maybe even better than—when we first married."

Gary had several characteristics that are crucial to success. Based upon research and clinical experience, we've summarized the factors which make a man a good candidate for an implant. Gary had many of them. You should too before having the surgery.

In general, a good candidate for implant surgery is emotionally stable. Like Gary, he is not severely depressed, though of course, some depression is common. Some doctors perform implant surgery only on men with physically caused potency problems, but other physicians find that men whose erection problems are attributed to psychological factors, if properly screened, can be quite satisfied and happy with the results of surgery. (These men may not have found that sex therapy improved their erections.) Whether physical factors are present or not, it's generally agreed that implant surgery should be considered only after any simpler treatments have been tried.

If a man has a regular partner, it's enormously helpful if, like Gary and Dottie, both lovers are motivated to solve the problem. And it's important that the couple continue to be warm toward each other and try to maintain good sexual communication.

One study shows that men interested in increasing their sexual enjoyment and that of their partners, as well as in regaining a feeling of being a "whole man," are much more satisfied with the results of surgery than those who are trying to improve relationships, change their marital status or the number of their sexual partners, or have children. And, not surprisingly, men in better health and with fewer complications after surgery are more likely to be pleased with their results.

A good candidate for implant surgery is not overly concerned with the size of his penis, because a penis erect from an implant usually will be slightly smaller in circumference and slightly shorter in length; he is healthy enough to withstand the operation, which sometimes requires a general anesthetic; he recognizes that he will experience pain following the operation, and that it will be weeks (and occasionally, months) before he is fully recovered and able to enjoy his newfound potency. Most important of all, perhaps, he is motivated by a strong desire to have intercourse and to get his problem fixed. He does not look upon the surgery as something to change his personality or make him more popular.

Of course, not all good candidates for surgery need to fit each of these criteria perfectly. Perhaps the most important factors are that a man who is considering such surgery be honest with himself, his partner and his doctor about his needs, wants, hopes and fears regarding the implant and the changes it will bring; that he gets answers to his questions (and a second opinion if he likes); and that his expectations are based on facts and information, not on myths and wishes.

The Power of Self-Sabotage

Sometimes a man's unrealistic (and often unarticulated) expectations will sabotage a technically perfect operation. Some doctors require all patients to be psychologically evaluated in the hopes of identifying just such patients.

An example of this problem is Zachary, a 53-year-old diabetic who had been divorced for many years. He was convinced his potency problem was to blame for his nonexistent social life. If he got himself into an intimate situation with a woman, he was afraid he would be "discovered." Zachary was convinced that once his potency was restored his problems interacting with women would be over. He could not admit to himself that his social difficulties were long-standing and preceded his potency problem.

Unfortunately, Zachary kept his hopes of a personality transformation completely private. He told his doctor that he wanted the surgery so he could have intercourse again. In terms of his health and general physical condition, Zachary appeared to be a good candidate for the operation. And as far as his doctor knew, he had realistic expectations.

The operation went without a hitch. During the recovery, however, Zachary complained of a great deal of pain. After several weeks, the pain subsided, but he was still displeased. He referred to the implant as "that thing." Nothing was right. Finally, quite upset, he let his hidden expectations come to light. He had expected the implant to take away his social ineptness and fear of women and make him a different man. Instead, after the operation he was the same man, except he was able to get an erection. And he was bitterly disappointed.

After several months, Zachary demanded to have his implant removed. He resisted all advice to get psychological and sex therapy to help him with his problems. Looking back on Zachary's situation, it's clear that he would have fared much better if counseling had helped him first develop his social skills, overcome his shyness and become more comfortable around women. Then his decision to get an implant would have been based on a desire to have intercourse—not on a wish to change his personality.

Styles of Implants

If you and your doctor decide you're a good candidate, you've got to choose the type of implant you want. Today, implants come in several basic types. The one that's been around the longest is called the semirigid implant. It works by artificially creating stiffness in the corpora cavernosa of the penis. The implant, made of plastic or silicone, replaces the rigidity that would normally be supplied by blood during an erection. Naturally, since a man has two corpora cavernosa running parallel to each other along the length of the penis, you get one implant for each cylinder. Each rod feels about as stiff as a soft carrot when you hold it in your hand. Of course, they are bendable. As men vary in size, the rods come in different lengths and circumferences. And just as a man may have slightly differently sized feet, so may his corpora cavernosa be different. This is no problem, because the doctor simply uses a different size in each chamber.

When the prosthesis is sized and inserted properly, it provides rigidity to the shaft of the penis and enough support to the base to allow intercourse. The implant provides stability to the head of the penis, although it does not make the head hard. It also increases the diameter of the penis, although not as much as a natural erection. And once the implant is in, the erection will not subside; it won't come and go like a regular erection. The prosthesis should be easily concealed under close-fitting underwear, but a man with a semirigid implant should realize that he will appear to have a partial erection when he is naked. This may be of concern to men who belong to athletic clubs or have other activities where nudity is common.

Comparing the Implants

SEMIRIGID IMPLANTS

Benefits
- The surgery can be performed under a local anesthetic, often on an outpatient basis.
- The recovery time is typically shorter than with the inflatables, because the surgery is less extensive.
- There is less chance of complications.
- There are no mechanical parts which can fail.
- These implants usually cost less.

Drawbacks
- The implant is more difficult to conceal since it is always erect. Some men may be embarrassed in locker room situations.
- Generally, the semirigid implants are less firm and smaller in circumference than an inflatable prosthesis when erect.

Comparing the Implants (continued)

- Although the overall complication rate is lower than for inflatables, there is a small chance that the semirigid implant will "travel" within the penis, popping out of the corpora cavernosa. This situation can be corrected, but it does require removal of the implant and another operation.

STANDARD INFLATABLE IMPLANTS
Benefits
- The size of the prosthesis changes as it is pumped up, so a man can control the amount of erection he wants.
- The erection is closer in appearance to a natural erection.
- The implant has less chance of popping out of the corpora cavernosa and "traveling" within the penis.
- For men with recurring bladder tumors that may require repeated surgery, inflatable implants are easier for the surgeon to operate around.

Drawbacks
- There is a higher failure rate because of the moving parts. However, the mechanical failure rate should continue to drop as implant design improves.
- The implant is more expensive. The device itself costs more, the hospital stay is usually longer and therefore more expensive, the surgeon's fee may be more and the operating time is longer and more costly.
- The man needs manual dexterity to operate the implant. Someone with a problem like severe arthritis or Parkinson's disease might find it unworkable. Of course, the partner can help.

NEWER INFLATABLE IMPLANTS:
HYDROFLEX AND FLEXI-FLATE
Benefits
- The implant is similar to the semirigid type in its advantages: a short operating time, minimal post-

> **Comparing the Implants (continued)**
>
> operative complications, a short hospital stay or surgery on an outpatient basis.
> - The implant is more concealable than the semirigid type.
> - Total cost for the surgery may run less than that of other inflatables because of reduced hospital time, although the prosthesis itself is more expensive than semirigids or other types of inflatables.
>
> *Drawbacks*
> - The mechanical parts of the implant can fail. These new types haven't been around long enough for anyone to know the long-term failure rate.
> - The Flexi-Flate is deflated by bending it down towards the stomach. This limits the number of positions in which to have intercourse. For example, the woman-on-top position may not work because it causes the penis to bend down and thus deflate.
> - The erection provided by the implant is like the erection of a semirigid prosthesis in that it doesn't increase the diameter of the penis or the length, but only makes it harder and more rigid.

The first of the modern semirigid prostheses was the Small-Carrion, named for the two doctors who developed it. It's been around since 1973 and is still being used by some physicians. Now, other variations on the same theme have been introduced. The newer models —the Flexirod, invented by Dr. Roy Finney, the Jonas Silicone-Silver prosthesis, named for its developer Dr. Udo Jonas, and the AMS 600—were designed to make the implant more concealable and bendable when not in the erect position.

The Small-Carrion prosthesis is bendable and allows the penis to be moved up, down or to the side. It has

Medical Solutions for Physical Problems

Semirigid Penile Implants

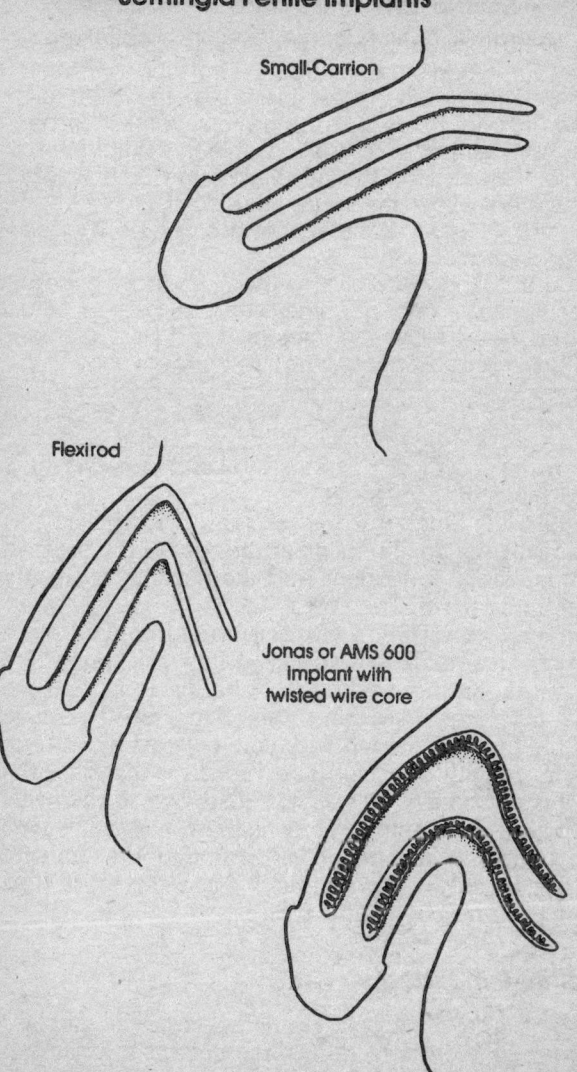

Small-Carrion

Flexirod

Jonas or AMS 600 implant with twisted wire core

> ### The OmniPhase and DuraPhase Implants
>
> The OmniPhase is a new type of implant which is a cross between the inflatable and the semirigid implants, but with a new twist. Like the inflatable type, it is rigid only when the man wants it to be. He must activate a cable within the implant to make it rigid. Like the semirigid type, it is wholly contained within the penis and does not have a reservoir. Best of all, the OmniPhase can be inserted using a local anesthetic.
>
> The DuraPhase is similar to the OmniPhase except that it does not become flaccid. Instead, the cables inside allow the implant to be bent (something like a gooseneck lamp) for concealment.

no portion specifically designed to bend, however. It is uniformly stiff throughout.

Unlike the Small-Carrion implant, the Flexirod was specifically designed to bend at the base of the penis to be more easily concealed. And the Flexirod is slightly stiffer along the shaft.

Yet another variation of the semirigid implant has a kind of memory: When you bend it, it will stay where you put it, and not snap back. Both the Jonas and the AMS 600 prostheses have this characteristic, made possible by their twisted wire core covered by silicone rubber. The advantage of these models is that once the penis is bent down, it will stay that way, so the penis won't always look erect. The one drawback to this type is that rarely, a wire may break, and although the wire is still covered by the silicone rubber, the penis then becomes more floppy at the base.

Putting It in Place

Here's what to expect from the semirigid implant surgery. To avoid infection, some doctors ask patients to shower with a special antiseptic soap for several days before the operation. This procedure helps to decrease surface bacteria and may reduce the chance of infection. For the same reason, some doctors put patients on antibiotics for a period before and after the operation.

Although infections with prostheses are rare, caution is in order, because any time you have a wound with a foreign body in it, like a penile implant, it takes fewer bacteria to cause an infection than in a simple incision without a foreign body.

With semirigid implant surgery, you might have a general, local or spinal anesthetic, depending on your general health and the preferences of your doctor. In any case, you won't experience pain during the procedure, although with a local anesthetic you might feel some pulling and pressure.

There are different ways the surgeon can get access to the corpora cavernosa, where the implants are placed. The skin incision can be made around the head of the penis, at the base or along the length. (Uncircumcised men may need to have their foreskin removed during surgery.) The surgeon can also cut in or under the scrotum. Once the doctor is in the area, an additional cut into the corpora cavernosa is made so that the two parts of the implant can be positioned.

The implants come in several different lengths and widths, and the correct size will be determined when you're opened up.

Once the implants are in place, they fit snugly inside the corpora cavernosa and don't have to be sewn in place. The incisions are sewn shut, and the procedure is over. From start to finish, this type of operation routinely takes about an hour.

Recovery from this type of surgery is usually very uneventful. When you first check out the results, you'll find yourself with a swollen penis. You may have a catheter in your bladder, and as anyone knows who's had one, the sensation isn't terribly pleasant. Once the catheter comes out (usually in about a day), you may feel a burning sensation when you urinate. The penis

> ### How to Quiz Your Doctor about Implants
>
> Be sure your doctor gives you clear answers to these questions before you make any firm decisions:
> - Is there any other treatment which will help? If yes, should I try that first?
> - What types of implants would you recommend for me? Why?
> - Is there anything special about my physical condition that would make one type of implant better or worse?
> - How much experience do you have doing implant operations? How about with this particular type of implant?
> - Is there anything about my general health that makes me at higher risk than usual for certain complications? If so, which ones?
> - How long will it take to recover from the surgery? How long a hospital stay do you expect? How long will I have to stay home from work?
> - How much does the operation cost?

may temporarily turn purple from bruising about one day after the surgery.

Most men require some pain medication for several days, sometimes longer. You'll want to take a week or more off from work, and in general, the whole genital area will be sore and tender. There's a lot of variation in how much pain men feel during the recovery period; some men find themselves feeling pretty good in just a few days, others are in pain that requires medication for six weeks or so.

Often it will be difficult to bend the prosthesis in the first few weeks because of soreness and pain, even if it was designed to bend easily. (After surgery, it may take some types of implants 12 weeks or longer to bend easily and be easily concealed.) As time goes on, it becomes easier. Usually men are told to wait about 6 weeks before having intercourse. To be truthful, most men are not in the mood for love during the first few weeks of recovery, anyway.

While semirigid implants do seem to work miracles for some men, they also have drawbacks. If the implant is too long for the penis, the penis can curve, with painful results. Left uncorrected, the implant can actually work its way out of the corpora cavernosa, damaging the penis. And implants that are too short cause problems too. The head of the penis may bend down because it isn't getting proper support—the result is often termed an SST deformity, after the jet airplane that's famous for its turned-down nose. Obviously, too short a prosthesis can make intercourse difficult.

On a person with a very stretchy penis, selecting the right size can be a judgment call. In such a situation, the surgeon may opt for a little too short vs. a little too long because complications from too long an implant are the riskiest.

Men who have extensive scarring in their penises may have corpora cavernosa which resist implants, because the space where the prosthesis fits is scarred partially shut. In this case, a smaller (especially in diameter) prosthesis may be required.

A man who has very poor tissue surrounding the prosthesis is at risk for a "traveling" implant. Rarely, the implant may move out of the end of the penis into the urethra or out the back of the corpora cavernosa. Pressure from the implant just wears a hole in the weak tissue. A reasonably healthy man with a correctly sized implant needn't worry about this complication, and even men with diabetes or other problems which may cause weak tissue should take comfort from the fact that this problem is quite rare.

Another rare complication is when a man finds his penis is less sensitive to pleasure and to pain after surgery. If the nerves on top of his penis are scarred and must be stretched during surgery to implant the prosthesis, they may be damaged. Normal sensations may return to this area after several months or the numbness may be permanent.

On the other hand, after recovery, a few patients continue to experience pain without any obvious cause. In such rare cases, removal of the prosthesis may be the only alternative.

The Inflatable Implant

Inflatable prostheses, available since 1973, come the closest to approximating a normal erection. Unlike most types of semirigid implants, an inflatable prosthesis does not leave the man permanently erect. The penis increases in girth and length only when the implant is inflated. It comes closer to achieving about the same circumference as the man once had with his natural erection. However, as with the semirigid implant, a man's erection with this type of implant will be slightly shorter in length than his natural erection would be, and the head of his penis will not be erect.

It is virtually impossible to tell whether or not a man has an inflatable implant when he is not erect. That's why men who often are naked around others prefer this type of device. The prosthesis has three basic components: the two cylinders which occupy the corpora cavernosa; a reservoir of fluid which is placed under the muscles in the lower abdomen just in front of the bladder; and a pump which is placed in the scrotum. The cylinders are fundamentally different from the semirigid variety, because they are simply shells (made of silicone or a type of plastic) into which fluid can be pumped. Think of an inner tube totally deflated and then pumped up, and you get the picture. When a man squeezes the pump located in the scrotum, fluid is transferred from the reservoir into the cylinders, traveling along small tubes that connect all the components. How many times a man has to pump to achieve an erection varies a little, but usually 10 or 20 pumps does the job.

Inflatable Penile Implant

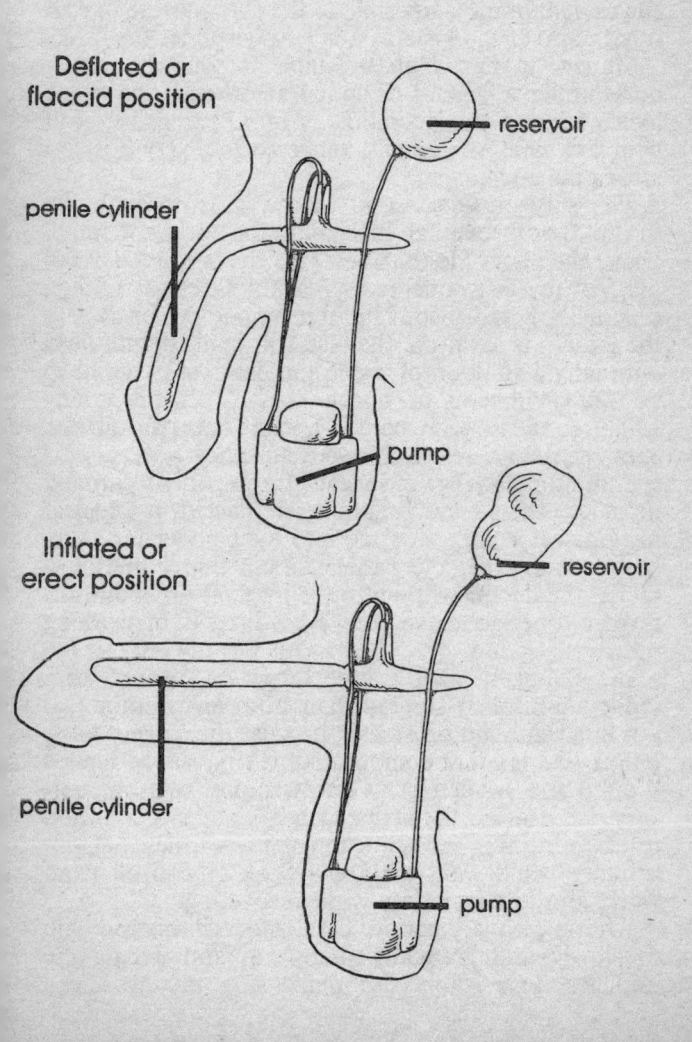

Deflated or flaccid position

- penile cylinder
- reservoir
- pump

Inflated or erect position

- reservoir
- pump
- penile cylinder

When he wants to deflate the erection, he simply depresses a release valve under the skin and holds it down. The result: The fluid goes back into the reservoir, and the man has a flaccid penis. The release valve can be felt, but it is invisible to the eye, because like all other parts of the system, it is located under the skin.

Surgery to install an inflatable implant is usually done under a general or spinal anesthetic, and not a local, because the operation is more extensive. And with this type of implant, a two to four day hospital stay is the norm.

The surgeon gets access to the body through the scrotum, or through an incision in the lower abdomen, above the penis. He then cuts into the corpora cavernosa. All the components are usually inserted through one incision and placed in their proper locales. Before the patient is sewn up, the reservoir is filled with fluid —usually a solution of water and contrast material so the fluid will show up on an X-ray. Then the tubing which connects each part is hooked up. And all the components are tested to make sure they work.

Some surgeons prefer to leave the prosthesis partially inflated, others leave it completely flaccid. It's typical for a catheter to be inserted into the bladder for a day or so. And while the patient is still under the anesthetic, the doctor will pump the implant up and down several times to make sure everything is in working order.

In general, it takes a little longer to recover from inflatable implant surgery than from an operation to put in a semirigid prosthesis, because the surgery takes longer and is more complicated. It's typical to have a bruised and swollen penis and scrotum following surgery (ice bags on the area can help), and it's common to feel a burning sensation the first few times that you urinate. You'll want to take a week or two off from work, and to take it easy while recovering.

After a recovery period, the doctor will instruct you to slowly and gradually pump up and deflate the implant. This is only to make sure the prosthesis inflates evenly as healing progresses. You should wait until your doctor gives the okay before attempting to have sex. It's important not to jump the gun and try inflating the implant too soon. Some men are so tender they don't even want to think about doing this for several weeks.

Typically, a man has to wait six weeks before he can have intercourse, and even then it's important to proceed slowly and gently. It will be a lot more comfortable, at least at first, to inflate the implant to about 75 percent of capacity at the most. It's important that the implant be completely deflated most of the time. If it remains partially inflated, scar tissue can form around the reservoir and prevent it from filling completely. The end result can be a penis that is partially inflated all the time. Surgery is necessary to correct this avoidable and relatively uncommon complication.

Of course the inflatable implant has drawbacks. A leak in the system is probably one of the most common problems. It takes just a tiny hole to sabotage the prosthesis. Usually, removal and repair is necessary—requiring additional surgery. Twisted tubing which prevents the fluid from traveling between the reservoir and the cylinders is a rarer occurrence. But if it does happen, surgery is necessary to straighten out the kinks. A weakness in the corpora cavernosa can result in a lopsided erection—because the implant balloons out to fill up the space. When most of the fluid ends up in one area, less is available to go elsewhere. The man finds himself with a mostly soft penis that has a big, stiff lump. Again, surgery can correct this condition; the physician replaces the cylinders with specially designed ones which won't balloon, but also aren't quite as big in diameter.

Two very new designs of implants, the Flexi-Flate and the Hydroflex, represent something of a cross between the inflatable and the semirigid types. Like the semirigid implant, these consist of two cylinders placed in the corpora cavernosa. But like the inflatable type, these cylinders actually inflate and the penis can be flaccid or rigid. To inflate the implant, a man pushes on the part of the prosthesis near the head of the penis. This transfers all the fluid from one chamber into another, causing an erection. The beauty of this design is that the reservoir is actually contained inside the cylinders themselves.

On the plus side, this type of inflatable implant is easier to put in than the other kinds of inflatables, requires less extensive surgery and is still very concealable. For a man who runs a greater-than-average risk from general anesthesia but who prefers the inflatable implant, these newer models present a viable compromise, because often a local anesthetic is all that's required.

The drawbacks to this crossbreed are that the penis never reaches a completely relaxed state, and it doesn't increase in girth as much as the more traditional type of inflatable implant. That's because the reservoir has to be smaller since it is located inside the corpora cavernosa. And it may be two to three months after surgery before you can operate the implant fully.

Recently, two more models of inflatable implants have become available. Surgitek's Uniflate and the Mentor Mark II both combine the reservoir and the pump, and place these in the scrotum. They can be inserted under a local anesthetic; because abdominal surgery is not required, these models are especially suited for someone who has had a pelvic operation such as a radical prostatectomy or a bladder removal. These models are not as rigid and do not provide as full an erection as some of the older types of inflatables. However, the implants do allow a physician to adjust the amount of fluid in the implant after surgery if the man wants to change the fullness of his erection.

What Type Is Right for You?

There's a lot to consider when choosing an implant, and you should discuss your options in detail with your physician and your partner. Remember, no one model is right for everyone. The best one for you depends on your particular health needs, physical condition, personal preferences and lifestyle.

Once you've been evaluated by a physician and it's been determined that your best treatment would be an implant, it's time to consider the different types. In most cases your physician will make specific recommendations. It's important to weigh all the factors, to involve your partner and to actually see and touch the different models, if possible.

You may find it helpful to talk to men who've had the different types of implants (and your wife may benefit from talking with their partners). Support groups (see chapter 6) can be helpful, and your doctor may be able to put you in touch with patients who have had the surgery, and their partners. But remember, your needs are uniquely yours. What's right for one man won't necessarily be right for you.

The importance of personal preference was emphasized to us when we talked with two different patients on the same day. In the morning, a man with a semirigid implant said he "couldn't imagine" why anyone would want an inflatable prosthesis. Just a few hours later, another gentleman, happy with his inflatable, declared he would never even consider the semirigid type. Each was sure he had made the right decision—and each was correct.

Take all the time you need to make a decision. Some couples decide rather quickly. Robert and Greta, for example, married for almost 50 years, didn't take months to choose. "Both of us went to the doctor and both of us decided," Robert explains. This 74-year-old gentleman wanted the inflatable, and that's what he got.

Gabe, a 52-year-old office manager, found the choices more difficult than Robert. Gabe's potency problem was due to a case of Peyronie's disease. He was fortunate, however, because the scarring from the disease was moderate, and the inflatable prosthesis was an option for him. Gabe took a year to make up his mind, and during that time the newest type of inflatable implant with the reservoir in the penis became available. He calls the results "fantastic. I'm like a young man, and my wife can attest to that."

Medical Problems Can Limit Choices

Sometimes medical problems determine the type of implant you should have. A man in poor health, for example, isn't a good candidate for a general anesthetic, and for that reason his physician may quite rightly refuse to put in an inflatable prosthesis. A man with extensive scarring in his penis may not be able to have an inflatable implant because the prosthesis can't expand properly if the corpora cavernosa are severely scarred. Jonathan, for example, a 47-year-old government official, has systemic lupus, a disease which, among other things, injures the small blood vessels. His illness was a major factor in his potency problem, because the effects of the disease made it impossible for blood to get into his penis in sufficient quantities to produce an erection.

Jonathan's physician recommended a semirigid implant, and as it turned out, that was the only option for him. "They thought it would be a 45- to 90-minute operation. It was a 3-hour operation. Both urologists on the case said they had never seen a case of scarring like mine," Jonathan reports. In fact, Jonathan's scarring was so extensive that the surgeons were forced to use a slightly smaller sized prosthesis, because there wasn't more room in the penis.

Some men with nerve injuries suffer from partial numbness in their penises. A man with this condition is more prone to the problem of the traveling semirigid implant, because he can hurt his penis without realizing it. So, for him, an inflatable implant, which puts less pressure on the penis when it's not erect, may be preferable.

Doctors, like patients, have their own preferences. What's important is that you understand your doctor's recommendations and the reasons for them. Some doctors put in only one type of prosthesis; some have a particular manufacturer they prefer.

If you're confused or unsure about your options, be sure you get all the information you need. And consider getting a second opinion. You and your lover are the people who are going to live with your implant—not your physician. Your happiness and peace of mind are most important.

The Bottom Line

Implant surgery is not cheap. Hospital charges and surgeon's fees vary a great deal throughout the country. In 1986, the semirigid prosthesis cost about $1,000; the inflatables about twice that; and the semi-inflatables about $3,000—surgery, hospital and doctors' fees not included. Manufacturers do offer some warranty protection, but that's for the prosthesis alone, not the surgeon or the hospital fees.

You have to figure in the cost of the hospital stay, medications, time spent in the operating room, surgeon's fees, anesthesiologist's fees and the markup the hospital charges on the prosthesis.

A man who has a semirigid prosthesis put in on an outpatient basis, with no complications, may end up with a bill under $5,000. On the other hand, a man who gets an inflatable prosthesis and stays in the hospital several days may find himself owing $10,000 or more.

Many patients are fortunate to have all or a large part of their health insurance cover the cost of the operation. Be sure to check with your insurance company first. In 1986, Medicare paid 80 percent of the cost of implant surgery, if the patient's potency problem was caused by a physical condition (see chapter 7 for additional insurance tips).

Making the Most of Your Implant

For most implant patients, adjusting to the prosthesis involves healing, learning how the device works and becoming comfortable enough with it to forget it. And if the couple has remained physically and emotionally close in spite of the problem, their adjustment will be easier.

"I was pretty sore, and very uncomfortable," recalls Henry, a retired dentist. "At first it hurt to pump the implant up. As time progresses, you can pump more and relax more. After three or four months I forgot it was there."

Michael echoes Henry's thoughts. "There was a lot of discomfort and frustration in learning to use the implant." Now, a year later, he's adjusted to it. "We don't even consider that I have an implant."

Some fortunate men experience little pain, and adjustment for them is easy. Paul, a 69-year-old owner of a landscape business, had a fast and uneventful recovery from surgery. "I had no trouble adjusting to the implant, not after the swelling went down. It just seemed like a part of me, like my eyeglasses. It made me whole again. And my wife felt it was very satisfying and very natural."

Jeffrey, a 61-year-old plumber, knew his erection problems were caused by the prostate surgery necessary to get rid of his cancer. And he was eager to have the implant surgery for his own satisfaction, and for his wife's. Jeffrey's doctor found him to be a good candidate for surgery, and Jeffrey was given a semirigid implant. "The doctor recommended no sex for at least six weeks—I was ready in three."

The amount of pain just after surgery doesn't tell you anything about the success of the operation. Ralph, a 46-year-old businessman, recalls his recovery. "The first time the doctor pumped it up—a month after surgery—the pain was incredible! I've only experienced such pain once before, when I was hit in the testicles with a baseball."

Ralph went home and, taking his doctor's advice, soaked in a hot tub. "Within an hour and a half the pain was gone. While soaking in the tub, I pumped it up." Ralph—and his wife—were pleased. But he was initially surprised when his penis got wider and harder, not longer. Once his soreness disappeared, it took the couple about four weeks to get adjusted to the implant. Ralph had to learn to hit the release button in exactly the right way to deflate it.

Sometimes adjustment is a bit more of a problem.

"I was in the hospital three days, and home for eight weeks recovering. It was eight weeks until I used it the first time. It takes a full year to adjust. It took me a year to learn how to pump it up and release it without pain. You need practice," says Carl, a 54-year-old draftsman.

It's common to have certain fears and anxieties about a new prosthesis. A man may be concerned he will hurt himself or his partner with the implant. Having slow, gentle intercourse a few times will help him realize he doesn't have to worry. The prosthesis is designed to be sturdy, and is quite resistant to breaking. (The mechanical failures of the inflatable are not directly related to vigorous intercourse, and there's really not much you or your partner can do to break it. Anything that doesn't hurt you won't hurt the implant itself.) You may, however, find that you need to modify your positions during intercourse. Some couples find sex more comfortable with the woman on top.

A woman who has gone without intercourse for a while may find sex a little uncomfortable at first, because her vagina may have tightened. But taking intercourse very slowly can really help. Enough lubrication is a must, and a water-soluble lubricant can be helpful. If pain persists, a woman should see her gynecologist.

Part of the adjustment process is becoming so comfortable that you forget about the implant. Just because you are always able to get an erection doesn't mean you will always want to have intercourse. In fact, for

Preventing Infection

Infection is a concern with any surgery. But when a foreign object like an implant is involved, the risk increases. Serious infection after an implant operation is quite unusual. But because the body often can't fight an infection as efficiently with the object in place, removal of the implant may be necessary.

To minimize the risk, pay careful attention to your doctor's instructions regarding rest, care of the genital area and medication. In addition, if any of the following occur, contact your physician immediately.
- You develop a fever of more than 100 degrees.
- Increased swelling, redness or soreness occurs around the incision or the implant.

---

some men, body image is a major factor in their satisfaction with the implant. For example, Gilbert recovered from the surgery, but later developed health problems which prevented him from having intercourse. However, "just the look and size of the penis helps our morale," he says, referring to the satisfaction he and his wife feel. "We think this is an important point even though we are not using it for actual intercourse." This elderly man also reports that his wife makes him feel good. "She praises the way I look. She enjoys touching and holding me."

What is important is that you feel comfortable and secure using the implant, and feel that it is a part of your body. If you and your partner have trouble adjusting, ask your physician to recommend a sex therapist, preferably one who is experienced in dealing with implant patients and their partners.

The Partner's Reaction

"I'm an optimistic person. At first it was new. You think 'oh my God.' Now I don't even think about it. It

> ### Getting Used to the New You
>
> It's normal to have some adjustment problems after implant surgery. Most couples solve these without much difficulty. Just knowing what to expect can make it easier.
>
> Each couple is different but it's not uncommon to:
> - Have some anxiety about being able to have intercourse.
> - Notice that the penis looks somewhat different.
> - Take some time to adjust to the fact that erection is no longer physical evidence of arousal—that desire can be shown in other ways.
> - Need to try out different positions.
> - Need to spend time getting comfortable to the point where the implant is no longer an issue.

just takes a little practice, like with everything new," says Janice, a real estate agent whose high energy is reflected in her vibrant voice. "It took at least a couple of months to adjust to it. After a while it was the same as natural," she explains. Janice and her husband, Bill, have been married more than 30 years.

Jane, a 48-year-old self-described "retired Mom" who's been married 20 years, is also satisfied with the results of her husband's surgery. "I'm definitely pleased. It's 90 percent as good as when he was in his 20's, and that's terrific. And no more premature ejaculations! Even if he does ejaculate, he can go longer. You do have to change positions. The woman-on-top works better because of the bend of the prosthesis." The only change Jane noticed is a slight reduction in the circumference of the erect penis. "That's where he loses about 10 percent," she says.

For Jane, a clear-headed look at the potency problem and the solution was helpful. "We've adjusted. It's like false teeth, or a false arm. I look at it like this: You lose something, you replace it."

Studies have found that, generally, women are satisfied with the results of the implant. Not surprisingly, there is a correlation between the partners' satisfaction: Usually, when one is happy, so is the other. And the more involved the partner is from the beginning, the more likely she is to be pleased with the results.

Artery Repair

Artery surgery is an option for some men who don't get enough blood into the penis to produce and maintain an erection because their arteries are partially blocked.

Sometimes the blood-flow problem can be corrected by replacing the narrow artery with a new, artificial one; sometimes the solution is to insert a tiny, deflated surgical balloon into the partially blocked artery and inflate the balloon to dilate the artery. Both types of surgery offer a real chance of restoring potency.

Another option for men whose potency problems can be blamed on malfunctioning arteries is to bring in a new blood supply to the penis. There are two basic ways to do this.

One method involves taking an artery, usually from the abdominal wall, and rerouting it so it carries blood into the penis. One end of the artery stays in the normal position, while the other is cut and swung around so it supplies the penis. The operation qualifies as major surgery and takes several hours.

The other option is to remove a well-functioning vein from the leg and hook it into an artery which normally supplies the leg. The vein then actually carries some of the blood meant for the leg into the penis. It's a type of bypass operation, and the replaced vein actually functions as an artery.

This type of surgery may sound fairly straightforward, but actually it is quite complicated and prone to problems. Sometimes too much blood is routed into the penis, and this unfortunate situation can lead to priapism, a serious condition. Another problem is that the newly constructed avenue for the blood flow may

> ### A Satisfying Experience
>
> Just how satisfied are men with their implants? Most are pretty satisfied, according to several studies.
>
> For example, reactions to the semirigid penile implant were favorable at a Seattle hospital. Eighty-three percent of the men who responded were satisfied. Most felt that their expectations had been met, and most said they would choose to have the operation if they had to make the choice again. However, five men specifically stated that they would not repeat the procedure—two because their partners did not like the results, one because he suffered prolonged and severe pain and the two others because the results didn't measure up to their expectations.
>
> Doctors at the Mayo Clinic asked their inflatable prosthesis patients to report their reaction. Sixty-one patients answered.
>
> About half of all respondents reported that they were very satisfied with the implant; another 15 were fairly satisfied. According to the patients, their partners felt approximately the same way.
>
> Eight patients complained of mechanical problems. When these were fixed, the patients were satisfied with their erections and with sexual intercourse.
>
> After the repairs were made, the total results indicated that almost 90 percent of the inflatable implant patients were satisfied.

not remain open, causing the potency problem to return.

Although these last two procedures are now relatively uncommon in the U.S., some very experienced European surgeons have reported success rates of 60 to 80 percent with them. The operations may become more popular as surgeons here become more experienced with them.

The best candidates for surgery which brings in a new blood supply to the penis are relatively young men who have blood-flow problems from trauma, such as a pelvic fracture. It's important, however, that nerve damage not be a factor in their potency problem, because the operation will do nothing for nerve injuries. Also, men whose problems result from blockage of the small arteries caused by arteriosclerosis are not likely to have good results, because other tissues in the penis may be damaged also. But if you think you might be a good candidate, consult your physician. He can refer you to the few major medical centers in the U.S. where such operations are performed.

Sealing Leaky Veins

As you know, a man with leaky veins can find his erection sabotaged with amazing and disheartening efficiency. Until recently, leaky veins have been largely ignored by the medical profession, but now surgical solutions to this problem are receiving increased attention. One solution is to surgically tie off or remove the leaky veins, thus removing the source of the problem.

Belgian doctors have demonstrated just how effective vein surgery can be on certain patients. Out of 80 patients with potency problems, 20 were found to have impressive vein leaks. Significantly, the leak involved the deep dorsal vein, a major source of blood flow out of the penis. The surgeons tied off the vein. Results were dramatic: 16 men found themselves with enough restored potency to allow intercourse. The 4 men who didn't benefit from such improvement were found to have serious artery problems.

The best candidate for vein surgery has only his veins to blame for his potency difficulty; his arteries and nerves are normal. Usually the surgeon will make an incision somewhere along the side of the scrotum, find the offending veins (which have previously been identified by a type of X-ray) and remove or tie them off, thus preventing them from carrying blood out of the penis. At the time of surgery, the doctor can actually measure the extent of the leak by infusing fluid into the penis and measuring how fast it leaves. This

Yohimbine: Hope for the Future?

Yohimbine, a drug that's extracted from the bark of a tree, is credited by some experts with increasing erection. Some doctors prescribe yohimbine pills to men who have potency problems and low libido.

One theory holds that yohimbine works by affecting parts of the nervous system which control erection. But the jury is still out on whether this theory is correct. Researchers are still trying to determine whether or not the drug actually does enhance erection and sexuality.

In one study, researchers gave yohimbine to 23 men who were thought to have physically caused potency problems because they didn't get erections in their sleep. These men, who ranged in age from 32 to 72 years, took the yohimbine three times a day for at least ten weeks.

What happened? For most, unfortunately, nothing. More than half of the men experienced no change in potency. However, six men found their erections were restored to normal and they could have intercourse. Four men reported improvement, but still found their erections "unsatisfactory."

And one man found his potency only temporarily restored. Unfortunately, after five months on yohimbine, he again experienced potency problems.

The side effects were minimal: One man became nauseous and two complained of dizziness. Reducing the dosage and then increasing it again slowly took care of the vertigo.

Another study, this time of men reported to have erection problems caused by psychological difficulties, provided some interesting results. Sixty-two percent of men receiving yohimbine reported improved erections; only 16 percent of the men ingesting a sugar pill said their potency increased. Researchers did not report whether yohimbine provided lasting relief.

If the results with human subjects turn out to be the same as with laboratory rats, yohimbine may

> ### Yohimbine: Hope for the Future? (continued)
>
> prove to be beneficial for men with low sexual desire and chronic testosterone deficiency. Researchers at Stanford University divided rats into two groups: The unfortunate ones got nothing, while the others received yohimbine. Twenty minutes after the shots, the yohimbine-treated rats were engaged in the rodent version of an orgy, exhibiting twice the sexual behavior of the rats who didn't get yohimbine.
>
> The success with the rats could be due in part to their large dose and the fact that the yohimbine was injected. Humans are given smaller doses in a pill form that isn't as easily absorbed as the injections.
>
> The best advice is to look upon yohimbine as something of a long shot. Discuss your options in detail with your physician, and remember that other treatments, like penile implants and shots, are available.

way, he can gauge when enough veins have been tied off. Depending on where the veins are located, the procedure can be major or relatively minor surgery.

How successful are operations on penile veins? It helps to pick a surgeon experienced in this procedure; as many as three quarters of the men operated on by experts in this field can achieve normal erections after surgery.

Unfortunately, no one knows how likely it is that a man with some leaky veins will develop others at some future time. Nevertheless, vein surgery holds the promise of a real advance in the treatment of some potency problems, making implants less necessary for some men.

Repairing a "Bent" Penis

Peyronie's disease produces scarring, lumps and bumps in the penis. These abnormalities can cause the penis to bend when erect. No one knows what causes this disease, which generally affects middle-aged and older men. Sometimes a man with Peyronie's disease, upset by the appearance of his penis, becomes psychologically unable to get an erection, although his physical system is still working well. Sex therapy and counseling may help.

The good news about Peyronie's is that usually it gets better by itself, over time. Sometimes medical treatment seems to improve matters. For some men, however, Peyronie's gets worse. The bend in the penis can become so severe that intercourse is difficult. For a few unfortunate men, the scarring in the penis causes them to lose their ability to get an erection.

In such advanced cases, surgical treatment may help. For men still able to become erect, the doctor can cut out the scar and patch the area with tissue taken from another part of the body. If the scarring is extensive, however, the penis may be damaged and erectile ability lost after the procedure.

Another option is for the surgeon to take a tuck on the opposite side from the bend, and literally try to straighten out the penis surgically. For men who can't get an erection at all, the most reliable surgery is to straighten the penis and put in an implant. For many men with Peyronie's disease who are impotent, the implant is the only alternative.

Although the different treatments discussed in this chapter provide successful solutions to many patients, they are by no means the only options. It's always important to explore whatever treatments are available and applicable to your case. Even after surgery restores potency, some couples find they need help adjusting. Sex therapy can be a real help to such patients.

In Search of Potency-Producing Medications

Many researchers are studying medications which may help erection problems. Drugs that block spasms in the arteries (including those in the penis) are being tried and may prove beneficial to men with reduced blood flow. Several drugs, currently being tested and not yet on the market, may increase sexual desire.

For some men, naturally anxious about their sexual difficulties, an antianxiety medication may provide relief from performance anxiety and result in improved erections. Be sure to discuss the benefits and side effects of any medication with your doctor.

9

Sex Therapy for Sexual Success

John, a 45-year-old married man, visited his doctor complaining that his erections were no longer satisfactory. He couldn't get a "good" erection, he said—one that was sufficiently firm to allow him to have intercourse.

Trying to find out what was causing John's poor erections, his doctor gave him a penile shot. The injection produced an erection that was adequate for intercourse, and quite normal as far as the physician could tell. John, however, was distinctly unimpressed. "This is as good as I get when I try to have intercourse, and it's not good enough," he lamented.

Obviously, something was wrong. John was physically able to have intercourse—but he was very uncomfortable doing so. His insistence on what he unrealistically considered a "perfect" erection, combined with his fear of disappointing his partner, was ruining his sex life. Emotionally unable to examine his attitudes, he had labeled his penis and his erections as the problem. In John's view, it was not that he did not want to have intercourse; no, it was just that his penis was not cooperating.

The physician suggested that sex therapy could improve John and his wife's sexual relationship. It could also help John achieve his goal of more frequent and satisfactory intercourse. But John was clearly unimpressed with the suggestion. "I know I'm not crazy," he declared. "I don't want to see any therapist, and I sure don't need a psychiatrist." That's too bad, because the therapy might have solved his problem. And it might have shattered a few myths he has about sex therapy.

Unfortunately, many men share John's attitude: They take advice to see a sex therapist as an indication that someone thinks they are crazy. In fact, nothing could be further from the truth. Sex therapy is for people who want to overcome habits and attitudes which sabotage their sex lives—it's usually not for people with serious emotional or mental problems, because often they can't benefit from it. Generally, a sex therapist will not focus on your unconscious, or attempt to analyze you. A sex therapist will help you define your goals and possibly revise them so they are more attainable; identify problem areas and suggest solutions; and provide suggestions and exercises for making positive changes.

The fact is, sexual problems affect most people at some point in their lives. Think about it: Why would this emotionally packed area of human behavior be any more immune from disturbance than other parts of life? And sex therapy doesn't take a lifetime. Sometimes, just a brief period of help can make a very positive and rewarding difference.

Although there are lots of variations of sex therapy, modern-day sex therapy began with the work of Masters and Johnson. As the term is usually used, sex therapy is designed to focus on the needs, concerns and expectations of the client. It can be a highly structured, short-term program lasting a few weeks or months, or it may be more flexible in design.

Different forms of sex therapy can benefit men and women with a wide variety of sexual difficulties, but we're going to concentrate on how sex therapy can help men who experience erection problems.

Some people become anxious and uptight just hearing the words "sex therapy," because they don't understand what sex therapy involves.

Paying for Sex Therapy

How much you pay for sex therapy depends on where you live, which therapist you see, the length of treatment and the type of program. Hourly rates may be the same or close to those charged for other types of therapy. Intensive programs may cost $1,500 to $2,000, or substantially more. Some therapists do offer sliding scales based on the client's ability to pay, and some university training programs may occasionally offer therapy at reduced prices.

What's important is that you understand, up front, how much the therapy will cost. Get an estimate as to the number of sessions. And ask if at any point in the program you decide not to continue—or if the therapist decides you should stop—do you get a partial refund of any money you've paid in advance?

Many health insurance policies will not pay for sex therapy, so be sure to check out your coverage in advance.

Try to look at it this way. Imagine that you are someone who is afraid of public speaking. You get extremely anxious and tense before you have to talk in front of a group of people. You're afraid your speech will fall flat, your audience will be bored, or someone will ask you a question you have no idea how to answer. You feel your throat closing up as your nervousness increases. All the witticisms you so carefully rehearsed, the jokes and anecdotes you collected for this occasion, desert you in your moment of need. This is performance anxiety. It's the same thing that sometimes hits a man when he gets in bed with a lover. He worries that he won't get or maintain a good erection and that his partner will be disappointed. Maybe he's been rehearsing the encounter over and over in his head, and feels like he's about to go onstage.

What Makes a Good Sex Therapist

Finding a sex therapist who is qualified, experienced and trained to handle problems like yours is important. We believe that a personal recommendation from a qualified professional is one of the best ways to find someone to help you. Ask the urologist who examined you for physical problems for a recommendation.

Another good source of referral is a university which has a sex therapy clinic, or a program to train sex therapists. Even if the clinic itself is too far away or otherwise inconvenient for you to use, many will provide referrals to graduates or other qualified sex therapists who practice near you.

The American Association of Sex Educators, Counselors and Therapists (AASECT) gives referrals. Some therapists choose to be certified by this organization, and you can get the names of those who practice in your area by calling AASECT at 202-462-1171 or by writing to them at 11 Dupont Circle, N.W., Suite 220, Washington, D.C. 20036. To be certified, a therapist must have satisfied educational and training requirements.

The American Board of Family Psychology has stringent requirements for certifying psychologists in marital and family therapy, and in marital and sex therapy. The Board will provide referrals to members practicing in your area. Call 817-776-6081 or write to Dr. George Nixon, American Board of Family Psychology, 6501 Sanger, Suite 15, P.O. Box 7977, Waco, TX 76714.

It's important to realize that, unlike some other professions, there is no one university degree that a sex therapist has which will tell you he or she is trained, qualified or experienced. Sex therapists have vastly different levels of training and experience. And they come with different professional educations and degrees: Some are medical doctors; some are psychiatrists or psychologists; others are nurses; still others are social workers or coun-

> ### What Makes a Good Sex Therapist (continued)
> selors. Some have no degrees in the helping professions. Sexual problems can sometimes be a part of other difficulties, like depression, so thorough professional training is important. In all cases, we recommend you ask the therapist these questions before beginning treatment:
> - What professional education, training, and degrees do you have? Specifically, what training in sex therapy have you completed?
> - Do you belong to any professional organizations? Which ones?
> - Have you treated many patients with problems like mine? (Some sex therapists have experience with many patients with erection problems; others do not.)
> - What kind of a treatment plan or program would you recommend in my case? Why? What are the alternatives?

There are professionals who can teach you to relax and be a better, more confident public speaker. Well, a sex therapist can offer the same kind of help for some men with erection problems. Specifically, sex therapy can help men whose erection problems are caused by anxiety, nervousness or other psychological distress; and men whose erection problems have a physical cause or a physical contributing factor, but who want to learn how to increase their sexual pleasure, and possibly improve their erections, as much as possible. Sex therapy can teach you how to pleasure yourself and your partner; how to enjoy other types of sexual contact besides intercourse; and how to communicate better with your partner.

Can sex therapy help you? The best answer to that question comes from some self-evaluation and from an assessment by a trained, experienced sex therapist. In general, however, there are certain characteristics which make someone more likely to benefit from sex therapy, and more able to learn solutions to correct an erection problem.

Are You Suited for Sex Therapy?

A good candidate for sex therapy is someone interested in finding out more about himself. Therefore, he is somewhat introspective, has some insight into himself and wants to learn more. He will have functioned well sexually in the past, and his problem will have developed recently. This is particularly important, because men with erection problems may become extremely depressed, and solving the problem early can help men avoid the cycle of rejection and despair that can develop over time.

Some therapists require that a man with an erection problem already have a partner in a relationship. The reason for such a rule is that because sex is something which concerns both partners, both should participate in any resolution of a sexual problem. The two partners don't have to be married or to have been together for a long time, but it's important that they feel good about each other. Other therapists will work with men who do not have a steady partner, or don't have a partner at all.

Perhaps most important of all, a good candidate for sex therapy is someone who is motivated: He wants to improve his sexual functioning and his sexual relationship and learn more about his body. He is willing to do the homework the therapist assigns; he wants to change.

There are also key characteristics a good candidate does *not* have. He doesn't suffer from persistent, long-term, low sexual desire, even though the erection problem may have recently reduced his interest in sex. He's not seeking help just because he's being pressured to change by his lover. He doesn't have very restricted and firmly fixed ideas about what is "normal" sex; he

Is the Therapist on the Level?

Just as important as checking out credentials and getting recommendations is knowing what should and should not happen in sex therapy. Here's a list of general guidelines.
- A sex therapist should answer your questions fully.
- A sex therapist should explain the treatment program to you.
- A sex therapist should not promise a "cure," but the therapist can offer you encouragement and support.
- A sex therapist should not suggest having sex with you or your partner. (If this happens, leave immediately. And then report the practitioner to the appropriate professional organization or licensing board.)
- A sex therapist should not blame you or your lover for the problem.

If you don't feel comfortable with a particular therapist, regardless of his or her professional qualifications, you may always seek care elsewhere.

---

will consider sexual behavior besides intercourse, and he's willing to experiment. He does not carry within him a strong prohibition against sex. For example, a man who says, "I avoid sex until I can't stand it" will need to spend additional time in sex therapy examining and reconsidering his attitudes.

Along the same lines, someone who remarks, "I masturbate only when I can't stop myself" isn't going to be comfortable stimulating himself as part of a sex therapy program. Working on his attitudes toward self-pleasure would be an important first step, and a good sex therapist would be able to help him examine and possibly change those feelings.

Just as the wife or lover plays an important role in diagnosis and treatment, she can be crucial to successful sex therapy. In the best situation, the partner is interested, involved and supportive of therapy. She wants the sexual relationship to improve. She is willing to experiment. She genuinely likes her partner, and he feels the same way about her. In short, there is a feeling of good will and affection in the relationship.

Sometimes a woman is afraid of what sex therapy involves, so she sends her husband on what one therapist called "a scouting mission." Once he reports back that things are okay, that the therapist seems reasonable and the treatment may help, she then decides to become involved. She's often pleased to discover that her feelings and reactions are considered worthy of attention.

Of course, we want to emphasize that these guidelines are general; some people who start sex therapy with significant obstacles can be helped to overcome them. What's important is that you and your partner honestly share your feelings and concerns with the therapist.

Marvin and Caroline are an example of a couple who are likely to benefit from sex therapy. Marvin, a 53-year-old executive for a large corporation, has been married to Caroline, his second wife, for almost eight years. They have a strong, caring relationship and always thought they communicated quite well. When they went for help they were supportive of each other's needs and able to talk about their concerns. They wanted to improve their sex life together.

Marvin first noticed a problem after he and Caroline had been together for five years. "Almost overnight I stopped getting erections. It started out, it would just go soft quickly. Then, in the space of about two months, nothing." Until this happened Marvin and Caroline had been enjoying, in her words, "a very full sex life."

Marvin went to his doctor, and tests revealed no physical problem. The erection difficulty continued, and after several months Marvin's physician recommended that he go to a sex therapy clinic at a nearby university. Their experience is just one example of sex therapy. Other therapists proceed with treatment differently.

Marvin and Caroline entered a structured, medical school-based sex therapy program which lasted for three months. Follow-up visits were available after they completed treatment. Each week, they had a session with their two therapists, a man and a woman. (The male-female sex therapy team is based on the ideas of Masters and Johnson. But recent research suggests that a single therapist—male or female—may be just as effective. And certainly, many successful therapists work alone.)

Thorough tests had found no physical cause for Marvin's erection problem, so that part of the process was finished. Marvin and Caroline filled out questionnaires. They answered questions about their past and present sexual habits and about how they felt about certain types of sexual behavior. Then they were interviewed separately and the therapists discussed their answers in detail. In addition, the therapists obtained even more medical and personal information.

Some interesting facts emerged during the couple's discussions with the therapists. Marvin realized his body was sending him a message: He was very uncomfortable about on-the-job developments, and said he was under a lot of stress. "My problem coincided almost exactly with a job change I wasn't happy about."

Upset about his work situation, Marvin had begun drinking heavily. He had been a social drinker for many years, without suffering any apparent ill effects. But as his unhappiness at work increased, his alcohol consumption did likewise. Obviously, adding large amounts of alcohol to this already-pressured situation just made his erection problem worse. But it wasn't until he entered sex therapy that Marvin realized the extent of his self-sabotage.

Therapy helped him make these connections. But it did more for the couple. It improved their communication.

Learning to Talk

Caroline came to some realizations of her own. "We worked through a lot of feelings about sex and things other than sex. We found out we had never really argued, were really polite and had lots of repressed anger," Caroline explains. "We learned to give 'I' messages—this is what I like, this is what I don't like."

Breaking down communication barriers they didn't even know existed helped Marvin and Caroline feel closer, and they began to want to express this intimacy physically. They felt the pressure subsiding and were able to relax more easily and to say more clearly what they wanted, in bed and out. They were ready for the next step in the treatment program: sensate focus.

Focus on Pleasure

Sensate focus was an important component of Marvin and Caroline's sex therapy program. Sensate focus is a fancy term which simply refers to a series of graduated exercises designed to increase physical pleasure while keeping anxiety to a minimum. It begins with nongenital touching and progresses, after several sessions, to intercourse. The aim of sensate focus is to increase pleasure and knowledge of your own and your partner's body, to remove any performance pressure to have intercourse (usually intercourse is prohibited during the first several exercises) and to move away from feeling that intercourse is the only "good" form of sex. Sensate focus helps lovers change their definition of a good, satisfying sexual experience to include a variety of behaviors, attitudes and pleasures.

Like many couples these days, Marvin and Caroline had found it difficult just to have enough time for sex, let alone intimacy. They both worked at demanding jobs and often felt exhausted when they came home. Because they were so fatigued, it was difficult to recharge and concentrate just on each other. The sex therapy program, with its homework assignments, required Marvin and Caroline to devote time and energy to their relationship, to each other and to physical intimacy.

After the initial interviews and a discussion of expectations and goals, Marvin and Caroline were ready to begin the sensate focus exercises. The first week they were instructed to caress, touch and enjoy each other, but avoid any genital and breast touching. The exercises progressed week by week until intercourse was allowed. Some couples, like Marvin and Caroline, find that erections occur early in the program. Sex therapy clients are typically instructed not to take advantage of such events, but to continue with the program as instructed. That's because the exercises are supposed to teach partners to enjoy each other and to learn what feels good without having intercourse, or the pressure to perform. If such enjoyment can be learned, future occasional bouts of "erectile failure" will not stand in the way of sexual pleasure.

Learning to have pleasurable sex without intercourse is a good way to expose some myths about sex. Many men think that an erection is necessary for a woman's sexual pleasure, but in fact it is not. A woman can experience much joy and achieve orgasm without an erect penis being in the picture. That does not mean that a woman won't enjoy intercourse, just that it's not always necessary. Like many of us, Caroline felt that intercourse was "real sex," and other pleasures didn't quite qualify. Learning otherwise made her feel better and enjoy sex more. And realizing that sex and pleasure don't require an erection is reassuring—and reenergizing—to many men.

Once genital touching is permitted, the therapist might explain that the woman should gently caress the man's penis until he gets an erection. Then she stops touching until the erection goes away—without the man ejaculating. The lovers can then repeat the exercise. Doing this several times gives the man practice in getting, losing and regaining an erection. It's reassuring

> ### A Visit to a Sex Therapist
>
> Remember, in almost all cases, you should have a thorough medical evaluation specifically aimed at detecting any physical causes for your potency problem before you seek sex therapy.
>
> Once you visit the therapist, you can expect to:
>
> - Be interviewed in some detail about your physical, medical, personal, marital and sexual history.
> - Have your partner (if you have one) interviewed and involved.
> - Discuss what you want to achieve in therapy.
> - Be prohibited from attempting intercourse for a period of time.
> - Be given exercises to do at home while away from the therapist.
> - Learn from discussions, written materials and films about the male and female capabilities for sexual pleasure and arousal.
> - Use fantasy, alone and with a partner, to increase enjoyment.

to both partners to realize that an erection once lost is not gone forever.

Or the man might caress the woman. Some men have always been the more active partner in sexual encounters, and they may find it difficult to relax and let their partner give pleasure to them, as the exercises require. One way around this is for the man to caress and stroke his lover first. Initiating the exercise may make it easier for him to then let his companion take the lead.

Once you're comfortable with sexual pleasure that doesn't involve intercourse, and with the experience of losing and regaining an erection, the therapist may suggest that you're ready for intercourse. Often sex therapists recommend that the woman be on top, because this makes it easier for her to be the more active partner. Such an arrangement may help the man because he has less pressure to perform and can more easily relax and enjoy himself.

An important part of a sex therapy program is for each partner to be responsible for his or her own pleasure—and to communicate his or her feelings. Marvin and Caroline welcomed this change. Focusing on different ways to have sensual pleasure was a wonderful development. "This helped us take the emphasis away from intercourse," she says. Initially, the ban on intercourse was difficult, but the process of going through the exercises provided an unexpected bonus for Caroline. She found herself learning to be more comfortable with enjoying sensual and sexual pleasures which did not involve intercourse. Like many of us, although she "knew" such behavior was okay, she had not quite accepted it emotionally. But having Marvin caress her for a period of time without any expectation of intercourse helped her overcome her inhibitions about "that kind" of touching.

What Are Your Expectations?

Getting expectations clear and discussing them in detail with the therapist and your partner is an essential part of sex therapy. If you can get erections in some situations but not others, it's realistic to explore what is happening in the situations when you don't become erect. For example, a man who feels he "should" have sex whenever his partner is willing may discover that just removing that requirement solves the problem. If you have a physical illness which plays a role in your potency, your expectations of what constitutes success must, of course, be defined with those facts in mind. A sex therapist will probe and help you define what constitutes success for you. It's important to get this clear before you embark on a program of therapy, so everyone knows the goals and objectives of the program.

Sometimes a couple comes in for one problem, and in the process of defining the man and woman's expectations, different concerns emerge. Harry's announced reason for wanting sex therapy was his inability to consistently maintain an erection. This 57-year-old man suffered from high blood pressure and had to take medication for this condition. He also had been diagnosed recently as diabetic, a fact he found very difficult to accept.

Harry's first marriage had ended in divorce. In discussions with the therapist it became clear that Harry blamed his erection problem for the breakup of this relationship. He was convinced that the same thing might happen again with his second wife, Shirley, a vivacious 54-year-old who also had been married before. For the most part, Harry and Shirley considered themselves a happy couple. But increasingly, Harry was fixated on his "sexual failures." He was convinced that Shirley would reject him just as his first wife had—and that his erectile problems were to blame.

Harry felt an erect penis was necessary to satisfy a woman, and he was quite surprised when the therapist explained in detail that this was not true. He was even more surprised when Shirley, encouraged by the therapist, explained that she was not overly concerned with Harry's erection problem.

When Harry lost potency, Shirley's usual comment was, "Don't worry about it." Harry interpreted this remark as a well-intended solace for his failure. But Shirley meant her words, and more. Her first husband had been, she explained, a "slam-bam thank you ma'am" kind of guy, and Shirley was quite happy to be cuddled, kissed and caressed. She wanted to be physically close to Harry, but she did not feel especially deprived by Harry's loss of potency. What she did want was physical affection. Harry's preoccupation with intercourse as the only "real" sex was troubling her.

What Harry and Shirley learned in sex therapy helped their fundamentally sound relationship. They learned to communicate more clearly and directly. Each learned to say what was wanted without confusing the other. Relieved of the self-induced pressure to always produce an erection, Harry relaxed and found his erections improved. He also began taking better care of himself, because he could accept more easily the changes his diabetes required in his life.

It's important to realize that success and expectations are unique and individual definitions. For one man, success may be accepting the physical constraints an illness or injury has given him, and learning new ways for sexual and sensual pleasure. Doctors told Gerald, a 38-year-old man with multiple sclerosis, that his illness would prevent him from having intercourse. Gerald and his wife discussed all their options, and decided that a penile implant was not for them. They decided to give sex therapy a try. In Gerald's case, the doctors' pessimism proved to be at least premature, maybe unwarranted. Gerald ended up getting erections about half the time when he became aroused, and sex therapy taught him and his wife other ways they could enjoy each other.

For Jeffrey, a 49-year-old marketing executive, redefining his expectations was crucial. Jeffrey was suffering from stress-overload brought on by numerous changes in his life. His professional activities had increased dramatically; a teenaged son was giving him problems; his wife had started a new and demanding career. Jeffrey found himself having fewer and fewer erections. He felt the ones he did have were inadequate. He found his "inability to perform" frustrating, and he was a man who had always taken special pride in his endurance and persistence in all aspects of his life, sex included.

Jeffrey came to therapy alone. As it turned out, the solutions were quite simple. He needed to learn to relax. He needed to identify the pressures in his life, and to make some "deals" with himself to forget them —especially in the bedroom. And he needed to make the time he spent with his wife private and safely secure from intrusions by his son.

Once Jeffrey put his new solutions into practice, his

erections returned to normal. He was able to enjoy intercourse. And he also learned an important lesson: His body was sending him a message to stop pushing quite so hard.

For Marvin and Caroline, improving erections was a realistic goal, but it was only part of the story. "I would call the sex therapy a success since we could start having intercourse," Marvin says. But learning the connections between his physical and emotional state was important for the future. When financial pressure beset the couple, Marvin reacted. "The immediate effect was I lost my erectile ability. It's more in my head than anything else." Does this incident tell Marvin sex therapy didn't work? Far from it. "Now we have the attitude toward the problem of working together; now we have direction," Marvin explains. His expectations for himself are firmly rooted in reality.

Self-Help Sex Therapy

You can apply the techniques we discuss in this chapter yourself, and also check out other sources, such as *Male Sexuality,* by Bernie Zilbergeld, Ph.D., and *All about Sex Therapy,* by Peter R. Kilmann and Katherine H. Mills. Many sex therapists don't see any harm in trying sex therapy on your own. If you do decide to proceed, be sure you discuss what you want to do, and why, with your partner before beginning. Take things very slowly. Don't push yourself to do something you feel unready to do. Make sure you have a private, comfortable environment in which to practice your exercises, and set aside special time for this purpose.

If you make progress on your own, congratulations! And don't let one setback throw you off course. If, however, you eventually decide to seek professional help, don't feel that your time has been wasted. Because you are so well informed, you may be able to proceed a little faster than someone else. If you do seek out a professional, be sure to share your self-help experiences with the therapist.

Self-help sex therapy requires thought and careful progression. You have to start at the beginning, with communication, and not just jump right into the exercises. Sex therapy is a little like taking a course: You have to put in study time, you have to do your homework, and sometimes a teacher or therapist is not only helpful, but essential. That's why we think it's important to emphasize that if your attempt at self-help isn't satisfying, you shouldn't necessarily give up on sex therapy itself. An experienced professional may help you overcome the roadblocks to success that you couldn't overcome on your own.

Sex Therapy and the Single Man

As we've noted, some sex therapy programs are designed to work only with couples. But research has shown that men without partners can also make significant improvements with sex therapy.

First, let's look at what we mean by men without partners. This is not a homogeneous group. A man who is recently divorced may be without a partner, but he has a history of social contact and intimacy with at least one woman. On the other hand, a man whose partner refuses to participate in therapy is alone in his quest for improvement, but is in a very different situation from the divorced man. Some therapists have noted that men in long-standing relationships whose lovers will not participate in treatment are least likely to improve. Problems in the relationship itself may be preventing the couple from dealing with sexual difficulties successfully.

And single men with erection problems who are socially inhibited can improve their communication skills and their potency in group therapy. For example, California therapists gave group members homework assignments emphasizing sensual pleasure (at first without intercourse), social skills and fantasy exercises.

> ### Masturbation Exercises
>
> For men without partners, masturbation is often an integral part of sex therapy, although those with lovers can benefit from it also. Attitudes about masturbation have changed a lot, but many people still regard it as sinful, selfish, dirty or distasteful—even if they don't believe that masturbation will cause blindness, warts or hairy palms. In fact, most people engage in self-pleasuring; one study found that almost all men and more than 80 percent of women masturbate. But just because everybody does it doesn't mean we all accept it as normal and healthy.
>
> So, someone who feels uncomfortable with masturbation will need to examine his attitudes before beginning any exercises. A good sex therapist should be able to help him do that.
>
> Self-stimulation is an important part of sex therapy for erection problems. Learning that a lost erection can be restored is reassuring. A man may be instructed to stimulate himself until he is aroused, then to let his penis become flaccid. Once he is no longer erect, he begins self-pleasuring again. Learning how to do this when he's alone will help him accomplish the same thing when he is with his lover.

Learning about normal changes in erections was an important component of the therapy. Because female therapists participated, the men were able to role-play situations with women and then use their newly-developed communication skills in their private lives. At the conclusion of the therapy, 90 percent of the men said their erections were improved. Because these men had learned how to communicate more freely, the authors say, their erection problems decreased.

When it comes down to basics, communication is the primary key to satisfying sex. And if a therapist can help improve your style of communication, he can probably improve your sex life too.

10

For Women Only: How to Help Yourself (As You Help Your Partner)

Potency isn't just a man's issue. When your partner's erection is absent you feel the loss as much as your partner. One of the first ways you may react to your lover's trouble with erections is to doubt yourself and your relationship.

You might feel lonely, isolated and deprived of much-wanted physical and emotional attention. You might be frightened about sharing your problem even with your closest friends. Perhaps your partner has told you not to tell anyone—even your family doctor—about his erection difficulties. Perhaps the subject upsets him so much that he won't even let you discuss your concerns with him.

You might begin to believe that your only choice is to ignore the problem. You might cling to the hope that if you bury your head in the sand everything will miraculously resolve itself.

But deep inside you know the problem will probably only continue—and might worsen.

These feelings are common. Many women whose partners have erection problems feel inadequate and sometimes blame themselves. And many women feel responsible for the solution. Some women cling to the romantic notion that love conquers all. But while love can be powerful, it can't unclog blocked blood vessels, diagnose illnesses or remove all stress and pressure in life.

How can you help yourself and your partner? How can you cope with your own feelings while still being a support system for your husband?

There aren't any simple solutions; what works for one woman might not work for you. But there are some basics to making the most of a tough situation. And there are ways to make it better.

Working Together for Pleasure

Here is some advice that can help you and your partner through this difficult time:
- Remember, no one is to blame. Assigning blame is always unproductive and often unjustified. Look to the future, not the past. Use your time and energy to get appropriate help solving the problem.
- Think in terms of we—not just he, or me. People who successfully overcome their difficulties work together as a team. They grow stronger as a couple as they confront and solve the problem.

Just examine Marianne's story to find out how important these guidelines are.

Marianne, a 35-year-old personnel manager, has been happily married to Jack for almost a decade. If you asked her, she'd make no bones about describing herself as aggressive, smart and capable. She and Jack have had their ups and downs, but generally their marriage has been strong. Their friends call them a happy couple.

But their friends haven't seen their private side. When Jack lost his ability to get an erection, Marianne felt threatened and blamed herself. Although she usually communicated well with her husband, she knew this subject upset him. Rather than make him more worried, she kept her feelings a secret for a long, painful time. The results were far-reaching. "I thought it was my fault—initially," says Marianne. She had always been quite secure about her relationship with

How to Help Your Lover

Here are some pointers on how you can help your situation:

- Be warm, friendly and physical towards your lover. Let him know you want to hug, kiss and cuddle him—but that you don't expect intercourse now.
- Tell him that you want him to hold you, that you need him. Communicate directly, but gently. You might say, for example, "I want to be close to you. Please touch me. I don't need you to use your penis, I just want us to lie here together and be close."
- Do not tell your lover that intercourse doesn't matter. If he believes you, he may question just how much you liked intercourse before. And if he doesn't believe you, he'll say to himself, "She thinks I'm so fragile that she can't tell me the truth anymore."
- Sometimes a couple unconsciously gets into arguments so they'll be angry and won't want to have sex. Try to avoid this self-defeating trap, and if you think your partner is falling into it, point it out.
- Don't assign blame for the problem. Don't say, "It's your problem, you fix it." Remember, the problem affects both of you. And the solution needs to come from both of you, too.
- Encourage him to have a medical evaluation as soon as possible. The longer a serious potency problem persists, the more strain it can put on the relationship—and delay might seriously damage his health.
- If he resists getting medical help, suggest that he go to a support group. And go yourself, even if he won't. Just seeing that there are lots of people with similar problems—and good solutions—might propel him to do something.
- Participate in the diagnosis and treatment. Make your needs and concerns known to the physician or sex therapist.

> **How to Help Your Lover (continued)**
> - Focus on solving the problem, not on the lack of erection. Like many men, your partner may be extremely sensitive about his condition and his self-esteem can be seriously threatened. Your reassurance and calm support is important.
> - Continue to enjoy nonsexual activities together. Don't let the erection problem be the focus of your life.

Jack. But the potency problem drove a wedge into her self-confidence and filled her with doubt. "Was he losing interest in me?" And she even wondered if he was having an affair.

"I would use all the ways I could find to blame myself. I had bouts of low self-esteem and self-loathing that would come and go in cycles." She and Jack had always enjoyed an active, exciting sexual life, and she hadn't ever considered that it would change. She was afraid that Jack's erection problem might mean the end of something important that she enjoyed, that also brought them close emotionally.

But in many ways, Marianne was fortunate. Jack, although hurting and depressed himself, was able to reach out to her and reassure her that she was not to blame for his difficulty, and that he still found her attractive and wanted her sexually. And Marianne had other responsibilities, like her job, that demanded much of her energy and prevented her from becoming obsessed with the sexual problem. And even though she was emotionally hurt, Marianne was determined not to let the erection difficulty create a barrier between her husband and herself. She made special efforts to let Jack know she cared about him and wanted to be physically close to him—intercourse or not.

Although Marianne was careful not to spend all of her time concentrating on the lack of potency, neither did she withdraw from her husband. She gave him plenty of affection and didn't shy away from being physical with him.

And perhaps as important, she took an active role in getting help. She urged him to check whether there was a physical cause. As it turned out, tests showed that Jack did not have a physical cause for his lack of erection. What he did have was an overload of stress, anxiety and tension—feelings he had been keeping bottled up inside. Sex therapy turned out to be the right treatment.

Marianne's openness and willingness to help were important to the sex therapy. She didn't regard the erection problem as Jack's alone, and she did not withdraw sexually. She examined her own expectations and beliefs. She worked to keep her tendency to blame herself from overwhelming her by encouraging her husband to seek a solution.

Marianne and Jack had a number of important things in their favor:
- They were very committed to each other.
- They had a history of a mutually satisfying and pleasurable sexual relationship.
- They made efforts to communicate with each other, although both felt bad.
- They sought help early on in the situation.

In short, they took an active stance instead of a passive approach.

Encouraging Jack to get an evaluation was a smart move on Marianne's part. Sometimes knowing the cause makes it easier to cope with the problem, because it removes the stress of being in a state of limbo.

Although knowing the cause helps, you can still expect some bumps on the road to sexual recovery; after all, you still have needs of your own.

For example, Annie and Phil had been married for about 15 years when he started to have erection problems. Annie was sure that Phil's diminished response was linked to a blood pressure medicine he was taking,

> ### Oversympathetic Response
>
> Women whose husbands suffer potency problems may develop sexual problems themselves. Of 151 such women, more than 60 percent reported sexual problems in a study done at Loyola University's Sex Clinic. Only 8 percent of these women reported that their sexual problem developed before their husband's. The author, Domeena C. Renshaw, M.D., notes that most of the men had an erection problem for anywhere from two years to as much as a decade before they went for help. Early treatment of an erection difficulty may prevent many women from developing sexual problems of their own.
>
> Most of the women did not blame their husbands for the sexual problems. They were, says Dr. Renshaw, "supportive, sensitive and concerned."

but knowing that fact didn't solve the problem or satisfy her sexual needs. Annie recalls: "It was very frustrating for me. I was getting sick, I was plagued with headaches. I didn't blame myself, because we always had a good relationship, but I felt depressed, like someone had taken something away from me. I've heard of people getting divorced because of sexual problems, but we didn't desert each other." Annie, a woman of 46, didn't let her depression immobilize her. Instead, she took an active role. She had him try the stamp test (see chapter 7). She also looked in the telephone book for the number of a local support group, and encouraged her husband to contact them. Her efforts eventually paid off, and Annie and Phil are happy with the results. Other couples don't find a solution so easily.

For some, answers come more slowly. Coping with a long period of impotence can be very difficult, especially when the cause is unknown and the prospect of restoring potency is uncertain. (This situation is becoming less common as diagnoses and treatments improve.) Marjorie and Bert had been married almost 20 years. Before they were married, Bert explained to Marjorie that he had a persistent erection problem. For the first years of their relationship, Marjorie was able to accept the situation, but as the years went on, she found it increasingly difficult to adjust.

Bert's condition was such that sometimes he could get an erection, only to lose it before he could attempt intercourse. Some therapists think that this situation may be more difficult for a woman to accept than when the man is simply unable to get any erection at all. This is because when there is an erection, the woman becomes hopeful. She thinks, "Maybe this time things will work," and she allows herself to become aroused. If she feels intercourse is the only acceptable expression of her desire, she's frustrated when her partner loses his erection. And, like Marjorie, despite efforts to "not take it personally," she may do just that. Her anger may build and feed on itself.

The years without a good sexual relationship have hurt both Bert and Marjorie. Her pain shows in her face, in her voice and in the way she twists and kneads her hands as she speaks. "We're fortunate with other aspects of our relationship," she says. "But I do have anger, and it is a lot deeper than Bert realizes. The last few months we've been withdrawn because of me. Hugging or kissing is okay, but fondling or anything else, no. I enjoy lying in his arms, but I don't want to start anything we can't finish."

Marjorie has been deprived of something most married women take for granted. The lack of successful treatment and her self-blame and frustration have taken their toll. And because, like many of us, Marjorie regarded intercourse as the only "real" sex, perhaps she suffered even more. Allowing herself to explore other ways of having sex would keep her from being locked into a life without any sexual contact. She doesn't want to leave Bert and he doesn't want to leave her. Right now they're in a standoff, both in pain. As in most sexual battles, there are no winners.

Is His Erection a Sign of Your Attractiveness?

Some women attach enormous significance to their lover's ability to get an erection. They think that a firm erection is a sign of genuine love. A woman who believes the penis is some type of emotional-sexual lie detector will feel threatened and rejected by a man with an erection problem. She may doubt herself intensely, and she may jump to all types of conclusions about the cause of his problem.

If the above scenario strikes a chord in you, you should probably explore your feelings further, perhaps with the help of a counselor. It's important to recognize just what messages you give yourself about the situation, and what you express to your lover. A woman who feels that erections are proof of a man's love may feel too hurt to participate in treatment. She may resist facing the problem, fearing that ultimately, her husband is going to leave her. But our research indicates that couples who deal directly with potency problems often fare extremely well, both in resolving the sexual difficulty and in maintaining, and even strengthening, their relationship.

Whatever course of treatment you and your lover choose, get started as soon as you can. It is much better to get to the problem early. Even in the best of situations, the void left by not knowing what is causing a potency problem is often filled with anxiety, depression and debilitating self-doubt—for both the man and the woman. That's why we recommend that you take care of yourself—and help your partner—by getting qualified professional help early. You wouldn't want a painful stomachache to go untreated, and the emotional pain that potency problems can cause is just as, or more, debilitating and serious.

Six Ways to Feel Better about Yourself

- Learn all you can about erections and impotence problems by reading this book and talking to your doctor.
- Don't give up on sexual pleasure even if your partner isn't interested. Try to maintain physical contact with him, and give yourself pleasure by masturbating.
- Don't let the problem control your life. Put energy into having some positive experiences. Don't withdraw from friends, family and activities you enjoy.
- Take care of yourself. This is a difficult, stressful time for you, and you need extra amounts of support—which your partner, preoccupied with his own feelings, is probably unable to give. Talk to a close friend, or seek professional help with coping. Eat well and exercise to combat stress.
- Part of taking care of yourself is recognizing that most cases of impotence have nothing to do with the man's attraction to his partner. Love may be strong, but it can't open clogged blood vessels or overcome other physical conditions.
- Examine your attitudes towards erection. One woman said about her husband, "If I can't give him an erection, I don't want anything to do with him." Her insecurity caused a lot of pain for herself and her husband. She was a victim of the myth that her partner's erection would validate her worth as a woman.

11

Staying Potent: Six Guidelines for Future Sexual Success

There's no reason why most men can't enjoy potency well into old age. Your chances of enjoying intercourse in your later years are determined largely by your genetic heritage, your daily habits and your emotional well-being. While there's nothing you can do about your gene pool, you do have a lot of control over your lifestyle. You can live in a way that puts the odds for maintaining potency in your favor, or you can set yourself up for problems. The choice is yours.

If you want to prolong your potency, try to follow these essential guidelines:
- Eat a low-cholesterol, low-fat, high-fiber diet.
- Maintain your proper weight.
- Keep your blood pressure normal.
- Exercise regularly—at least three times a week.
- Don't smoke, chew or sniff tobacco.
- If you drink alcohol, drink moderately.

Let's take a closer look at these suggestions.

Eating for Sexual Success

We know that a well-functioning blood-flow system is essential for erections. Over a long period of time, what you eat can mean the difference between a

Six Guidelines for Future Sexual Success 221

> ### The Potent Lifestyle
>
> The link between lifestyle habits and loss of potency is supported by the work of some French physicians who studied 440 men with erection problems. The doctors found that men with erection problems are likely to have one or more of the following: diabetes, high cholesterol levels, high fat levels and high blood pressure. Many also smoke. In fact, the doctors found that every man they studied who had two or more of these major risk factors also had low blood pressure in his penis, which indicates poor blood flow, one cause of erection problems.

healthy or blocked flow of blood to your penis—the difference between erection and impotence.

The keys to good blood flow are your penile arteries. Keeping them working well is essential if you want to enjoy intercourse throughout your life. While there are only a few studies of the arteries in the penis, these arteries seem to follow the same rules of operation as the body's other arteries, which have been examined extensively. Medical research has found many ways to keep arteries functioning healthily, and these methods can help maintain potency. Probably the most important way is to maintain a diet low in cholesterol and saturated fat.

Foods that contain large amounts of cholesterol (a waxy, fatlike substance), can harm potency because they can clog up the penile arteries, blocking the flow of blood. While the body produces some cholesterol naturally, for most people the problem develops from eating high cholesterol foods like eggs and fatty meats. Some people can eat practically anything and still maintain low cholesterol and healthy arteries, but most of us need to watch what we eat.

Saturated fats can also raise the level of cholesterol in your blood. They tend to be found in the same foods that have cholesterol: red meats, dairy products (except for no-fat varieties) and different types of shortening. On the other hand, small amounts of polyunsaturated fats, found in vegetables such as corn, soybeans and safflower seeds, are good for your arteries. They can help reduce the level of cholesterol-depositing substances called low density lipoproteins (LDLs).

Lipoproteins come in two forms: low density lipoproteins (LDLs) and high density lipoproteins (HDLs).

Both substances carry cholesterol in the blood, but with a crucial difference. LDLs appear to clog the arteries by depositing cholesterol that narrows these essential pathways. But nature has provided a counterpart to LDLs: HDLs help clean cholesterol out of the body, opening the arteries.

The higher your level of HDLs, and the lower your level of cholesterol and LDLs, the better off you are.

Arteries don't become clogged with fats and cholesterol overnight. Instead, the clogging takes place gradually—and silently. And this process can begin early in life. In fact, researchers have found fatty deposits in the arteries of children as young as 6, and in young men.

More evidence that impotence-causing arterial blockage can begin early in life comes from Czechoslovakia, where doctors examined the penile arteries of deceased men whose ages at death ranged from 19 to 85. All men 38 years of age and older had some blockage in these arteries.

This research makes it clear that a man who wants to keep enjoying intercourse must keep his penile arteries clean. The type of diet which will help to protect your penile arteries is one which will be healthy for your entire blood-flow system, including your heart.

But suppose you've spent most of your life enjoying hearty meals loaded with fat and cholesterol: bacon and eggs for breakfast, a double cheeseburger for lunch and, as one man put it, "anything for dinner, as long as it's fried." Will switching your diet do anything for potency and the health of your penile arteries?

There is little doubt that some individuals who change their diet can reduce their cholesterol levels and, over a period of time, even decrease arterial

Diet for Healthy Blood Flow

This diet is recommended by the Stanford University Heart Disease Prevention Program as a good way to lower your intake of saturated fat, cholesterol and salt.

- Reduce by one-half the number of weekly servings of whole milk, ice cream, cheese (except low-fat varieties) and fatty meats (beef, lamb, bacon, spareribs, sausage and luncheon meats). In their place, substitute fish, poultry and complex-carbohydrate foods.
- Switch from ice cream to ice milk, from whole to nonfat milk and from regular to nonfat yogurt.
- Trim the fat off meat and broil or roast instead of frying.
- Rarely, if ever, eat organ meats like liver, sweetbreads and brains.
- Switch from butter or hard margarine to soft tub margarine, and instead of lard or shortening, use unhydrogenated vegetable oil.
- Cut back on egg yolks to no more than four a week, but use egg whites liberally.
- Switch from peanut butter made with hydrogenated fat to peanut butter without hydrogenated fat.
- Cut back on fast foods, processed or convenience foods and commercial baked goods.
- Drastically reduce your intake of high-salt foods, such as bacon, ham, sausage, frankfurters, luncheon meats, sauerkraut, salted nuts, pickles and salted snack foods.
- Gradually eliminate your use of salt at the table, and cut your use of salt in cooking by two-thirds. Use salt substitutes to help you make the transition, and experiment with spices, herbs, lemon, wine and vinegar.
- Increase your intake of whole fruits and vegetables and lightly milled or whole grains (for example, whole-wheat bread, cracked wheat, rolled oats, bulgur, brown rice and rye).

blockages. (Sometimes medication combined with diet is needed.) Canadian doctors, for example, put 50 patients with blockages in their leg arteries on a low-cholesterol, low-fat diet. Some used the American Heart Association's program, others the Pritikin maintenance plan. Despite their leg pain, all participants were supposed to exercise regularly, cut out smoking as much as possible, reduce their intake of salt and caffeine (both of which can raise blood pressure) and limit alcohol consumption.

After one year on the program, all participants had lower levels of cholesterol and blood fats, and higher levels of high-density lipoproteins (HDLs), an all-important cholesterol-remover. The researchers also found that the more *fiber* an individual ate, the more likely he was to have lowered his cholesterol. As an additional benefit, everyone lost weight. All were better able to exercise, as measured on a treadmill. This improvement may reflect increased blood flow to the legs, resulting from fewer blockages in the arteries. Many participants said they felt better. Unfortunately, the researchers did not report the program's effect on erection.

Obesity is bad for your arteries because it promotes increased fats in your blood, high cholesterol, and keeps your body from producing enough HDLs. And if you are prone to diabetes, overweight will make you more susceptible to it—and the erection difficulties that can follow. So, for heavy men, taking off pounds is a necessary part of any plan for improving the health of the arteries and prolonging potency. A high-fiber diet can help you lose weight, and oat bran in particular may help lower your cholesterol. In addition to limiting your fat intake, exercise is important to losing weight.

Losing weight and keeping faithful to a low-salt, low-fat diet can also help lower your blood pressure. High blood pressure and many medications used to treat it can sap potency. You should have your blood pressure checked at least once a year, more often if possible. Another aid to controlling high blood pressure is exercise.

Exercise for Potency

Exercise can boost potency by increasing your sense of well-being and your ability to handle stress. It also helps keep your arteries functioning well. So it's important that you exercise regularly. Your doctor can help you plan an exercise program that will be safe and beneficial.

Ask him to focus on aerobic exercise—steady exercise over a prolonged period of time which increases your heart rate and makes your body produce more HDLs. Many activities qualify as aerobic exercise, including jogging, bicycling and walking briskly. To be really helpful, however, most of these exercises need to be done for 20 to 30 minutes at a time, at least three times a week. You don't need to start out at this pace. Begin slowly and work your way up gradually. Exercise activities with a lot of stops and starts, such as handball, tennis and weight lifting, won't do your arteries as much good as a less strenuous, but continuous workout. The key is to get your heart rate up to 80 percent of its maximum, and keep it there for 12 to 15 minutes. Ask your doctor what your maximum heart rate should be. Then, when you exercise, stop periodically to check your pulse to see what your rate is.

Faithfully following an exercise program for several months also tends to lower your blood pressure. Doctors know that high blood pressure is a major cause of clogged arteries, so lowering your blood pressure can help your arteries, your heart—and your erections.

Sometimes men who enjoy exercise believe that all they have to do to protect their health and their potency is work out. Some people believe in the tooth fairy, too. The truth is that all the other elements of the potency program—diet, normal weight, normal blood pressure, no smoking and moderate use of alcohol, if any—are essential, too. If you jog five miles and then reward yourself with a double cheeseburger and fries, followed by a cigarette, your arteries are still susceptible to trouble.

Smoking Can Dampen Your Fire

It's not just the immediate negative effects of smoking that you should worry about when you light up. The long-term results of smoking can be even worse—over time smoking can silently sabotage your sex life.

Smokers' arteries are harder, thicker and more clogged than those of nonsmokers. And smoking seems to mess up peripheral arteries even more than those supplying the heart. That means it may be particularly bad for the arteries in your penis. Smoking can also cancel the positive effects of exercise, leaving you at square one.

Our best advice: What is good for your lungs and heart is also good for your penis. So don't smoke. If you do, stop. There are many programs that help people give up tobacco. Don't hesitate to get help if the thought of going cold turkey makes you tremble.

Avoid Stiff Drinks

Long-term drinking can also sap your potency. Many men know firsthand that drinking too much makes them unable to get an erection, at least temporarily. What isn't as well known is that long-term heavy drinking can sabotage potency. While no one fully understands just how this works, we do know that excessive alcohol can severely reduce the production of testosterone in the testicles. Whatever small amounts of the hormone a chronically heavy drinker does manage to produce may be rendered ineffective by his damaged liver, which has to metabolize the hormone. Large amounts of alcohol can also hurt the nervous system, which plays an important role in erection.

The effects of this type of self-sabotage can remain undetected for years, finally recognized only after serious damage to potency has occurred. Limit your use of alcohol now so you'll enjoy sex in the future.

You don't need to give up liquor altogether; you just need to be moderate. In small amounts—such as one beer or one 4-ounce glass of wine or one shot of hard liquor per day—alcohol may actually increase the cholesterol-removing HDLs in your body, and thus help prevent clogs in your arteries. There's no question, however, that large amounts of alcohol will do you and your erections much more harm than good.

The Power of Potent Thinking

The most important factor in lifelong sexual success is attitude. All the information and medical advice in the world won't help you unless you want it to. If you feel that sex is important and you want it to be a vital part of your life, chances are you'll find a way to make it so.

Remember: About 90 percent of men with erection problems can find a solution.

References

CHAPTER 1

Aldridge, G.J., and Aldridge, R.G. "Sexuality and the Practicing Physician: A Review of the Literature." *Corrective and Social Psychiatry* 30 (1984): 107–8.

Bancroft, J. "Erectile Impotence—Psyche or Soma." *International Journal of Andrology* 5 (1982): 353–55.

Freeman, J.T. "Sexual Capacities in the Aging Male." *Geriatrics* 16 (1961): 37–43.

Greenberg, M. "Sex after 50: Frank Talk about a Formerly Taboo Subject." *Transition,* February 1984, 37–57.

Kofoed, L., and Bloom, J.D. "Geriatric Sexual Dysfunction: A Case Survey." *Journal of the American Geriatrics Society* 30 (1982): 437–40.

Kolodny, R.C. et al. *Textbook of Sexual Medicine.* Boston: Little, Brown and Company, 1979.

Martin, C.E. "Factors Affecting Sexual Functioning in 60- to 79-Year-Old Married Males." *Archives of Sexual Behavior* 10 (1981): 399–420.

Masters, W.H., and Johnson, V.E. *Human Sexual Inadequacy.* New York: Bantam, 1980.

Pfeiffer, E., and Davis, G.C. "Determinants of Sexual Behavior in Middle and Old Age." *Journal of the American Geriatrics Society* 20 (1972): 151–58.

Schover, L.R. *Prime Time: Sexual Health for Men over Fifty.* New York: Holt, Rinehart and Winston, 1984.

Silber, S.J. *The Male.* New York: Charles Scribner's Sons, 1981.

Solnick, R.L., and Birren, J.E. "Age and Male Erectile Responsiveness." *Archives of Sexual Behavior* 6 (1977): 1–9.

Verwoerdt, A. et al. "Sexual Behavior in Senescence." *Geriatrics* 24 (1969): 137–54.

Zilbergeld, B. *Male Sexuality: A Guide to Sexual Fulfillment.* New York: Bantam, 1978.

CHAPTER 2

Barry, J.M. *Evaluation of the Impotent Male.* American Urological Association Update Series, vol. 2, lesson 5. Houston: AUA Office of Education, 1983.

References

Bennett, A.H., ed. *Management of Male Impotence.* International Perspectives in Urology, vol. 5. Baltimore and London: Williams and Wilkins, 1982.

Creed, K.E., et al. "Autonomic Control and Vascular Changes during Penile Erection in Monkeys." *British Journal of Urology* 61 (1988): 510–515.

Crowe, R., et al. "Spinal Cord Lesions at Different Levels Affect Either the Adrenergic or Vasoactive Intestinal Polypeptide-immunoreactive Nerves in the Human Urethra." *The Journal of Urology* 140 (1988): 1412–1414.

deGroat, W.C., and Booth, A.M. "Physiology of Male Sexual Function." *Annals of Internal Medicine* 92 (1980): 329–31.

Federman, D.D. "Impotence: Etiology and Management." *Hospital Practice,* March 1982, 155–59.

Fournier, G.R., Jr., et al. "Mechanisms of Venous Occlusion During Canine Penile Erection: An Anatomic Demonstration." *The Journal of Urology* 137 (1987): 163–167.

Furlow, W.L., guest ed. *Symposium on Male Sexual Dysfunction.* Urologic Clinics of North America, vol. 8, no. 1. Philadelphia: W.B. Saunders Company, 1981.

Goldstein, I. *Impotence.* American Urological Association Home Study Course, series 7, no. 1. Houston: AUA Office of Education, 1984.

Hedlund, H., and Andersson, K.E. "Contraction and Relaxation Induced by Some Prostanoids in Isolated Human Penile Erectile Tissue and Cavernous Artery." *The Journal of Urology* 134 (1985): 1245–1250.

Juenemann, K.P., et al. "The Role of Vasoactive Intestinal Polypeptide as a Neurotransmitter in Canine Penile Erection: A Combined In Vivo and Immunohistochemical Study." *The Journal of Urology* 138 (1987): 871–876.

Kimoto, Y., and Ito, Y. "Autonomic Innervation of the Canine Penile Artery and Vein in Relation to Neural Mechanisms Involved in Erection." *British Journal of Urology* 59 (1987): 463–472.

Kolodny, R.C. et al. *Textbook of Sexual Medicine.* Boston: Little, Brown and Company, 1979.

Krane, R.J. et al., eds. *Male Sexual Dysfunction.* Boston: Little, Brown and Company, 1983.

Lavoisier, P., et al. "Reflex Contractions of the Ischiocavernosus Muscles Following Electrical and Pressure Stimulations." *The Journal of Urology* 139 (1988): 396–399.

Lue, T.F. Presentation at Update on Impotence and Infertility, San Francisco, October 1985.

Masters, W.H., and Johnson, V.E. *Human Sexual Inadequacy.* New York: Bantam, 1981.

Newman, H.F., and Northup, J.D. "Mechanism of Human Penile Erection: An Overview." *Urology* 17 (1981): 129–38.

Silber, S.J. *The Male.* New York: Charles Scribner's Sons, 1981.

Valji, K., and Bookstein, J.J. "The Veno-Occlusive Mechanism of the Canine Corpus Cavernosum: Angiographic and Pharmacologic Studies." *The Journal of Urology* 138 (1987): 1467–1470.

Van Arsdalen, K.N. et al. *Physiology of Erection.* Monographs in Urology: Erectile Physiology, Dysfunction and Evaluation, part 1, vol. 4, no. 4. Princeton: Custom Publishing Services, 1983.

———. *Etiology and Evaluation of Erectile Dysfunction.* Monographs in Urology: Erectile Physiology, Dysfunction and Evaluation, part 2, vol. 4, no. 4. Princeton: Custom Publishing Services, 1983.

Vardi, Y., and Siroky, M.B. "A Canine Model for Hemodynamic Study of Isolated Corpus Cavernosum." *The Journal of Urology* 138 (1987): 663–666.

Wagner, G., and Green, R. *Impotence: Physiological, Psychological, Surgical Diagnosis and Treatment.* New York: Plenum Press, 1981.

Wespes, E., et al. "Penile Deep Dorsal Vein Cushions and Erection." *British Journal of Urology* 60 (1987): 174–177.

CHAPTER 3

Brass, E.P. "Effects of Antihypertensive Drugs on Endocrine Function." *Drugs* 27 (1984): 447–58.

Chopra, I.J. et al. "Estrogen-Androgen Imbalance in Hepatic Cirrhosis." *Annals of Internal Medicine* 79 (1973): 198–203.

Cocores, J.A., and Gold, M.S. "Substance Abuse and Sexual Dysfunction." *Medical Aspects of Human Sexuality* Feb (1989): 24–33.

Cornely, C.M. et al. "Chronic Advanced Liver Disease and Impotence: Cause and Effect?" *Hepatology* 4 (1984): 1227–30.

Council on Scientific Affairs. "Drug Abuse in Athletes: Anabolic Steroids and Human Growth Hormone." *Journal of the American Medical Association* 259 (1988): 1703–1705.

Crenshaw, T.L. et al. "Alcohol, Antihypertensives, and Sexual Dysfunction: A Common Problem." *Medical Aspects of Human Sexuality* 19 (1985): 87–89.

Forsberg, L. et al. "Impotence, Smoking and Beta-blocking Drugs." *Fertility and Sterility* 31 (1979): 589–91.

Fraunfelder, F.T., and Meyer, S.M. Letter to editor. *Journal of the American Medical Association* 253 (1985): 3092–93.

Glina, S., et al. "Impact of Cigarette Smoking on Papaverine-Induced Erection." *The Journal of Urology* 140 (1988): 523–524.

Goldstein, I. et al. "Radiation-Associated Impotence." *Journal of the American Medical Association* 251 (1984): 903–10.

"How Prescription Drugs Can Affect Male Sexual Function." *Drug Therapy,* August 1981, 81–84.

Juenemann, K.P., et al. "The Effect of Cigarette Smoking on Penile Erection." *The Journal of Urology* 138 (1987): 438–441.

Kolodny, R.C. et al. *Textbook of Sexual Medicine.* Boston: Little, Brown and Company, 1979.

Lieberman, M. *The Sexual Pharmacy: The Complete Guide to Drugs with Sexual Side Effects.* New York: New American Library, 1988.

Lin, S.N., et al. "Local Suppressive Effect of Clonidine on Penile Erection in the Dog." *The Journal of Urology* 139 (1988): 849–852.

Lipman, A.G. "Drugs Associated with Impotence." *Modern Medicine,* May 1977, 81–82.

Lue, T.F. et al. "The Effect of Cigarette Smoking on Penile Erection." Presented at the Western Section, American Urological Association, Seattle, July 1986.

Schover, L.R. *Prime Time: Sexual Health for Men over Fifty.* New York: Holt, Rinehart and Winston, 1984.

Snyder, S., and Karacan, I. "Effects of Chronic Alcoholism on Nocturnal Penile Tumescence." *Psychosomatic Medicine* 43 (1981): 423–30.

Tan, E.T. et al. "Erectile Impotence in Chronic Alcoholics." *Alcoholism: Clinical and Experimental Research* 8 (1984): 297–301.

Van Arsdalen, K.N., and Wein, A.J. *Drugs and Male Sexual Dysfunction.* American Urological Association Update Series, vol. 3, lesson 34. Houston: AUA Office of Education, 1984.

Van Thiel, D.H. et al. "Alcohol and Sexual Function." *Pharmacology, Biochemistry & Behavior* 13 (1980): 125–29.

———. "Recovery of Sexual Function in Abstinent Alcoholic Men." *Gastroenterology* 84 (1982): 677–82.

Virag, R. et al. "Is Impotence an Arterial Disorder? A Study of Arterial Risk Factors in 440 Impotent Men." *Lancet,* January 1984, 181–84.

Wagner, G., and Green, R. *Impotence: Physiological, Psychological, Surgical Diagnosis and Treatment.* New York: Plenum Press, 1981.

Wilson, G.T. "The Effects of Alcohol on Male and Female Sexual Function." *Sexual Medicine Today,* December 1984, 6–15.

Wilson, G.T. et al. "Alcohol, Selective Attention and Sexual Arousal in Men." *Journal of Studies on Alcohol* 46 (1985): 107–15.

Zilbergeld, B. *Male Sexuality: A Guide to Sexual Fulfillment.* New York: Bantam, 1978.

CHAPTER 4

Abber, J.C., et al. "Priapism Induced by Chlorpromazine and Trazodone: Mechanism of Action." *The Journal of Urology* 137 (1987): 1039–1042.

Bauer, J.J. et al. "Sexual Dysfunction Following Proctocolectomy for Benign Disease of the Colon and Rectum." *Annals of Surgery* 197 (1983): 363–67.

Bennett, A.H., ed. *Management of Male Impotence.* International Perspectives in Urology, vol. 5. Baltimore and London: Williams and Wilkins, 1982.

Benson, R.C. "An Updated Approach to Correcting Impotence in Elderly Men." *Geriatrics* 40 (1985): 87–102.

Bolt, J.W., et al. "Sexual Dysfunction after Prostatectomy." *British Journal of Urology* 58 (1986): 319–322.

Braunstein, G.D. "Endocrine Causes of Impotence." *Postgraduate Medicine* 74 (1983): 207–17.

Broderick, G.A., and Lue, T.F. "Priapism and the Physiology of Erection." *AUA Update Series* Vol 7, lesson 29 (1988): 226–231.

Carson, C.C., and Mino, R.D. "Priapism Associated with Trazodone Therapy." *The Journal of Urology* 139 (1988): 369–370.

Castleman, M. *Sexual Solutions*. New York: Simon and Schuster, 1983.

Cooper, A.J. "Advances in the Diagnosis and Management of Endocrine Impotence." *The Practitioner* 228 (1984): 865–70.

Davidson, J.M. et al. "Hormonal Replacement and Sexuality in Men." *Clinics in Endocrinology and Metabolism* 2 (1982): 599–624.

Davis, S.S. et al. "Evaluation of Impotence in Older Men." *Western Journal of Medicine* 142 (1985): 499–505.

Delcour, C. et al. "Investigation of the Venous System in Impotence of Vascular Origin." *Urologic Radiology* 6 (1984): 190–93.

Deutsch, S., and Sherman, L. "Previously Unrecognized Diabetes Mellitus in Sexually Impotent Men." *Journal of the American Medical Association* 244 (1980): 2430–32.

"Diabetic Impotence—Of Mind or Matter?" *Transition*, May 1983, 51–62.

Dormont, P. "Life Events That Predispose to Erectile Dysfunction." *Medical Aspects of Human Sexuality* 23 (1989): 17–19.

Elist, J. et al. "Evaluating Medical Treatment of Impotence" *Urology* 23 (1984): 374–75.

Ellenberg, M. "Sexual Function in Diabetic Patients." *Annals of Internal Medicine* 92 (1980): 331–333.

Ficher, M., et al. "Do Endocrines Play an Etiological Role in Diabetic and Nondiabetic Sexual Dysfunctions?" *The Journal of Andrology* 5 (1984): 8–16.

Furlow, W.L. Response to reader question. *Medical Aspects of Human Sexuality* 19 (1985): 13–16.

Gendel, E.S., and Bonner, E.J. "Sex, Angina, and Heart Disease." *Medical Aspects of Human Sexuality* 20 (1986): 18–36.

Goldstein, I. *Impotence*. American Urological Association Home Study Course, series 7, no. 1. Houston: AUA Office of Education, 1984.

Goldstein, I. et al. "Radiation-Associated Impotence." *Journal of the American Medical Association* 251 (1984): 903–10.

Hargreave, T.B., and Stephenson, T.P. "Potency and Prostatectomy." *British Journal of Urology* 49 (1977): 683–88.

Hellerstein, H.K., and Friedman, E.H. "Sexual Activity and the Post-Coronary Patient." *Medical Aspects of Human Sexuality* 3 (1969): 70.

Jameson, R.M. "Impotence and Prostatectomy." *The Practitioner* 226 (1982): 1969.

Jonas, P. et al. "Postprostatectomy Impotence in Elderly Patients." *Geriatrics* 38 (1983): 113–17.

Keene, J.S. et al. "Undetected Genito-Urinary Dysfunction in Vertebral Fractures." *Journal of Bone and Joint Surgery* 62-A (1980): 997–99.

Kolodny, R.C. et al. *Textbook of Sexual Medicine*. Boston: Little, Brown and Company, 1979.

Krane, R.J. et al., eds. *Male Sexual Dysfunction*. Boston: Little, Brown and Company, 1983.

Kursh, Elroy D., and Bodner, Donald R. "Alternative Method of Nerve-Sparing When Performing Radical Retropubic Prostatectomy." *Urology* 32 (1988): 205–209.

Lehman, T.P., and Jacobs, J.A. "Etiology of Diabetic Impotence." *Journal of Urology* 129 (1983): 291–94.

Libman, E., and Fichten, C.S. "Prostatectomy and Sexual Function." *Urology* 29 (1987): 467–478.

Lincoln, R., et al. "Changes in the Vipergic, Cholinergic and Adrenergic Innervation of Human Penile Tissue in Diabetic and Non-Diabetic Impotent Males." *The Journal of Urology* 137 (1987): 1053–1060.

Lue, T.F. et al. "Potential Preservation of Potency after Radical Prostatectomy." *Urology* 22 (1983): 165–67.

———. "Neuroanatomy of Penile Erection: Its Relevance to Iatrogenic Impotence." *Journal of Urology* 131 (1984): 273–80.

Maatman, T.J., et al. "Erectile Dysfunction in Men with Diabetes Mellitus." *Urology* 29 (1987): 589–592.

McCulloch, D.K. et al. "The Natural History of Impotence in Diabetic Men." *Diabetologia* 26 (1984): 437–40.

Mahajan, S.K. et al. "Sexual Dysfunction in Uremic Male: Improvement Following Oral Zinc Supplementation." *Contributions to Nephrology* 38 (1984): 103–11.

Michal, V. "Arterial Disease as a Cause of Impotence." *Clinics in Endocrinology and Metabolism* 2 (1982): 725–48.

Michal, V., and Ruzbarsky, V. "Histological Changes in the Penile Arterial Bed with Aging and Diabetes." In *Vasculogenic Impotence*, edited by A.W. Zorgniotti and G. Rossi. Springfield, Ill.: Charles C. Thomas, 1980.

Miller, L. "Nonsurgical Treatment of Sexual Dysfunction Associated with Penile Curvature." *Medical Aspects of Human Sexuality*. April (1989): 65–70.

Morse, W.I., and Morse, J.M. "Erectile Impotence Precipitated by Organic Factors and Perpetuated by Performance Anxiety." *Canadian Medical Association Journal* 127 (1982): 599–601.

Papadopoulos, C. "Sexuality Following Heart Surgery." *Medical Aspects of Human Sexuality* 20 (1986): 40.

Renshaw, D.C. "Diabetic Impotence: An Important Organic-Psychogenic Interface." *Chicago Medicine* 87 (1984): 956–60.

Rodger, R.S.C. et al. "Zinc Metabolism Does Not Influence Sexual Function in Chronic Renal Insufficiency." *Contributions to Nephrology* 38 (1984): 112–15.

Rossman, B., and Zorgniotti, A.W. "Progressive Systemic Sclerosis (Scleroderma) and Impotence." *Urology* 33 (1989): 189–192.

Rousseau, Paul. "Impotence in Elderly Men." *Postgraduate Medicine* 83 (1988): 212–219.

Schiavi, R., and Schreiner-Engel, P. "Physiologic Aspects of Sexual Function and Dysfunction." *Psychiatric Clinics of North America* 3 (1980): 81–95.

Slag, M.S. et al. "Impotence in Medical Clinic Outpatients." *Journal of the American Medical Association* 249 (1983): 1736–40.

Spark, R.F. et al. "Impotence Is Not Always Psychogenic." *Journal of the American Medical Association* 243 (1980): 750–55.

Sprenger, K.B.G. et al. "Zinc and Sexual Dysfunction." *Contributions to Nephrology* 38 (1984): 119–25.

Surya, B.V., et al. "Experience with Potency Preservation During Radical Prostatectomy." *Urology* 32 (1988): 498–501.

Vircburger, M.I., et al. "Testosterone Levels after Bromocriptine Treatment in Patients Undergoing Long-term Hemodialysis." *The Journal of Andrology* 6 (1985): 113–116.

Wagner, G., and Green, R. *Impotence: Physiological, Psychological, Surgical Diagnosis and Treatment.* New York: Plenum Press, 1981.

Walsh, P.C., and Donker, P.J. "Impotence Following Radical Prostatectomy: Insight into Etiology and Prevention." *Journal of Urology* 128 (1982): 492–97.

Walsh, P.C., and Mostwin, J.L. "Radical Prostatectomy and Cystoprostatectomy with Preservation of Potency: Results Using a New Nerve-sparing Technique." *British Journal of Urology* 56 (1984): 694–97.

Walsh, P.C., et al. "Potency Following Radical Prostatectomy with Wide Unilateral Excision of the Neurovascular Bundle." *The Journal of Urology* 138 (1987): 823–828.

Weldon, V.E., and Tavel, F.R. "Potency-Sparing Radical Perineal Prostatectomy: Anatomy, Surgical Technique and Initial Results." *The Journal of Urology* 140 (1988): 559–562.

Wespes, E., and Schulman, C.C. "Venous Leakage: Surgical Treatment of a Curable Cause of Impotence." *Journal of Urology* 133 (1985): 796–98.

Whitehead, E. et al. "Male Sexual Dysfunction and Diabetes Mellitus." *New York State Journal of Medicine*, October/November 1983, 1174–79.

Williams, W. "Psychogenic Erectile Impotence—A Useful or a Misleading Concept?" *Australian and New Zealand Journal of Psychiatry* 19 (1985): 77–82.

Yesavage, J.A. et al. "Plasma Testosterone Levels, Depression, Sexuality, and Age." *Biological Psychiatry* 20 (1985): 222–25.

Zorgniotti, A.W., and Rossi, G., eds. *Vasculogenic Impotence.* Springfield, Ill.: Charles C. Thomas, 1980.

CHAPTER 5

Berger, R.E. et al. Unpublished results of a survey of impotence patients, 1982.

Castleman, M. *Sexual Solutions.* New York: Simon and Schuster, 1983.

Daniel, D.G. et al. "Correlations between Female Sex Roles and Attitudes toward Male Sexual Dysfunction in Thirty Women." *Journal of Sex and Marital Therapy* 10 (1984): 160–69.

Renshaw, D.C. "Inflatable Penile Prosthesis." *Journal of the American Medical Association* 241 (1979): 2637–38.

———. "Wives of Impotent Men." *Consultant* 19 (1979): 41–48.

———. "Coping with an Impotent Husband." *Illinois Medical Journal* 159 (1981): 29–33.

CHAPTER 6

Castleman, M. *Sexual Solutions.* New York: Simon and Schuster, 1983.

Crenshaw, T.L. et al. "Alcohol, Antihypertensives, and Sexual Dysfunction: A Common Problem." *Medical Aspects of Human Sexuality* 19 (1985): 87–89.

Elist, J. et al. "Evaluating Medical Treatment of Impotence." *Urology* 23 (1984): 374–75.

Forsberg, L. et al. "Impotence, Smoking, and Beta-blocking Drugs." *Fertility and Sterility* 31 (1979): 589–91.

Hartman, W., and Fithian, M. *Any Man Can: The Multiple Orgasmic Technique for Every Loving Man.* New York: St. Martin's Press, 1984.

Kilmann, P.R., and Auerbach, R. "Treatments of Premature Ejaculation and Psychogenic Impotence: A Critical Review of the Literature." *Archives of Sexual Behavior* 8 (1979): 81–100.

Kilmann, P.R., and Mills, K.H. *All about Sex Therapy.* New York: Plenum Press, 1983.

LoPiccolo, J., and Lobitz, W.C. "The Role of Masturbation in the Treatment of Orgasmic Dysfunction." *Archives of Sexual Behavior* 2 (1972): 163–71.

LoPiccolo, J., and LoPiccolo, L., eds. *Handbook of Sex Therapy.* New York: Plenum Press, 1978.

Lowe, J.C., and Mikulas, W.L. "Use of Written Material in Learning Self-Control of Premature Ejaculation." In *Handbook of Sex Therapy,* edited by J. LoPiccolo and L. LoPiccolo. New York: Plenum Press, 1978.

Lue, T.F. et al. "The Effect of Cigarette Smoking on Penile Erection." Presented at the Western Section, American Urological Association, Inc., Seattle, July 1986.

McCulloch, D.K. et al. "The Natural History of Impotence in Diabetic Men." *Diabetologia* 26 (1984): 437–40.

Raley, P.E. *Making Love*. New York: Avon, 1976.

Renshaw, D.C. "Brief Consultation: Premature Ejaculation." *Consultant* December (1978): 99–100.

Rosenthal, S.H., ed. "Sex over Forty." Newsletters. San Antonio, Texas.

Tan, E.T. et al. "Erectile Impotence in Chronic Alcoholics." *Alcoholism: Clinical and Experimental Research* 8 (1984): 297–301.

Turnbull, J.M., and Weinberg, P.C. "Psychological Factors Involved in Impotence." *Journal of Andrology* 4 (1983): 59–66.

Van Thiel, D.H. et al. "Alcohol and Sexual Function." *Pharmacology, Biochemistry & Behavior* 13 (1980): 125–29.

———. "Recovery of Sexual Function in Abstinent Alcoholic Men." *Gastroenterology* 84 (1982): 677–82.

Wilson, G.T. "Alcohol, Selective Attention and Sexual Arousal in Men." *Journal of Studies on Alcohol* 46 (1985): 107–15.

Zilbergeld, B. *Male Sexuality: A Guide to Sexual Fulfillment*. New York: Bantam, 1978.

Zilbergeld, B., and Kilmann, P.R. "The Scope and Effectiveness of Sex Therapy." *Psychotherapy* 21 (1984): 319–26.

CHAPTER 7

Abber, J.C. et al. "Diagnostic Tests for Impotence: A Comparison of Papaverine Injections with the Penile Brachial Pressure Index and Nocturnal Penile Tumescence." *Journal of Urology* 133 (1985): 188A.

Abel, G. et al. "Differential Diagnosis of Impotence in Diabetics: The Validity of Sexual Symptomatology." *Neurology and Urology* 1 (1982): 57–69.

Anders, E.K. et al. "Nocturnal Penile Rigidity Measured by the Snap-Gauge Band." *Journal of Urology* 129 (1983): 964–66.

Annoni, F., et al. "Evaluation of Penile Circulation with the Doppler Technique." *Journal of Andrology* 5 (1984): 131–134.

Barrett, D.M., and Wein, A.J., eds. *Controversies in Neuro-Urology*. New York: Churchill Livingstone, 1984.

Bennett, A.H., ed. *Management of Male Impotence*. International Perspectives in Urology, vol. 5. Baltimore and London: Williams and Wilkins, 1982.

Beutler, L.E. et al. "Diagnosis and Treatment of Male Erectile Dysfunction." *Arizona Medical* 38 (1981): 351–56.

Blaivas, J. et al. "Comprehensive Laboratory Evaluation of Impotent Men." *Journal of Urology* 124 (1980): 201–4.

Bohlen, J.G. *Sleep Erection Monitoring in the Evaluation of Male Erectile Failure*. Urologic Clinics of North America, vol. 8, no. 1. Philadelphia: W.B. Saunders Company, 1981.

Bookstein, J.J., et al. "Penile Pharmacocavernosography and Cavernosometry in the Evaluation of Impotence." *The Journal of Urology* 137 (1987): 772–776.

——. "Pharmacoarteriography in the Evaluation of Impotence." *The Journal of Urology* 137 (1987): 333–337.

Bradley, W.E. "New Techniques in Evaluation of Impotence." *Urology* 29 (1987): 383–388.

Buvat, J., et al. "Is Intracavernous Injection of Papaverine a Reliable Screening Test for Vascular Impotence?" *The Journal of Urology* 135 (1986): 476–478.

Carter, J.N. et al. "Prolactin-Secreting Tumors and Hypogonadism in 22 Men." *New England Journal of Medicine* 299 (1978): 847–52.

Collins, J.P., and Lewandowski, B.J. "Experience with Intracorporeal Injection of Papaverine and Duplex Ultrasound Scanning for Assessment of Arteriogenic Impotence." *British Journal of Urology* 59 (1987): 84–88.

Collins, W.E. et al. "Multidisciplinary Survey of Erectile Impotence." *Canadian Medical Association Journal* 128 (1983): 1393–99.

Condra, M., et al. "Screening Assessment of Penile Tumescence and Rigidity." *Urology* 29 (1987): 254–257.

——. "The Unreliability of Nocturnal Penile Tumescence Recording as an Outcome Measurement in the Treatment of Organic Impotence." *The Journal of Urology* 135 (1986): 280–282.

Desai, K.M., et al. "Neurophysiological Investigation of Diabetic Impotence. Are Sacral Response Studies of Value?" *British Journal of Urology* 61 (1988): 68–73.

Deutsch, S., and Sherman, L. "Previously Unrecognized Diabetes Mellitus in Sexually Impotent Men." *Journal of the American Medical Association* 244 (1980): 2430–32.

Earls, C.M., et al. "Penile Sufficiency: An Operational Definition." *The Journal of Urology* 139 (1988): 536–538.

Ellis, D.J., et al. "Snap-Gauge Band Versus Penile Rigidity in Impotence Assessment." *The Journal of Urology* 140 (1988): 61–63.

Fanous, H.N. et al. "Radioisotope Penogram in Diagnosis of Vasculogenic Impotence." *Urology* 20 (1982): 499–502.

Fisher, C. et al. "Evaluation of Nocturnal Penile Tumescence in the Differential Diagnosis of Sexual Impotence." *Archives of General Psychiatry* 36 (1979): 431–37.

Gerstenberg, T.C. "Nerve Conduction Velocity Measurement of Dorsal Nerve of Penis in Normal and Impotent Males." *Urology* 21 (1983): 90–92.

Gerstenberg, T.C., et al. "Standardized Evaluation of Erectile Dysfunction in 95 Consecutive Patients." *The Journal of Urology* 141 (1989): 857–862.

Goldstein, I. et al. "Vasculogenic Impotence: Role of the Pelvic Steal Test." *Journal of Urology* 128 (1982): 300–306.

———. "Dorsal Nerve Impotence: A Clinical Study of the Mechanism." *Journal of Urology* 133 (1985): 187A.

Hatch, J.P., et al. "Psychometric Differentiation of Psychogenic and Organic Erectile Disorders." *The Journal of Urology* 138 (1987): 781–783.

Herzberg, Z. et al. "Method, Indications and Results of Corpus Cavernosography." *British Journal of Urology* 53 (1981): 641–44.

Jones, W.J. *The Evaluation and Treatment of Psychosexual Dysfunction in Men.* American Urological Association Update Series, vol. 3, lesson 33. Houston: AUA Office of Education, 1984.

Kaneko, S., and Bradley, W.E. "Penile Electrodiagnosis: Penile Peripheral Innervation." *Urology* 30 (1987): 210–212.

———. "Penile Electrodiagnosis. Value of Bulbocavernosus Reflex Latency Versus Nerve Conduction Velocity of the Dorsal Nerve of the Penis in Diagnosis of Diabetic Impotence." *The Journal of Urology* 137 (1987): 933–935.

Karacan, I. "Sleep Environment Important in Assessing NPT." *Urology* 32 (1988): 180.

———. "Nocturnal Penile Tumescence as a Biological Marker in Assessing Erectile Dysfunction." *Psychosomatics* 23 (1982): 349–60.

Karacan, I., and Salis, P. "Diagnosis and Treatment of Erectile Impotence." *Psychiatric Clinics of North America* 3 (1980): 97–111.

Karacan, I. et al. "Sleep-Related Penile Tumescence as a Function of Age." *American Journal of Psychiatry* 132 (1975): 932–37.

———. "Penile Blood Flow and Musculovascular Events During Sleep-Related Erections of Middle-Aged Men." *The Journal of Urology* 138 (1987): 177–181.

Kedia, K.R., "Penile Plethysmography Useful in Diagnosis of Vasculogenic Impotence." *Urology* 22 (1983): 235–39.

Kerstein, M.D. "Thermography as a Diagnostic Measure of Vasculogenic Impotence." *The Journal of Urology* 137 (1987): 322–323.

Krane, R.J. et al., eds. *Male Sexual Dysfunction.* Boston: Little, Brown and Company, 1983.

Lavoisier, P., et al. "Bulbocavernosus Reflex: Its Validity as a Diagnostic Test of Neurogenic Impotence." *The Journal of Urology* 141 (1989): 311–314.

Lue, T.F. et al. "Erection Cavernosography." *Journal of Urology* 133 (1985): 189A.

———. "Functional Evaluation of Penile Arterial Blood Flow During Erection." *Journal of Urology* 133 (1985): 218A.

———. "Functional Evaluation of Penile Veins by Cavernosography in Papaverine-Induced Erection." *The Journal of Urology* 135 (1986): 479–482.

Marshall, P. et al. "Unreliability of Nocturnal Penile Tumescence Recording and MMPI Profiles in Assessment of Impotence." *Urology* 17 (1981): 136–39.

———. "Nocturnal Penile Tumescence Recording with Stamps: A Validity Study." *Journal of Urology* 128 (1982): 946–47.

———. "Importance of Electromyographic Data in Interpreting Nocturnal Penile Tumescence." *Urology* 22 (1983): 153–56.

Marshall, S. "Evaluation and Management of Simple Erectile Dysfunction in Office Practice." *Medical Aspects of Human Sexuality* 23 (1989): 4–8.

Martin, L.M. et al. "Psychometric Differentiation of Biogenic and Psychogenic Impotence." *Archives of Sexual Behavior* 12 (1983): 475–87.

Mellinger, B.C., et al. "Correlation Between Intracavernous Papaverine Injection and Doppler Analysis in Impotent Men." *Urology* 30 (1987): 416–419.

Melman, A., et al. "Evaluation of First 406 Patients in Urology Department Based Center for Male Sexual Dysfunction." *Urology* 32 (1988): 6–10.

Metz, P. et al. "Ultrasonic Doppler Pulse Wave Analysis versus Penile Blood Pressure Measurement in the Evaluation of Arteriogenic Impotence." *VASA* 12 (1983): 363–66.

Nickel, J.C. et al. "Endocrine Dysfunction in Impotence: Incidence, Significance and Cost-Effective Screening." *Journal of Urology* 132 (1984): 40–43.

Nseyo, U. et al. "Penile Xenon Washout: A Rapid Method of Screening for Vasculogenic Impotence." *Urology* 23 (1984): 31–34.

Podell, R.M. "Point of View: Sexual Science—Bridging the Disciplines." *Urology* 31 (1988): 90–93.

Pressman, M.R., et al. "Problems in the Interpretation of Nocturnal Penile Tumescence Studies: Disruption of Sleep by Occult Sleep Disorders." *The Journal of Urology* 136 (1986): 595–598.

Puyau, F., and Lewis, R.W. "Corpus Cavernosography Pressure Flow and Radiography." *Investigative Radiology* 18 (1983): 517–22.

Rajfer, J., et al. "Prevalence of Corporeal Venous Leakage in Impotent Men." *The Journal of Urology* 140 (1988): 69–71.

Renshaw, D.C. "Coping with an Impotent Husband." *Illinois Medical Journal* 159 (1981): 29–33.

Robiner, W.N. et al. "The Role of Minnesota Multiphasic Personality Inventory in Evaluation of Erectile Dysfunction." *Journal of Urology* 128 (1982): 487–88.

Robinson, L.Q., et al. "Results of Investigation of Impotence in Patients with Overt or Probable Neuropathy." *British Journal of Urology* 60 (1987): 583–587.

Roose, S.P. et al. "Reversible Loss of Nocturnal Penile Tumescence during Depression: A Preliminary Report." *Neuropsychobiology* 8 (1982): 284–88.

Rydin, E. et al. "Cystometry and Mictometry as Tools in Diagnosing Neurogenic Impotence." *Acta Neurologica Scandinavica* 63 (1981): 181–88.

Sarica, Y., and Karacan, I. "Bulbocavernosus Reflex to Somatic and Visceral Nerve Stimulation in Normal Subjects and in Diabetics with Erectile Impotence." *The Journal of Urology* 138 (1987): 55–58.

Saypol, D.C. et al. "Impotence: Are the Newer Diagnostic Methods a Necessity?" *Journal of Urology* 130 (1983): 260–62.

Schwartz, D.T. "Role of Confrontation in Performance and Interpretation of Nocturnal Penile Tumescence Studies." *Urology* 22 (1983): 240–42.

Schwartz, M.F. et al. "Hyperprolactinemia and Sexual Disorders in Men." *Biological Psychiatry* 17 (1982): 861–76.

Shabsigh, R., et al. "Evaluation of Erectile Impotence." *Urology* 32 (1988): 83–90.

Slag, M.F. et al. "Impotence in Medical Clinic Outpatients." *Journal of the American Medical Association* 249 (1983): 1736–40.

Spark, R. F. et al. "Impotence Is Not Always Psychogenic." *Journal of the American Medical Association* 243 (1980): 750–55.

Stief, C.G. "Functional Evaluation of Penile Hemodynamics." *The Journal of Urology* 139 (1988): 734–737.

———. "Primary Erectile Dysfunction." *The Journal of Urology* 141 (1989): 315–318.

Strachan, J.R., and Proyor, J.P. "Diagnostic Intracorporeal Papaverine and Erectile Dysfunction." *British Journal of Urology* 59 (1987): 264–266.

Tulloch, A.G. S. et al. "Impotence—The Team Approach to Investigation and Surgical Treatment." *British Journal of Urology* 54 (1982): 755–58.

Velcek, D. et al. "Penile Flow Index Utilizing a Doppler Pulse Wave Analysis to Identify Penile Vascular Insufficiency." *Journal of Urology* 123 (1980): 669–73.

Wabrek, A.J. "Bulbocavernosus Reflex Testing in 100 Consecutive Cases of Erectile Dysfunction." *Urology* 25 (1985): 495–498.

Wagner, G., and Green, R. *Impotence: Physiological, Psychological, Surgical Diagnosis and Treatment.* New York: Plenum Press, 1981.

Wasserman, M.D. et al. "Theoretical and Technical Problems in the Measurement of Nocturnal Penile Tumescence for the Differential Diagnosis of Impotence." *Psychosomatic Medicine* 42 (1980): 575–85.

Weinberg, J.J., and Badlani, G.H. "Utility of Rigiscan and Papaverine in Diagnosis of Erectile Impotence." *Urology* 31 (1988): 526–529.

Wespes, E., et al. "The Erectile Angle: Objective Criterion to Evaluate the Papaverine Test in Impotence." *The Journal of Urology* 138 (1987): 1171–1173.

Wesson, L.E. et al. "A New Approach to Evaluating Impotence in Outpatients." *North Carolina Medical Journal* 43 (1982): 562–67.

Zorgniotti, A.W., and Rossi, G., eds. *Vasculogenic Impotence.* Springfield, Ill.: Charles C. Thomas, 1980.

Chapter 8

Abber, J.C. et al. "Diagnostic Tests for Impotence: A Comparison of Papaverine Injections with the Penile Brachial Pressure Index and Nocturnal Penile Tumescence." *Journal of Urology* 133 (1985): 188A.

———. "Diagnostic Tests for Impotence: A Comparison of Papaverine Injection with Penile-Brachial Index and Nocturnal Penile Tumescence Monitoring." *Journal of Urology* 135 (1986): 923–25.

Althof, S.E., et al. "Intracavernosal Injection in the Treatment of Impotence: A Prospective Study of Sexual, Psychological and Marital Functioning." *Journal of Sex and Marital Therapy* 13 (1987): 155–167.

American Medical Systems product information. Minnetonka, Minn., 1985.

Antoniou, L.D. et al. "Reversal of Uremic Impotence by Zinc." *Lancet*, October 1977, 895–98.

Apte, S.M. et al. "The Inflatable Penile Prosthesis, Reoperation and Patient Satisfaction: A Comparison of Statistics Obtained from Patient Record Review with Statistics Obtained from Intensive Follow-Up Search." *Journal of Urology* 131 (1984): 894–95.

Bahnson, R.R., and Catalona, W.J. "Papaverine Testing of Impotent Patients Following Nerve-Sparing Radical Prostatectomy." *The Journal of Urology* 139 (1988): 773–774.

Bar-Moshe, O., and Vandendris, M. "Treatment of Impotence Due to Perineal Venous Leakage by Ligation of Crura Penis." *The Journal of Urology* 139 (1988): 1217–1219.

Barry, J.M. "Prediction of SemiRigid Penile Prosthesis Diameter from Saline Erection." *Journal of Urology* 131 (1984): 281.

Beaser, R.E. et al. "Experience with Penile Prosthesis in the Treatment of Impotence in Diabetic Men." *Journal of the American Medical Association* 248 (1982): 943–48.

Bennett, A.H., et al. "Reconstructive Surgery for Vasculogenic Impotence." *The Journal of Urology* 136 (1986): 599–603.

Benson, G.S. "Intracavernosal Injection Therapy for Impotence." *The Journal of Urology* 138 (1987): 1262.

Benson, R.C., Jr. "Vacuum Cleaner Injury to Penis: A Common Urologic Problem?" *Urology* 25 (1985): 41–44.

Benson, R.C. et al. "The Jonas Prosthesis—Technical Considerations and Results." *Journal of Urology* 130 (1983): 920–22.

Berg, R. et al. "Penile Implants in Erectile Impotence: Outcome and Prognostic Indicators." *Scandinavian Journal of Urology and Nephrology* 18 (1984): 277–82.

Betram, R.A., et al. "Severe Penile Curvature After Implantation of an Inflatable Penile Prosthesis." *The Journal of Urology* 139 (1988): 743–745.

Beutler, L.E. et al. "Women's Satisfaction with Partners' Penile Implant." *Urology* 24 (1984): 552–58.

Blake, D.J. et al. "Psychiatric Assessment of Penile Implant Recipient." *Urology* 21 (1983): 252–56.

Bookstein, J.J., and Lurie, A.L. "Selective Penile Venography: Anatomical and Hemodynamic Observations." *The Journal of Urology* 140 (1988): 55–60.

Bookstein, J.J., et al. "Production of Penile Veno-Occlusive Insufficiency by Arterial Occlusion in a Canine Model." *The Journal of Urology* 137 (1987): 1283–1286.

Boyd, S.D. "Two-Stage Technique for Implantation of Inflatable Penile Prosthesis in Pelvic Cancer Surgery." *Urology* 33 (1988): 1–4.

Boyd, S.D., and Schiff, W.M. "Inflatable Penile Prostheses in Patients Undergoing Cystoprostatectomy with Urethrectomy." *The Journal of Urology* 141 (1989): 60–62.

Boyd, S. et al. A report of the clinical trials for the AMS Hydroflex self-contained penile prosthesis. Publication 50512-E, American Medical Systems, 1985.

Breda, G., et al. "Long-term Follow-up of Peyronie's Disease." *Journal of Andrology* 5 (1984): 145–147.

Brook, A.C. et al. "Absence of a Therapeutic Effect of Zinc in the Sexual Dysfunction of Haemodialysed Patients." *Lancet*, September 1980, 618–19.

Brooks, M.B. "42 Months of Experience with the Mentor Inflatable Penile Prosthesis." *The Journal of Urology* 139 (1988): 48–50.

Buffum, J. "Pharmacosexology Update: Yohimbine and Sexual Function." *Journal of Psychoactive Drugs* 17 (1985): 131–32.

Bullard, D.G. et al. "Sex Counseling and the Penile Prosthesis." *Sexuality and Disability* 1 (1978): 184–89.

Carmignani, G., et al. "Cavernous Artery Revascularization in Vasculogenic Impotence: New Simplified Technique." *Urology* 30 (1987): 23–26.

Castaneda-Zuniga, W.R. et al. "Transluminal Angioplasty for Treatment of Vasculogenic Impotence." *American Journal of Radiology* 139 (1982): 371–73.

Clark, J.T. et al. "Enhancement of Sexual Motivation in Male Rats by Yohimbine." *Science* 225 (1984): 847–49.

Collins, G.F., Jr., and Kinder, B.N. "Adjustment Following Surgical Implantation of a Penile Prosthesis: A Critical Overview." *Journal of Sex and Marital Therapy* 10 (1984): 255–71.

Collins, J.P. "Experience with Lyophilized Human Dura for Treatment of Peyronie Disease." *Urology* 31 (1988): 379–381.

Crespo, E. et al. "Revascularization of the Cavernous Body in Vasculogenic Sexual Male Impotence with a New Microsurgical Technique." *Cardiovascular Research Center Bulletin* 22 (1983): 29–49.

Dacomed Corporation product information. Minneapolis, Minn., 1985.

Davidson, J.M. et al. "Hormonal Replacement and Sexuality in Men." *Clinics in Endocrinology and Metabolism* 2 (1982): 599–624.

Dennis, R.L., and McDougal, W.S. "Pharmacological Treatment of Erectile Dysfunction After Radical Prostatectomy." *The Journal of Urology* 139 (1988): 775–776.

Desai, K.M., and Gingell, J.C. "Saline-induced Artificial Erection without Papaverine: A Potential Source of Error in Diagnosing Cavernosal Venous Leakage." *British Journal of Urology* 62 (1988): 176–178.

Desai, K.M., et al. "Preliminary Report of a New Concept in the Pharmacological Treatment of Erectile Impotence Using an Implantable Drug Delivery System." *British Journal of Urology* 60 (1987): 267–270.

"Discussion: Zinc Metabolism." *Contributions to Nephrology* 38 (1984): 126–28.

Douglas, L. "Technique for Placement of Small-Carrion Prosthesis Post Priapism." *Urology* 30 (1987): 273–274.

Duffy, L.M., et al. "Vasoactive Intracavernous Pharmacotherapy—the Nursing Role in Teaching Self-Injection Therapy." *The Journal of Urology* 138 (1987): 1198–1200.

Ebbehoj, J., and Metz, P. "Congenital Penile Angulation." *British Journal of Urology* 60 (1987): 254–266."

Elist, J. et al. "Evaluating Medical Treatment of Impotence." *Urology* 23 (1984): 374–75.

Engle, R.M., et al. "Experience with the Mentor Inflatable Penile Prosthesis." *The Journal of Urology* 135 (1986): 1181–1182.

———. "Mentor Inflatable Penile Prosthesis." *Urology* 29 (1987): 498–500.

Fallon, B. et al. "Long-Term Follow-Up in Patients with an Inflatable Penile Prosthesis." *Journal of Urology* 132 (1984): 270–71.

Feighner, J.P. "Buspirone in the Long-Term Treatment of Generalized Anxiety Disorder." *The Journal of Clinical Psychiatry* 48 (1987): 3–6.

Fein, R.L. "Clinical Evaluation of Inflatable Penile Prosthesis with Combined Pump-Reservoir." *Urology* 32 (1988): 311–314.

Fein, R.L., and Needell, M.H. "Early Problems Encountered with the Mentor Inflatable Penile Prosthesis." *Journal of Urology* 134 (1985): 62–64.

Fovaeus, M., et al. "Effects of Some Calcium Channel Blockers on Isolated Human Penile Erectile Tissues." *The Journal of Urology* 138 (1987): 1267–1272.

Furlow, W.L. "Patient-Partner Satisfaction Levels with the Inflatable Penile Prosthesis." Letter. *Journal of the American Medical Association* 243 (1980): 1714.

Furlow, W.L., and Barrett, D.M. "Inflatable Penile Prosthesis: New Device Design and Patient-Partner Satisfaction." *Urology* 24 (1984): 559–63.

Furlow, W.L., and Goldwasser, Benad. "Salvage of the Eroded Inflatable Penile Prosthesis: A New Concept." *The Journal of Urology* 138 (1987): 312–314.

Furlow, W.L., and Motley, R.C. "The Inflatable Penile Prosthesis: Clinical Experience with a New Controlled Expansion Cylinder." *The Journal of Urology* 139 (1988): 945–946.

Furlow, W.L., et al. "Implantation of Model AMS 700 Penile Prosthesis: Long-term Results." *The Journal of Urology* 139 (1988): 741–742.

Gasser, T.C., et al. "Intracavernous Self-Injection with Phentolamine and Papaverine for the Treatment of Impotence." *The Journal of Urology* 137 (1987): 678–680.

———. "Penile Prosthesis Reimplantation." *The Journal of Urology* 137 (1987): 46–47.

Gelbard, M.K., et al. "The Use of Collagenase in the Treatment of Peyronie's Disease." *The Journal of Urology* 134 (1985): 280–282.

Gerstenberger, D.L. et al. "Inflatable Penile Prosthesis. Follow-Up Study of Patient-Partner Satisfaction." *Urology* 14 (1979): 583–587.

Gilbert, D.A., et al. "Phallic Reinnervation via the Pudendal Nerve." *The Journal of Urology* 140 (1988): 295–299.

Goldstein, M., and Blumberg, N. "Correction of Severe Penile Curves with Tunica Albuginea Autografts." *The Journal of Urology* 139 (1988): 1269–1270.

Goulding, F. "Fracture of Hydroflex Penile Implant." *Urology* 30 (1987): 490–492.

Gregory, J.G., and Purcell, M.H. "Penile Prostheses: Review of Current Models, Mechanical Reliability, and Product Cost." *Urology* 29 (1987): 150–152.

Hawatmeh, I.S. et al. "Management of Impotence by the Inflatable Penile Prosthesis." *Missouri Medicine* 78 (1981): 591–93.

Hollander, J.B., and Diokno, A.C. "Success with Penile Prosthesis from Patient's Viewpoint." *Urology* 23 (1984): 141–43.

Horton, C.E. et al. "Penile Curvative." *Plastic and Reconstructive Surgery* 75 (1985): 752–59.

Huisman, T.K., and MacIntyre, R.C. "Mechanical Failure of Omniphase Penile Prosthesis." *Urology* 31 (1988): 515–516.

Ishii, N., et al. "Intracavernous Injection of Prostaglandin E-1 for the Treatment of Erectile Impotence." *The Journal of Urology* 141 (1989): 323–325.

Kaufman, J.J. *Prevention and Management of Complications of Penile Prostheses.* American Urological Association Update Series, vol. 2, lesson 6. Houston: AUA Office of Education, 1983.

Kelami, A. "Congenital Penile Deviation and its Treatment with the Nesbit-Kelami Technique." *British Journal of Urology* 60 (1987): 261–263.

Kiely, E.A., et al. "Penile Function Following Intracavernosal Injection of Vasoactive Agents or Saline." *British Journal of Urology* 59 (1987): 473–476.

Kramarsky-Binkhorst, S. "Female Partner Perception of Small-Carrion Implant." *Urology* 12 (1978): 545–48.

Krane, R.J. et al., eds. *Male Sexual Dysfunction.* Boston: Little, Brown and Company, 1983.

Krauss, D.J. "Single Cylinder Penile Prosthesis." *Urology* 26 (1985): 466–467.

Krauss, D.J. et al. "The Failed Penile Prosthetic Implantation Despite Technical Success." *Journal of Urology* 129 (1983): 969–71.

Kudish, H.G. "Treatment of Impotence." *Postgraduate Medicine* 74 (1983): 233–40.

Lakin, M.M., and Montague, D.K. "Intracavernous Injections of Papaverine and Phentolamine: Correlation with Penile Brachial Index." *Urology* 33 (1989): 383–386.

Lange, P.H. "Vasoactive Intracavernous Pharmacotherapy for the Treatment of Erectile Impotence in Men with Spinal Cord Injury." *The Journal of Urology* 138 (1987): 539–542.

Lee, L.M., et al. "Prostaglandin E-1 Versus Phentolamine/Papaverine for the Treatment of Erectile Impotence: A Double-Blind Comparison." *The Journal of Urology* 141 (1989): 549–550.

Levine, S.B. "Benefits and Problems with Intracavernosal Injections for the Treatment of Impotence." *Medical Aspects of Human Sexuality* 23 (1989): 38–40.

Levine, S.B., et al. "Side Effects of Self-Administration of Intracavernous Papaverine and Phentolamine for the Treatment of Impotence." *The Journal of Urology* 141 (1989): 54–57.

Levinson, K., and Whitehead, E.D. "Omniphase Penile Prosthesis: Delayed Bilateral Central Cable Breakage." *The Journal of Urology* 141 (1989): 618–619.

Lewis, R.W., et al. "Another Surgical Approach for Vasculogenic Impotence." *The Journal of Urology* 136 (1986): 1210–1212.

Lue, T.F., and Tanagho, E.A. "Physiology of Erection and Pharmacological Management of Impotence." *The Journal of Urology* 137 (1987): 829–836.

McClellan, D.S., and Masih, B.K. "Gangrene of the Penis as a Complication of Penile Prosthesis." *Journal of Urology* 133 (1985): 862.

McCulloch, D.K. et al. "The Natural History of Impotence in Diabetic Men." *Diabetologia* 26 (1984): 437–40.

Mack, R.B. "Taljaribu Kila Dava Isifal: Yohimbine Intoxication." *North Carolina Medical Journal* 46 (1985): 229–30.

Maddock, J.W. "Assessment and Evaluation Protocol for Surgical Treatment of Impotence." *Sexuality and Disability* 3 (1980): 39–49.

Malloy, T.R., and von Eschenbach, A.C. "Surgical Treatment of Erectile Impotence with Inflatable Penile Prosthesis." *Journal of Urology* 118 (1977): 49–50.

Marmar, J.L. "Nonsurgical Treatment of Impotence." *Medical Aspects of Human Sexuality* 23 (1989): 44–48.

Marmar, J.L., et al. "Penile Plethysmography on Impotent Men Using Vacuum Constrictor Devices." *Urology* 32 (1988): 198–203.

Mentor Corporation product information, 1984.

Merrill, D.C. "Clinical Experience with Scott Inflatable Penile Prosthesis in 150 Patients." *Urology* 22 (1983): 371–75.

Metz, P., and Frimodt-Moller, C. "Epigastrico-Cavernous Anastomosis in the Treatment of Arteriogenic Impotence." *Scandinavian Journal of Urology and Nephrology* 17 (1983): 271–75.

Michal, V. et al. "Arterial Epigastricocavernous Anastomosis for the Treatment of Sexual Impotence." *World Journal of Surgery* 1 (1977): 515–20.

Morales, A. et al. "Nonhormonal Pharmacological Treatment of Organic Impotence." *Journal of Urology* 128 (1982): 45–47.

Muir, J.W. et al. "Bromocriptine Improves Reduced Libido and Potency in Men Receiving Maintenance Hemodialysis." *Clinical Nephrology* 20 (1983): 308–14.

Mulcahy, J.J. "The Hydroflex Self-Contained Inflatable Prosthesis: Experience with 100 Patients." *The Journal of Urology* 140 (1988): 1422–1430.

———. "The Self-Contained Inflatable and Mechanical Penile Prostheses." *AUA Update Series*, Vol 6, Lesson 20 (1987): 1–6.

———. "Tunica Wedge Excision to Correct Penile Curvature Associated with the Inflatable Penile Prosthesis." *The Journal of Urology* 138 (1987): 63–64.

Nadig, P.W., et al. "Noninvasive Device to Produce and Maintain an Erection-Like State." *Urology* 27 (1986): 126–131.

Nelson, R.P. "Nonoperative Management of Impotence." *The Journal of Urology* 139 (1988): 2–6.

Owen, J.A., et al. "Topical Nitroglycerin: A Potential Treatment for Impotence. *The Journal of Urology* 141 (1989): 546–548.

Padma-Nathan, H., et al. "Treatment for Organic Impotence: Alternatives to the Penile Prosthesis, Part I. *AUA Update Series*, Vol 6, Lesson 12 (1987): 1–7.

———. "Treatment for Organic Impotence: Alternatives to the Penile Prosthesis, Part II." *AUA Update Series*, Vol 6, Lesson 12 (1987): 1–7.

Palisades Pharmaceuticals, Inc., product information. Tenafly, N.J., 1984.

Pedersen, B. et al. "Evaluation of Patients and Partners 1 to 4 Years After Penile Prosthesis Surgery." *The Journal of Urology* 139 (1988): 956–958.

———. "Instability and Rotation of Silver Silicone Penile Prosthesis." *Urology* 31 (1988): 116–118.

Peterson, H.R. et al. "Attitudes of Diabetic Men after Implantation of a Semi-Rigid Penile Prosthesis." *Diabetes Care* 8 (1985): 156–60.

Porst, H. et al. "Dynamic Cavernosography: Venous Outflow Studies of Cavernous Bodies." *Journal of Urology* 134 (1985): 276–79.

Pressel, P. "Interview with Two Recipients of Penile Implants." *Journal of Enterostomal Therapy* 9 (1982): 34–35.

Reid, K. et al. "Double-Blind Trial of Yohimbine in Treatment of Psychogenic Impotence." *The Lancet* Aug 22 (1987): 421–423.

Reiss, H. "Improved Technique for Recording Cavernosometries." *Urology* 32 (1988): 115–118.

———. "Role of Spongiosography in Study of Penile Veins." *Urology* 29 (1987): 146–148.

Renshaw, D.C. Reply to Dr. Furlow's letter. *Journal of the American Medical Association* 243 (1980): 1714.

———. "Coping with an Impotent Husband." *Illinois Medical Journal* 159 (1981): 29–33.

———. "Diabetic Impotence: An Important Organic-Psychogenic Interface." *Chicago Medicine* 87 (1984): 956–60.

Rodger, R.S.C. et al. "Zinc Metabolism Does Not Influence Sexual Function in Chronic Renal Insufficiency." *Contributions to Nephrology* 38 (1984): 112–15.

Sarosdy, M.F., et al. "A Prospective Double-Blind Trial of Intracorporeal Papaverine Versus Prostaglandin E-1 in the Treatment of Impotence." *The Journal of Urology* 141 (1989): 551–553.

Savion, M., et al. "Pharmacological, Nonhormonal Treatment of Impotence." *Urology* 29 (1987): 510–512.

Scarzella, G.I. "Cylinder Reliability of Inflatable Penile Prosthesis." *Urology* 31 (1988): 486–489.

Schiffman, Z.J., et al. "Use of Dacron Patch Graft in Peyronie Disease." *Urology* 25 (1985): 38–40.

Schlamowitz, K.E. et al. "Reaction to the Implantation of an Inflatable Penile Prosthesis Among Psychogenically and Organically Impotent Men." *Journal of Urology* 129 (1983): 295–98.

Schover, L.R. *Prime Time: Sexual Health for Men over Fifty.* New York: Holt, Rinehart and Winston, 1984.

Schover, L.R., and von Eschenbach, A.C. "Sex Therapy and the Penile Prosthesis: A Synthesis." *Journal of Sex and Marital Therapy* 2 (1985): 57–66.

"Sexual Activity and Vaginal Atrophy." *Transition,* February 1984.

Sidi, A.A. et al. "Penile Prosthesis Surgery in the Treatment of Impotence in the Immunosuppressed Man." *The Journal of Urology* 137 (1987): 681–682.

———. "Vasoactive Intracavernous Pharmacotherapy for the Treatment of Erectile Impotence in Men with Spinal Cord Injury." *The Journal of Urology* 138 (1987): 539–542.

Sislow, J.G., et al. "Treatment of Congenital Penile Curvature Due to Disparate Corpora Cavernosa by the Nesbit Technique: A Rule of Thumb for the Number of Wedges of Tunica Required to Achieve Correction." *The Journal of Urology* 141 (1989): 92–93.

Somers, K.D., et al. "Chromosome Abnormalities in Peyronie's Disease." *The Journal of Urology* 137 (1987): 672–675.

Sprenger, K.B.G. et al. "Zinc and Sexual Dysfunction." *Contributions to Nephrology* 38 (1984): 119–25.

Stackl, W., et al. "Intracavernous Injection of Prostaglandin E-1 in Impotent Men." *The Journal of Urology* 140 (1988): 66–68.

Stanisic, T.H., et al. "Clinical Experience With a Self-Contained Inflatable Penile Implant: The Flexi-Flate." *The Journal of Urology* 139 (1988): 947–950.

Steers, W.D., et al. "Some Pharmacologic Effects of Yohimbine on Human and Rabbit Penis." *The Journal of Urology* 131 (1984): 799–802.

Stief, C.G., et al. "Mid-Term Results of Autoinjection Therapy for Erectile Dysfunction." *Urology* 31 (1988): 483–485.

Stief, C.G., and Wetterauer, U. "Erectile Responses to Intracavernous Papaverine and Phentolamine: Comparison of Single and Combined Delivery." *The Journal of Urology* 140 (1988): 1415–1416.

Surgitek product information. Racine, Wis.: Medical Engineering Corporation, 1985.

Thomas, R., et al. "Correction of Intrinsic Penile Chordee with a Ventral Penile Graft of Fascia Lata." *The Journal of Urology* 140 (1988): 191–193.

Turnbull, J.M., and Weinberg, P.C. "Psychological Factors Involved in Impotence." *Journal of Andrology* 4 (1983): 59–66.

University of California. Update on Impotence and Infertility. In syllabus book. San Francisco: Dept. of Urology, University of California, 1985.

van Andel, G. "Transluminal Iliac Angioplasty: Long-Term Results." *Radiology* 135 (1980): 607–11.

Virag, R. et al. "Vasculogenic Impotence: A Review of 92 Cases with 54 Surgical Operations." *Vascular Surgery* 15 (1981): 9–17.

Waldhauser, M., and Schramek, P. "Efficiency and Side Effects of Prostaglandin E-1 in the Treatment of Erectile Dysfunction." *The Journal of Urology* 140 (1988): 525–527.

Walther, M., and Foster, J.G. "Complications of Jonas Prosthesis." *Urology* 26 (1985): 64.

Watters, G.R. "Experience in the Management of Erectile Dysfunction Using the Intracavernosal Self-Injection of Vasoactive Drugs." *The Journal of Urology* 140 (1988): 1417–1419.

Weigel, J.W. "Inflatable Penile Prostheses: Troubleshooting and Management of Complications." *American Urological Association Update Series,* Vol 6, Lesson 34 (1987): AUA Office of Education, 1987.

Wespes, E., and Schulman, C.C. "Systemic Complications of Intracavernous Papaverine Injection in Patients with Venous Leakage." *Urology* 31 (1988) 114.

———. "Venous Leakage: Surgical Treatment of a Curable Cause of Impotence." *Journal of Urology* 133 (1985): 796–98.

Wiles, P.G. "Successful, Non-Invasive Management of Erectile Impotence in Diabetic Men." *Short Report from meeting of British Diabetes Association* (1987).

Williams, G., et al. "Diagnosis and Treatment of Venous Leakage: A Curable Cause of Impotence." *British Journal of Urology* 61 (1988): 151–155.

Wilson, S.K., et al. "Eleven Years of Experience with the Inflatable Penile Prosthesis." *The Journal of Urology* 139 (1988): 951–952.

Witherington, R. "Vacuum Constriction Device for Management of Erectile Impotence." *The Journal of Urology* 141 (1989): 320–322.

Zorgniotti, A.W., and Le Fleur, R.S. "Auto-Injection of the Corpus Cavernosum with a Vasoactive Drug Combination for Vasculogenic Impotence." *Journal of Urology* 133 (1985): 39–41.

Zorgniotti, A.W., and Rossi, G., eds. *Vasculogenic Impotence*. Springfield, Ill.: Charles C. Thomas, 1980.

CHAPTER 9

American Association of Sex Educators, Counselors, and Therapists. Requirements for sex therapist certification 11 Dupont Circle, N.W., Suite 220, Washington, D.C., 20036, July 1985.

American Board of Family Psychology. Membership information. P.O. Box 7977, Waco, Tex., 76714.

Chesney, A.P. et al. "A Comparison of Couples Who Have Sought Sex Therapy with Couples Who Have Not." *Journal of Sex and Marital Therapy* 7 (1981): 131–40.

Hampson, J.L. "Evaluation and Treatment of Psychogenic Male Erectile Dysfunction." In *Male Reproductive Dysfunction*, edited by R.J. Santen and R.S. Swerdloff. New York: Marcel Dekker, 1986.

Kaplan, H.S. *The New Sex Therapy*. New York: Brunner/Mazel, 1974.

Kilmann, P.R., and Auerbach, R. "Treatments of Premature Ejaculation and Psychogenic Impotence: A Critical Review of the Literature." *Archives of Sexual Behavior* 8 (1979): 81–100.

Kilmann, P.R., and Mills, K.H. *All about Sex Therapy*. New York: Plenum Press, 1983.

LoPiccolo, J., and Lobitz, W.C. "The Role of Masturbation in the Treatment of Orgasmic Dysfunction." *Archives of Sexual Behavior* 2 (1972): 163–71.

LoPiccolo, J., and LoPiccolo, L., eds. *Handbook of Sex Therapy*. New York: Plenum Press, 1978.

LoPiccolo, J. et al. "Effectiveness of Single Therapists Versus Cotherapy Teams in Sex Therapy." *Journal of Consulting and Clinical Psychology* 53 (1985): 287–94.

Lowe, J.C., and Mikulas, W.L. "Use of Written Material in Learning Self-Control of Premature Ejaculation." In *Handbook of Sex Therapy*, edited by J. LoPiccolo and L. LoPiccolo. New York: Plenum Press, 1978.

Masters, W.H., and Johnson, V.E. *Human Sexual Inadequacy*. New York: Bantam, 1980.

Mills, K.H., and Kilmann, P.R. "Group Treatment of Sexual Dysfunction: A Methodological Review of the Outcome Literature." *Journal of Sex and Marital Therapy* 8 (1982): 259–80.

Price, S.C. et al. "Group Treatment of Erectile Dysfunction for Men without Partners: A Controlled Evaluation." *Archives of Sexual Behavior* 10 (1981): 253–68.

Raley, P.E. *Making Love.* New York: Avon, 1976.

Reed, D.M. "Male Sexual Dysfunction and Counseling Techniques." In *Goldsmith's Practice of Surgery*, edited by A.R. Kendall and L. Karafin. Philadelphia: Harper and Row, 1982.

Reynolds, B.S. et al. "Dating Skills Training in the Group Treatment of Erectile Dysfunction for Men without Partners." *Journal of Sex and Marital Therapy* 7 (1981): 184–94.

Schiavi, R.C. "Psychological Treatment of Erectile Disorders in Diabetic Patients." *Annals of Internal Medicine* 92 (1980): 337–339.

Schoenberg, H.W. et al. "Analysis of 122 Unselected Impotent Men Subjected to Multidisciplinary Evaluation." *Journal of Urology* 127 (1982): 445–47.

Schover, L.R. *Prime Time: Sexual Health for Men over Fifty.* New York: Holt, Rinehart and Winston, 1984.

Schover, L.R., and von Eschenbach, A.C. "Sex Therapy and the Penile Prosthesis: A Synthesis." *Journal of Sex and Marital Therapy* 11 (1983): 57–66.

Seagraves, R.T. "Referral of Impotent Patients to a Sexual Dysfunction Clinic." *Archives of Sexual Behavior* 11 (1982): 521–28.

Seagraves, R.T. et al. "Characteristics of Erectile Dysfunction as a Function of Medical Care System Entry Point." *Psychosomatic Medicine* 43 (1981): 227–34.

Turnbull, J.M., and Weinberg, P.C. "Psychological Factors Involved in Impotence: A Review of the Literature." *Journal of Andrology* 4 (1983): 59–66.

Zilbergeld, B. "Group Treatment of Sexual Dysfunction in Men without Partners." *Journal of Sex and Marital Therapy* 1 (1975): 204–14.

———. *Male Sexuality: A Guide to Sexual Fulfillment.* New York: Bantam, 1978.

Zilbergeld, B., and Kilmann, P.R. "The Scope and Effectiveness of Sex Therapy." *Psychotherapy* 21 (1984): 319–26.

CHAPTER 10

Crenshaw, T.L. *Bedside Manners.* New York: Pinnacle, 1983.

Daniel, D.G. et al. "The Relationship between Beliefs about Men's and Women's Roles in Society and Views on Male Sexual Dysfunction in 135 Women." *Social Psychiatry* 19 (1984) 127–33.

Interviews with sex therapists, 1985–1986.

Renshaw, D.C. "Wives of Impotent Men." *Consultant* 19 (1979): 41–48.

———. "Coping with an Impotent Husband." *Illinois Medical Journal* 159 (1981): 29–33.

CHAPTER 11

Bailey, C. *Fit or Fat?* Boston: Houghton Mifflin Company, 1978.

Barndt, R., Jr., et al. "Regression and Progression of Early Femoral Atherosclerosis in Treated Hyperlipoproteinemic Patients." *Annals of Internal Medicine* 86 (1977): 139–46.

Berg, A., and Keul, J. "Influence of Maximum Aerobic Capacity and Relative Body Weight on the Lipoprotein Profile in Athletes." *Atherosclerosis* 55 (1985): 225–31.

Brown, G.D. et al. "Effects of Two 'Lipid-Lowering' Diets on Plasma Lipid Levels of Patients with Peripheral Vascular Disease." *Journal of the American Dietetic Association* 84 (1984): 546–50.

Clarkson, T.B. et al. "Psychosocial and Reproductive Influences on Plasma Lipids, Lipoproteins and Atherosclerosis in Nonhuman Primates." *Journal of Lipid Research* 25 (1984): 1629–34.

Fripp, R.R. et al. "Aerobic Capacity, Obesity, and Atherosclerotic Risk Factors in Male Adolescents." *Pediatrics* 75 (1985): 813–18.

Kannel, W.B., and Schatzkin, A. "Risk Factor Analysis." *Progress in Cardiovascular Diseases* 26 (1983): 309–32.

Newman, W.P., III, et al. "Relation of Serum Lipoprotein Levels and Systolic Blood Pressure to Early Atherosclerosis." *New England Journal of Medicine* 314 (1986): 138–44.

Oberai, B. et al. "Myocardial and Renal Arteriolar Thickening in Cigarette Smokers." *Atherosclerosis* 52 (1984): 185–90.

Ruzbarsky, V., and Michal, V. "Morphologic Changes in the Arterial Bed of the Penis with Aging." *Investigative Urology* 15 (1977): 194–99.

Stamford, B.A. et al. "Cigarette Smoking, Exercise and High Density Lipoprotein Cholesterol." *Atherosclerosis* 52 (1984): 73–83.

"The Stanford University Guide to a Healthier Heart." *Prevention*, February 1986, 33–62.

Virag, R. et al. "Is Impotence an Arterial Disorder? A Study of Arterial Risk Factors in 440 Impotent Men." *Lancet*, January 1984, 181–84.

Index

Page numbers in italic indicate chart.

AASECT. *See* American Association of Sex Educators, Counselors, and Therapists
Accutane, *58*
Acebutolol, *53*
Acetazolamide, *53*
Acne, *58*
Adipex, *59*
Adipost, *58*
Adolescence and early 20's, erection ease during, 15
Adrenal glands, 76–77
Adrenal problems, 76–77
Aging, normal changes in erection, 14–18, 22, 31, 48
AIDS, x
Akineton, *56*
Alcohol, 12, *57, 59,* 60–62, 69, 77, 112, 113, 134, 201, 220, 224, 226–227
    combined with drugs, 62, 112
Alcoholics, 12, 60–61
Aldactone, *54*
Aldomet, *54*
All about Sex Therapy (Kilmann and Mills), 208
Allergies, drugs for, *56, 58*
Alseroxylon, *53*
Altromid-S, *57*
American Association of Sex Educators, Counselors, and Therapists (AASECT), 196
American Board of Family Psychology, 196
American Heart Association, 224
Amicar, *57*
Amiloride, *53*
Amitriptyline, *54*
Amphetamines, 52, *59*

AMS 600 prosthesis, 170
Anal sphincter, 34, 138, 139
Androl-50, *58*
Anesthetic, 150–151, 164, 167, 170, 171, 176, 178, 180
Angina, *59*
Anhydron, *53*
Anisotropine, *55*
Anorex, *58*
Antabuse, *57*
Antianxiety medications, *54*
Antibiotics, 171
Antidepressants, *54,* 83
Antifungus, *58*
Antihistamines, *56*
Antihyperlipidemic, *57, 59*
Antihypertensives, *53–54, 57,* 62, 140
Antipsychotic, *57*
Antivert, *56*
Anus, 34
Anxiety, 6, 41–46, 71, 109, 114, 116, 183, 185, 192, 215
Aphrodisiacs, 128
Apo-Furosemide, *53*
Apresoline, *53*
Aquatag, *53*
Aquatensin, *54*
Aquazide, *54*
Artane, *56*
Arteries, 13, 19, 27, 30, 31, 62, 63, 67, 69, 72, 74, 75, 84, 87, 137, 138, 144, 145, 146, 147, 148, 155, 159, 186, 221, 222, 224, 225, 227
Arteriogram, 147
Arteriosclerosis, 67, 188
Arthritis, *58,* 168
Artificial insemination, 23
Asthma, medications for, *58*
Atropine, *55*
Aventyl, *55*

Index

Back injury, 136, 145, 150
Back problems, 79, 82
Back surgery, 156
Baclofen, 56
Banthine, 56
Barbiturates, 59
Benadryl, 56
Bendroflumethiazide, 53
Benzthiazide, 53
Benztropine, 56
Bethanidine, 53
Biothesiometer, 151
Biperidin, 56
Bladder, 21, 86, 150–151, 174
    cancer of, 63, 88
    drugs for spasms of, 55
    surgery for, 88
    tumors of, 168
Bleeding, abnormal
    medication for, 57
Blocadren, 59
Blood flow, 138, 146–151, 192, 220–221, 223
Blood-flow problems, 31, 49, 69, 72, 74, 106, 111, 133, 146–148, 155
Blood pressure, 50, 87, 112, 206, 220, 221, 224–225
    medication for, 53–54, 62, 112–113, 161
    penile, 146–147, 148
Blood tests, 134, 135
Blood vessel disease, 71–75, 133
Bonine, 56
Bowel, drugs for spasms of, 55
Bromocriptine, 75
Bulbocavernosus muscle, 138, 151
Buspar, 54
Buspirone, 54

Calan, 59
Calcium, 59
Cancer
    bladder, 63, 88
    hormones for treatment of, 57, 59
    penile, 88
    prostate, 30, 57, 58, 84, 85–86, 87, 89, 139–140, 182
    testicular, 24, 25, 89
Cantil, 56
Carbamazepine, 57

Catapres, 53
Cavernosogram, 149, 150
Cavernosography, 74–75
Chemotherapy, 77
Chlordiazepoxide, 54
Chlordinium, 55
Chlor-Iso TR, 56
Chlorpromazine, 55
Chlorprothixine, 55
Chlorthalidone, 53
Cholesterol, 57, 59, 220, 221–222, 223, 224
Cimetidine, 57
Cinnasil, 54
Circumcision, 21
Clindex, 55
Clinidium, 55
Clipoxide, 55
Clofibrate, 57
Clonidine, 53
Clopra-"Yellow," 58
Clorazepate, 54
Cocaine, 59
Cock rings, 125–127, 157–158
Cogentin, 56
Combagen, 56
Combid, 56
Combipres, 53
Communication, 90–108, 117, 122–123, 163, 202, 205, 206–207, 209, 210, 213, 214–215. *See also* Failure to communicate
Compazine, 55
Constricting ring, 157, 158
Corgard, 54
Corizide, 53
Corpora cavernosa, 20, 27, 33, 83, 146, 159, 160, 165, 171, 173, 174, 176, 177, 178, 180
Corpus spongiosum, 21, 160
Correctaid, 158–159
Corzide, 54
Counselors, 218
    as sex therapists, 196–197
Cyclathiazide, 53
Cyclobenzaprine, 56
Cycrimine, 56
Cyproterone acetate, 57
Cystometrogram, 150–151

Dantrium, 56
Dantrolene, 56

Darbid, 56
Dazamide, 53
Depletite, 57
Depression, 45, 46, 93, 142
Deserpidine, 57
Desipramine, 54
Desyrel, 55
Diabetes, 9, 45–46, 63, 66–70, 74, 111, 126, 133, 150, 161, 173, 206, 221, 224
Diamox, 53
Diazepam, 54
Dibenzaline, 54
Diet, 69, 72, 222, 223, 224, 225–226
   high-calorie, 63
   high-fat, 63, 74
   high-fiber, 220, 224
   low-cholesterol, 220, 221, 222, 223, 224
   low-fat, 38–39, 63, 220, 221, 222, 223, 224
   low-salt, 224
   pills, 57, 58, 59
Diethylpropion, 57
Dietic, 57
Digoxin, 57
Dilantin, 59
Dimenhydrinate, 56
Diphenhydramine, 56
Disease
   effect of on sperm production, 22
   sexually transmitted, x
Disopyramide, 57
Disulfiram, 57
Ditropan, 56
Diucardin, 53
Diurese, 54
Diuretics, 53–54
Diuril, 54
Diutensin-R, 54
Dolophine, 58
Dorsal vein, 188
Doxepin, 54
Dramamine, 56
Droperidol, 55
Drugs. *See also* Medications
   antianxiety, 54
   antidepressant, 54–55
   antihistamine, 56
   antihypertensive, 53–54
   for arthritis, 58
   for asthma, 58
   for bladder or bowel spasms, 55–56
   as cause of potency problem, 50–52, 52–59
   combined with alcohol, 62, 112
   for irregular heartbeats, 57
   as muscle relaxants, 56
   for Parkinson's disease, 56
   problem, 52–59
   as tranquilizers, 55
Dry ejaculation, 86–87
Duplex Doppler, 147
DuraPhase, 170

ECG. *See* Electrocardiogram
Edecrin, 53
Ejaculation, 14–15, 16, 17, 18, 20–21, 22, 23, 24, 30, 33, 34, 35, 73, 80, 120–121, 158, 159, 203
   dry, 86–87
   premature, 33–34, 68
      prevention of, 119–124
Ejaculatory control. *See* Ejaculation
Ejaculatory inevitability, 123
Elavil, 54
Electrocardiogram (ECG), 71
Enalapril, 53
Endocrinologist, 129
Enduron, 54
Enduronyl, 54, 57
Epididymis, 22, 24, 35
Epilepsy, 79–80
Epitol, 57
Epsilon aminocaproic acid, 57
Equanil, 54
Erecaid System, 157
Erectile dysfunction, 3
Erection
   anatomy of, 19–36
   guidelines for maintaining, 220–227
   illness's effect on, 66–89
   medical solutions for physical problems with, 152–192
   normal aspects of, 1–18
   prevention of, 37–65
   professional help for problems with, 129–151
   self-help for problems with, 109–128

sex therapy for problems with, 193–210
during sleep, 35–36, 134, 141, 142–143
women's role in, 90–108, 211–219
Esidrix, 54
Estrogens, 57
Ethacrynic acid, 53
Ethionamide, 57
Ethon, 54
Ethylestrenol, 57
Eutonyl, 55
Eutron, 54
Examination, physical, 133–134, 137–140, 150
Excitation phase, 32–33
Exercise, 22, 39, 63–64, 69, 72, 124, 210, 220, 224, 225–226
Exna, 53
Expectations, 205–208
unrealistic, 46–47, 164–165

Failure to communicate, 42–43. See also Communication
Fenfluramine, 58
Fertility, 23
Fiber, 220, 224
Finney, Dr. Roy, 169
Flagyl, 58
Flecainide, 57
Flexeril, 56
Flexi-Flate, 168–169, 177–178
Flexirod, 169–170
Fluidil, 53
Flumethiazide, 53
Fluphenazine, 55
Foreplay, 15, 16, 17, 46
Foreskin, 21, 171
Furazolidone, 58
Furosemide, 53
Furoxone, 58

General practitioners, 129
Ginseng, 128
Glans penis, 21, 33
Glaucoma, 59
Glucocorticoids, 58
Glucose tolerance, 135
Glycopyrrolate, 55
Goldstein, Dr. Irwin, 87

Guanadrel, 53
Guanethidine, 53

Haldol, 55
Haloperidol, 55
Harmonyl, 57
HDLs. See High-density lipoproteins
Headache, medications for, 58
Heart disease, 71–72, 133
Heart problems, medication for, 57
Heroin, 59
Hexabamate, 56
Hexocyclium, 55
High-density lipoproteins, 222, 224, 225, 227
Hormones, 19, 23–26, 32, 57, 58, 59, 61, 75–79, 139, 140. See also Luteinizing hormone, Testosterone
Hydralazine, 53
Hydrex, 53
Hydroflex, 168–169, 177–178
Hydroflumethiazide, 53
Hydro-Fluserpine, 53
Hydro-Ride, 53
Hydroxyzine, 56
Hygroton, 53, 54
Hylidone, 53
Hylorel, 53

IA. See Impotents Anonymous
I-ANON. See Impotents Anonymous
Illness, effects of on erection, 7
Imipramine, 54
Immunosuppressive agents, 58
Implant. See Penile implant
Impotence
chronic, 11–12
definition of, 3
ignorance about, 4–7
occasional, 11–12
primary, 3
secondary, 3
temporary, 12, 13
Impotents Anonymous (IA, I-ANON), 117–118, 131
Indapamide, 53
Indocin, 58
Indomethacin, 58

Infection, 22, 30, 44, 58, 77, 102, 170–171, 184
Injuries
    back, 136, 145, 150
    effect of, on sperm production, 22
    spinal cord, 79–80, 81–82, 150
Innovar, 55
Insulin, 66
Insurance coverage, 140, 181
Intercourse, 12, 18, 23, 30, 33–34, 35, 70, 71, 73, 74, 82, 83, 93, 96, 110, 111, 114, 115, 116, 118–119, 121, 122, 123, 124, 126, 137, 148, 156, 159, 160, 161, 162, 163, 164, 165, 173, 177, 182, 183, 184, 185, 187, 191, 193, 202, 203, 204, 205, 206, 213, 222
Inversine, 53
Irregular heartbeats, drugs for, 57
Ismelin, 53
Isocarboxazide, 54
Isopropamide, 56
Isoptin, 59
Isotretinoin, 58

Jonas, Dr. Udo, 169
Jonas Silicone-Silver prosthesis, 169–170

Kegel exercises, 124
Kemadrin, 56
Ketoconazole, 58
Ketoprofen, 58
Kidney dialysis, 75
Kidney disease, 75, 133
Kilmann, Peter R., 208
Klinefelter's syndrome, 78

Labetalol, 53
Lanoxin, 57
Larodopa, 56
Laxix, 53
LDLs. See Low-density lipoproteins
Leuprolide, 58
Levodopa, 56
Librax, 55
Librium, 54
Lidox, 55
Lioresal, 56
Lipoproteins, 222, 224, 225, 227
Lithium carbonate, 55

Liver damage, 79
Liver disease, 133, 135
Loniten, 54
Lopressor, 54
Lorelco, 59
Low-density lipoproteins, 222
Lozol, 53
Lubricant, water-based, 18, 183
Ludiomil, 55
Lue, Dr. Tom, 27, 147
Lupron, 58
Lupus, 58, 72
Luteinizing hormone, 26, 76

Male Sexuality (Zilbergeld), 124, 208
Maprotiline, 55
Marijuana, 52, 59
Marplan, 54
Masters and Johnson, 120, 139, 194, 201
Masturbation, 14, 73, 113, 116, 121, 122, 136
    exercises, 210
Matulane, 59
Maurazide, 53
Maxibolin, 57
Maxolon, 58
Mazanor, 58
Mazindol, 58
Mecamylamine, 53
Meclizine, 56
Medicare, 181
Medications, 11, 13, 69, 70, 112–113, 114, 134, 139. See also Drugs
    for adrenal problems, 77
    for anxiety, 192
    to block artery spasms, 192
    blood pressure, 53–54, 62, 161
    blood-thinning, 83
    combined with alcohol, 62, 112
    to increase desire, 192
    for pain, 172
    for Peyronie's disease, 83
    for pituitary tumor, 76
Mellaril, 55
Mentor Mask II, 178
Mepenzolate, 56
Meprobamate, 54
Mesoridazine, 55
Methadone, 58
Methandroid, 58

Index

Methandrostenolone, 58
Methantheline, 56
Methyclothiazide, 54
Methyldopa, 54
Methysergide, 58
Metoclopramide, 58
Metoprolol, 54
Metronidazole, 58
Mexiletine, 57
Mexitil, 57
Midamor, 53
Middle age, erections during, 16–17
Mills, Katherine H., 208
Miltown, 54
Minipress, 54
Minoxidil, 54
Moduretic, 53
Morphine, 59
Motion sickness, drugs for, 56
Multiple sclerosis, 80–81, 207
Mumps, 22, 77
Muscle relaxants, 56
Muscles, pelvic, 124
Myths
    about impotence, 9–14
    sexual, 203

Nadolol, 54
Naqua, 54
Narcotics, 52, 58, 59
Nardil, 55
Naturetin, 53
Navane, 55
Nerve damage, 67, 69, 75, 85–86, 88, 138, 142, 144, 145, 154, 155, 156
    tests for, 150–151
Nerve diseases, 79–82
Nerves, 13, 19, 84
Nervous system
    autonomic, 30
    parasympathetic, 30–31
    sympathetic, 30–31
Nicorette, 58
Nicotine, 58, 59, 110
Nizoral, 58
Nobesine, 57
Nocturnal Penile Tumescence Test, 146
    at home, 141, 142–143
    in lab, 141–142
Norflex, 56

Normodyne, 53
Norpace, 57
Norpramine, 54
Nortriptyline, 55
NPT tests. *See* Nocturnal Penile Tumescence Test
Numbness, 80, 151, 173–174, 180

Obephen, 59
Obesity, 63, 66, 224
Old age, erections during, 17–18
OmniPhase, 170
Opiates, 59
Oral sex, 17, 123
Orap, 55
Oreticyl, 57
Orgasm, 14, 15, 16, 34, 39, 48–49, 60, 86, 159
Orphenadrine, 56
Orudis, 58
Overweight. *See* Obesity
Oxybutynin, 56
Oxymetholone, 58

Pagitane, 56
Papaverine, 144, 153
Pargylene, 55
Parkinson's disease, 56, 80, 168
Parnate, 55
Partner involvement, 101, 106–108, 178–179, 184–186, 198–200
Pathilon, 56
Pelvic muscles, exercises for, 124
Pelvic steal syndrome, 137, 142, 148
Pelvic surgery, 30, 84–88, 159–191
Penile implant, 10, 49, 70, 72, 81, 82, 84, 106–108, 134, 159–186. *See also* Penile prosthesis
    adjusting to, 185
    choice of, 161–164, 178–181
    inflatable, 168–169, 170, 174–178
        benefits of, 168–169
        cost of, 181
        drawbacks of, 168–169, 177, 178
        surgical placement of, 174, 176
    satisfaction with, 187
    semirigid, 165–174, 177–181
        benefits of, 167
        cost of, 181

Penile implant, semirigid (cont.)
    drawbacks of, 167–168, 173–174
    surgical placement of, 170–172
Penile prosthesis, 75, 87, 132, 140, 150. *See also* Penile implant
    infections with, 171
Penile shots, 70, 81, 82, 87, 105, 111, 130, 134, 144–146, 147, 149, 152–157
Penile surgery, 88
Penile veins. *See* Veins, penile
Penis
    anatomy of, 19–22
    diseases of, 82–84
    muscle weakness in, 17
    size of, 13–14, 31, 163–164
Performance anxiety, 41–46, 64, 195
Peyronie's disease, 83–84, 98, 138, 179
    surgery for, 88, 191
Phenelzine, 55
Phenergan, 56
Phendimetrazine, 58
Phenmetrazine, 58
Phenoxybenzamine, 54
Phentermine, 59
Phentolamine, 54, 144, 153
Phenytoin, 59
Physical factors of erection problems, 7, 43, 49, 70, 71, 73–74, 113, 130, 139, 163
Physicians
    attitude of, 129–132
    and knowledge of erections, 7–9, 129
    as sex therapists, 196–197
Pituitary disease, 76
Pituitary gland, 26, 75–76
Pituitary tumors, 139
Plateau phase, 33–34
Polyunsaturated fats, 222
Pondimin, 58
Potency Restored, 118
PotenTest, 143
Prazosin, 54
Preludin, 58
Premature ejaculation, 33–34, 68, 119–124
Priapism, 82–83
Primozide, 55

Pritikin maintenance plan, 224
Proaqua, 53
Pro-Banthine, 56
Probucol, 59
Procarbazine, 59
Prochlorperazine, 55
Procyclidine, 56
Progestins, 59
Prolactin, 26, 75, 76, 135, 139
Prolixin, 55
Promazine, 55
Promethazine, 56
Propantheline bromide, 56
Propion, 57
Prostaglandin E-1, 144, 153
Prostate, 29–30, 34
    benign enlargement of, 84–85
    cancer of, 87, 89, 139–140, 182
    surgery of, 30, 84–87, 97
Protriptyline, 55
Psychiatrists, 129
    as sex therapists, 196–197
Psychological factors, 7, 10, 25, 48, 49, 73–74, 130, 140, 142, 155, 163
Psychological tests, 151
Psychologists, 130
    as sex therapists, 196–197
Pubococcygeus muscle (PC), 124

Quarzan, 55

Radiation treatment, 63, 77, 84, 87
Radical prostatectomy, 85–87
Rantidine, 59
Rapid eye movement stage of sleep (REM), 141
Rautensin, 53
Rautrax, 53
Rauwiloid, 53
Rauzide, 53
Recovery of Male Potency (ROMP), 117, 118
Recreational drugs, 52, 59, 113, 134
Rectal examination, 30, 89, 139
Rectal surgery, 88
Rectum, 138
Reflex test, 138
Refractory period, 35
Regibon, 57
Regitine, 54
Reglan, 58

Index

REM. *See* Rapid eye movement stage of sleep
Renshaw, Dr. Domeena C., 70, 216
Rescinnamine, 54
Reserpine, 54
Resolution phase, 34–35
Robinul, 55

Saluron, 53
Salutrensin, 53
Sandril, 54
Sanorex, 58
Sansert, 58
Saturated fats, 221–222
Scrotum, 22, 33, 34, 179, 174, 176
Sealets, 55
Sectral, 53
Seizures, medication for, 57, 59
Self-help, 109–128, 208–209
Self-sabotage, 38–41, 66, 164–165, 226–227
    how to stop, 110–113
Semans, Dr. James, 120
Semen, 16, 21, 34, 35, 122, 138
Seminal vesicles, 29, 34, 85
Sensate focus, 202–205
Sensual pleasure, 42, 47, 205
Serentil, 55
Serpasil, 54
Sex therapists, 22, 47, 118, 119, 120, 124, 130, 184, 194, 195, 196–197, 198, 199, 200, 204, 205, 208–210, 213
    qualifications of, 196–197
Sex therapy, 70, 134, 139, 165, 191, 193–210, 215
    cost of, 195
    for single men, 209–210
Sexual aids, 124–125
Sexual desire, 32, 35, 61, 76, 77, 80, 113, 140, 141, 160
Sexual energy, 11, 14
Sexual response cycle, 32–35
Sexual success, guidelines for, 220–227
Sickle cell anemia, 83
Sinemet, 56
Sinequan, 54
Sinuses, 27, 31, 33, 34, 74, 144, 153, 159
Sleep erections, 35–36, 134, 141–143

Slipped disc, 82
Small-Carrion, 169–170
Smoking, 13, 58, 62–63, 69–70, 74, 87, 110–112, 134, 220, 221, 225, 226
Snap-Gauge test, 143
Social workers, as sex therapists, 196–197
Spanish fly, 128
Sparine, 55
Spectatoring, 45
Sperm, 20, 22, 23, 33
Spinal cord injuries, 79–80, 81–82, 150
Spironolactone, 54
Squeeze technique, 119, 120, 122–123
SST deformity, 173
Stamp test, 143, 216
Stanford University Heart Disease Prevention Program, 223
Stanzolol, 59
Stelazine, 55
Steroids, 84
    anabolic, 57, 58, 59
Stop-start technique, 119, 120–121
Stress, 11, 32, 45, 46, 49–50, 112, 215
    reducing, 113–118
Suction devices, 157–159
Support groups, 117–118, 131, 179, 216
Surgery
    for adrenal problems, 77
    arterial, 72, 186–188
    bladder, 88
    for cancer, 63
    as cause of erection problems, 84–89
    implant, 159–186
    penile, 88
    for Peyronie's disease, 84, 191
    for pituitary tumor, 76
    prostate, 30, 84–87, 97, 182
    rectal, 88
    testicular, 88–89
    vein, 188, 190
Surmontil, 55

Tagamet, 57
Tambocor, 57

Taractan, 55
Tegretol, 57
Tenoretic, 53
Tension, 215
Tenuate, 57
Tepanil, 57
Testicles, 19, 33, 34, 61, 76, 102, 103, 134, 140, 226
  anatomy of, 22-26
  injury to, 79
  problems with, 77-79
  undescended, 22
Testicular self-exam, 24
Testicular surgery, 88-89
Testosterone, 23-26, 32, 61, 73, 75, 76, 88-89, 102, 134, 135, 226
Testosterone pills, 79
Testosterone shots, 79
Tetracycline, 44
Thalitone, 53
Thermography, 147-148
Thiazides, 54
Thioridazine, 55
Thiothixene, 55
Thorazine, 55
Thyroid glands, 76-77
Thyroid problems, 76-77, 135
Timolol maleate eye drops, and erection problems, 51, 59
Timoptic, 51, 59
Tobacco, 110, 112, 113, 220, 226
Tofranil, 54
Tral, 55
Trandate, 53
Tranquilizers, 55, 83
Transurethral prostatectomy (TURP), 85
Tranxene, 54
Tranylcypromine, 55
Trauma, 72, 153, 187-188
Trazadone, 55
Trecator, 57
Trichlormethiazide, 54
Tridihexethyl, 56
Trifluoperazine, 55
Trihexyphenidyl, 56
Trimipramine, 55
Tronac, 58
Tuberculosis, 57
Tybamate, 54
Tybatran, 54

Unrealistic expectations, 46-47, 164-165
Urethra, 20-21, 33, 34, 88, 122, 138, 160
Urine, 20, 22, 86
Urodynamic test, 150-151
Urologist, 8, 17, 24, 27, 63, 82, 107, 116, 129, 130, 145-146, 147-148, 150, 180, 196
  selection of, 130-132

Vacuum devices, 157-159
Valium, 54
Valpin, 55
Vascular problems. *See* Blood-flow problems; Blood vessel disease; Veins, leaky
Vasectomy, 13
Vaseretic, 53
Vasotec, 53
Vein problems, 75
Veins
  leaky, 74, 144, 149, 150, 154, 159
    surgery for, 188, 190
    tests for, 149-150
  penile, 13, 19, 27, 29, 34, 72-73
Verpamil, 59
Vistaril, 56
Vitamins, 127-128
Vivactil, 55

Walsh, Dr. Patrick C., 86
Winstrol, 59
Woman-on-top position, 121, 148, 185, 204-205
Women
  participation of, in therapy, 104-108
  reactions of, to impotence, 95-96
  self-help advice for, 211-219
  sexual problems of, 216

Xenon wash-out, 149-150

Yohimbine, 189-190

Zantac, 59
Zilbergeld, Dr. Bernie, 124, 208
Zinc, 75, 128